Sandra Holtgreve, Karlson Preuß, Mathias Albert (eds.)
Envisioning the World: Mapping and Making the Global

Global Studies

Sandra Holtgreve, born in 1989, is a doctoral researcher at Bielefeld University and part of the Research Training Group "World Politics". She studied Social Work, sociology, and Inter-American Studies. Her doctoral research deals with knowledge sociology and Social Work education.

Karlson Preuß, born in 1988, is a doctoral researcher at Bielefeld University and part of the Research Training Group "World Politics". He studied philosophy, sociology, French and Comparative Constitutional Law and is currently working on his PhD in the field of Sociology of Law.

Mathias Albert, born in 1967, is a professor of political science at Bielefeld University and Speaker of the Research Training Group "World Politics". In addition to his research in the history and sociology of world politics, he is active in youth studies (Shell Jugendstudie) and in polar research.

Sandra Holtgreve, Karlson Preuß, Mathias Albert (eds.)
**Envisioning the World:
Mapping and Making the Global**

[transcript]

We acknowledge support for the publication costs by the Open Access Publication Fund of Bielefeld University

Bibliographic information published by the Deutsche Nationalbibliothek
The Deutsche Nationalbibliothek lists this publication in the Deutsche Nationalbibliografie; detailed bibliographic data are available in the Internet at http://dnb.d-nb.de

This work is licensed under the Creative Commons Attribution 4.0 (BY) license, which means that the text may be be remixed, transformed and built upon and be copied and redistributed in any medium or format even commercially, provided credit is given to the author. For details go to http://creativecommons.org/licenses/by/4.0/
Creative Commons license terms for re-use do not apply to any content (such as graphs, figures, photos, excerpts, etc.) not original to the Open Access publication and further permission may be required from the rights holder. The obligation to research and clear permission lies solely with the party re-using the material.

First published in 2021 by transcript Verlag, Bielefeld
© **Sandra Holtgreve, Karlson Preuß, Mathias Albert (eds.)**

Cover layout: Maria Arndt, Bielefeld
Cover illustration: THEPALMER / istockphoto.com
Printed by Majuskel Medienproduktion GmbH, Wetzlar
Print-ISBN 978-3-8376-5529-2
PDF-ISBN 978-3-8394-5529-6
https://doi.org/10.14361/9783839455296

Printed on permanent acid-free text paper.

Contents

Acknowledgments 7

List of tables 9

List of figures 11

Introduction: Envisioning the World, Mapping the Global
Sandra Holtgreve, Karlson Preuß, Mathias Albert 13

From Region to World, and Back Again
How Latin Americans Envisioned the Global (1810-1840)
Gladys Vásquez 29

The World of Anti-Semitism
A Historical-Sociological Analysis of the Global Element of Hostility
Against Jews in Germany (1780-1925)
Marc Jacobsen and Tobias Werron 45

Envisioning a World Law
Reflections on the *Congrès international de droit comparé* (1900) and
the Latent Underpinnings of Comparative Legal Practice
Karlson Preuß 65

Determining *the Global* from a Social Work Perspective
Sandra Holtgreve and Cornelia Giebeler 87

The Revolution in Rojava and the International
Yasin Sunca 105

Resisting World Politics on 'Migration and Development'?
Tracing the Trajectory of Counter Discourses
and Movements in Latin America
Mustafa Aksakal 125

'Sovereignty' and 'Intervention'
Metaphors of Russia's Loneliness in a Global World
Sergei Akopov... 145

Russia and the EU in a Multipolar World:
Invoking the Global in Russian Terms
Aziz Elmuradov.. 165

Back from the USSR
Envisioning the Global Through Journey Narratives
Lucy Gasser 179

Beyond a Global Horizon
Vers la pensée planétaire (1964) and the Discourse
of Planetarity 1930-2020
Michael Auer 199

References 223

Notes on Contributors 259

Acknowledgments

This book is the outcome of collaborative work of the Research Training Group 'World Politics: The Emergence of Political Arenas and Modes of Observation in World Society' at Bielefeld University, funded by the German Research Council (GRK 2225). We are indebted to Stephen Curtis for his excellent language editing services. We also would like to thank the Institute for World Society Studies for generously supporting the publication of this book. We acknowledge support for the publication costs by the Open Access Publication Fund of Bielefeld University.

List of tables

Table 8.1: Employment of 'sovereignty' in 1994–2018 addresses of Russian presidents
Table 8.2: Numbers of symbolic representations of Russian sovereignty 1994–2020 projected onto 'internal' and 'external' political communities

List of figures

Figure 8.1: Metaphors of 'sovereignty' in addresses of Russian presidents 1994–2020

Introduction: Envisioning the World, Mapping the Global

Sandra Holtgreve, Karlson Preuß, Mathias Albert

Mapping and making the global through practices of observation

Visions of the world and descriptions of the global are based on *practices of observation*. Rather than working with an account of structures and connections, or with a fixed definition of 'the global', the contributions in this book seek to identify narratives, images and models that are used in practices of observation in order to address 'the world' or 'the global' and how they come to appear as a distinct realm of the social world. In addition to considering the conditions for the 'emergence' of the global in particular practices of observation, this book is also interested in the impact of these global modes of observation on field-related discourses, processes and agents. It focuses, therefore, on the *phenomenological* dimension of globalization processes. The individual contributions reconstruct how specific visions of the world emerge in different social fields and how various actors throughout time have tried to map, describe and make sense of the global, thereby contributing to its constitution, that is, to its 'making'.

This book brings together views from Sociology, History, Literary Theory and International Relations and takes up a range of discussions in world society/world polity as well as in global history research. Many disciplines involved in the field of globalization research are witnessing an increased interest in approaches that pursue the process of globalization at the level of local practices, discourses and strategies. Diverse as the disciplinary, theoretical and empirical backgrounds of the contributions gathered here may be, they converge in the effort to retrace 'practices of world making' (Bell 2013: 257) in various areas of society. The aim is to establish a connection between different areas in order to find underlying commonalities in observational practices that are not evident at first glance and consequently little addressed in the globalization literature. We particularly focus on two core issues: the practical driving forces of globalization and the relation between the global and the local. Regarding the former, a main concern is to complement accounts that focus on only one, or a few, 'grand' narratives – such as global capitalism, legalization, digitalization etc. – with reconstructions of how a global horizon emerges within the perspective of particular observers. As a corollary to this analytical approach, we also seek to demonstrate the ways in which the global and the local are to be understood as complementary sides of the same processes (Werron 2012: 110; see also Robertson 1998).

The growing unease with the grand narratives of globalization

'Grand' narratives of globalization are usually exactly that: impressive and also beautiful in their grandeur. The diversity of empirical reality quite often turns out to be less beautiful in its actual messiness. The grand narratives that seem to dominate globalization research (cf. Greve and Heintz 2005: 111; Sassen 2007: 6) focus on the emergence of institutions and organizations that operate on a worldwide scale, on global networks, interconnectedness through communication technology and global communicative structures. However, various fields of research are experiencing a growing unease about such narratives and criticize them for being biased towards structural or even structurally deterministic accounts of global social reality. Criticism has been levelled at, for example, world polity theory (of the so-called 'Stanford School') and its focus on 'the institutional conditions of diffusion' (Strang and Meyer 1993) when attempting to make sense of globally diffused cultural patterns or sociological systems theory that ascribes the spatial decontextualization of communicative acts to the problem-specific mode of operation of different function systems (economy, science, law etc.) while comprehending the emergence of a world society as a necessary corollary of the process of functional differentiation (Luhmann 1991: 60; Stichweh 2000: 18). Both world polity scenarios of the diffusion of global cultural goods (Greve and Heintz 2005: 111) and systems theory's narrative of universal functional differentiation have been pointed out for being rather insensitive towards specific empirical questions (Werron and Holzer 2009: 7). Likewise, in the field of global history the 'preoccupation with connectivity' (Conrad 2018: 824) has been countered by a research agenda that is more interested in 'the strategies of local actors' (ibid.: 825) towards the global as well as in concrete 'articulations of globality'

(Bell 2013: 257). Generally speaking, current debates on globalization reveal the impulse to empirically substantiate its grand narratives.

Different paths have been taken to theoretically articulate this general unease. In sociology, the distinction between 'micro' and 'macro' has turned out to be one of the most prominent pathways taken in this respect. In research on processes of globalization and the formation of a world society/world polity, it has become a frequent trope to juxtapose macro- and micro-sociological approaches to conceptualizing the global (Greve and Heintz 2005: 111; Knorr-Cetina and Bruegger 2002: 907). In line with this seeming conceptual divide, macro- and micro-oriented modes of analysis have been competing with each other both in addressing the drivers of globalization as well as in conceptualizing the relationship between the global and the local.

In contrast to 'macro-structural' accounts of a global social reality, sociologists from different theoretical backgrounds have attempted to cultivate a perspective that shifts attention to the local phenomena that are embedded in, and entangled with, processes of globalization. As Saskia Sassen (2007: 4) observes: 'Conceiving of globalization not simply in terms of interdependence and global institutions but also as inhabiting the national [we could add "the local" – authors] opens up a vast and largely unaddressed research agenda'. In trying to redress this situation, Sassen (ibid.: 193) has called attention to the 'microsites' and 'microspaces' in which global dynamics unfold. In this context, she (ibid.: 8) studies global cities as sites of local 'instantiations of the global'. Similarly, Karin Knorr-Cetina and Urs Bruegger (2002) speak of 'global microstructures' when studying specific orders and patterns of social interaction which maintain global financial markets. Efforts to provide stronger micro-foundations can also be observed within neo-institutionalist theory. As has been critically noted, however, a micro-perspective might be incompatible with a general research frame that still tends to overlook individual actors (cf. Powell and Colyvas 2008; Hasse and Schmidt 2010; Kirchner et al. 2015).

While it is generally regarded as plausible to split globalization research along the micro/macro distinction, there exist a number of attempts to employ more complex conceptual frameworks to adequately describe processes of globalization. Sassen (2007: 8), for instance, calls for 'different conceptual architectures' which require 'new categories that do not presuppose the customary dualities of national/global and local/global'.[1] In a similar manner, Rudolf Stichweh (2000: 16), building on Niklas Luhmann's reservations about the micro/macro distinction,[2] stresses that an interaction may be simultaneously attributed to both the micro- and macro-levels. According to this understanding, world society actualizes itself through particular local acts: 'The fusion of the global and the local takes places at the local level' (ibid.: 257).

The shortcomings of the micro/macro distinction have been addressed in different areas of globalization research and have inspired a variety of conceptual alternatives. In the field of migration studies (Faist 2018; Sassen 2001; Basch et al. 1997; Pries 2002), scholars have recognized that the dynamics of regular cross-border interactions sustain a space with its own right and rules. Thus, for example, *transnational social spaces* in which processes in the micro and macro dimensions intersect have come under the spotlight. In contrast to typical perspectives on globalization, the literature on transnational spaces primarily shifts the focus to the meso-level dynamics of everyday practices. In a similar sense, the concept of *glocalization* is probably the most prominent attempt to conceive of global and local processes as representing two sides of the same coin. Shifting the focus from top-down perspectives that consider globalization as separated from local, regional or national processes, the glocalization literature emphasizes the spatial multidimensionality of societal phenomena (Robertson 1998; Wellman 1999; Bauman 1998).[3] The literature on glocalization envisions modes of observing the global through the local that allow it to be shown that 'globalization is responsible both for homogeneity and heterogeneity' (Roudometof 2015: 9). The concept of glocalization has raised awareness of the fact that globalization does not take place beyond the local level, but operates through it.

Observation as a practice that conditions globalization

The present volume follows up on attempts to undermine the micro/macro distinction of conventional globalization research. We acknowledge that analysing globalization and dividing globalization research along micro/macro lines can be heuristically and analytically fruitful in many respects. However, we think it is useful to employ a distinction that has the advantage of covering both micro- and macro-phenomena and structures in processes of globalization: Bettina Heintz and Tobias Werron argue that globalization may unfold in two different, yet often related dimensions that both cover and span the micro/macro distinction. Firstly, globalization occurs on the dimension of global/transnational *networks* and *connections*. This means that, in various areas of society such as the economy, transport, law, entertainment etc., interconnections emerge that are not confined to the borders of the nation-state. Secondly, globalization takes place at the level of *description* and *observation* (Heintz and Werron 2011: 361f.). The field of law is globalizing, for example, not only through international treaties and supranational institutions, but also through judges taking account of legal developments in other countries and voluntarily aligning their decisions with foreign jurisprudence and the idea of a world law (see the chapter by Preuss, this volume). The discipline of Social Work does not react to an objective world in which it then establishes itself, but rather engenders the global in manifold ways in its own discourse and practices of observation (see the chapter by Holtgreve and Giebeler). Geopolitical world conflicts, such as the conflict between Russia and the West, can be traced back to competing ways of envisioning the world (see the chapters by Akopov, Elmuradov, Vásquez, and by Sunca).

This volume thus focuses on the descriptive dimension of globalization that has received far less attention in globalization research than the level of connectivity. With Werron (2012: 112), we agree that it is worthwhile to describe globalization processes independently of the dimension of connectivity. Globalization phenomena are also recognizable where connectivity is limited or even actively resisted. Phenomena such as the isolation of a state through border protection, anti-globalization resentments, concepts of global enemies (e.g. bankers, Jews, etc.) can thus be interpreted as globalization phenomena (see the chapters by Jacobsen and Werron and by Aksakal). Moreover, by focusing on the level of description, it is possible to identify models of worldmaking that elude the dominant globalization narratives by drawing on unorthodox epistemologies of the global and the world. Notably philosophy and literature offer the potential to counter the Eurocentrism of the current globalization discourse with multipolar and planetary alternatives (see the chapters by Gasser and by Auer).

Sharing the impression that there is a tendency in globalization research towards self-explanatory and universalistic narratives that are hard to pin down empirically, we follow up on the suggestion that processes of globalization materialize in specific local acts, discourses and practices of observation. From this perspective, the global as a spatial framework is not self-evident, but rather 'constructed' in concrete practices. The contributions gathered here capitalize on the insights of the spatial turn in sociology. Rather than starting from prefabricated spatial assumptions, they pursue the question of 'how the global is generated *socially* in each case' (Epple 2018: 395). Yet, despite their focus on concrete practices, they seek nonetheless to make a contribution to *globalization* research and attempt to avoid the shortcomings of many studies professing a 'micro-sociological' perspective that tend to concentrate on local practices of organization and interaction but neglect the question of how the *global* is envisioned and observed in these practices. Although the global is implicitly presupposed in many 'micro-founded' studies, it is not addressed as an object of investigation. Rather than confronting the grand narratives of globalization research with meticulous isolationist accounts of microsites, our goal is to add empirical and historical depth to these narratives by examining practices of worldmaking as empirical evidence of how narratives on the global and the world evolve and sustain themselves. The focus is thus directed towards the *conditioning* practices that underlie processes of institutionalization, diffusion, and functional differentiation among others.

There are various societal domains in which it is far from evident that agents would be likely to position themselves in relation to the global (Heintz and Werron 2011: 361). For instance, it seems highly unlikely that a Constitutional Court would transcend its national legal framework by quoting the decision of a foreign court. Likewise, a claim that educators all over the world take global educational standards into account when implementing reforms at local schools and universities would require explanation. The existence of global modes of observation visible in various social fields and areas comes with prerequisites attached and is, from a historical standpoint, relatively new. Stichweh stresses that (2019: 517): 'Observation was tied to closely circumscribed localities for a long time'. From this point of departure, globalization research has commonly called attention to the various ways in which new communications technologies have had deterritorializing effects on practices of communication and observation. While this is a valuable perspective, research tends to neglect to reconstruct *how exactly* modes of observation in specific social domains have transformed in the course of globalization dynamics. To which problem does the globalization of specific observational practices respond? How is the global conceived in these practices?

The aim of this book is to identify and contextualize specific modes of observation and communication by which the global is addressed. Each contribution analyses a 'special type of communications [...] that explicitly address the world as an issue and are thereby constitutive of the world' (Stichweh 2000: 240). Professing a broadly constructivist understanding of processes of globalization, we acknowledge that the world/the global is created in practices of communication and observation. We thus seek to retrace globalization on the level of these practices. In this context, the communicative conditions necessary for the perspective of the global are to be brought to the fore. We are interested in 'the way in which humans fabricated symbolic systems, how they constructed and reconstructed worlds' (Bell 2013: 258). Through which narratives, images and models have different agents created the discursive horizon of the global?

Fields and theories

By focusing on practices that envision the global from field-related standpoints we attempt to retrace how the global is created by different agents in different fields and discourses. Generally, this means that the global is inscribed as the relevant horizon of meaning, which needs to be distinguished from any structural definition of the global. It says nothing about the structural establishment of connections on a global scale (cf. Albert 2016: 27ff.). While, arguably, it has historically often been the case, there is no necessity for a 'phenomenological globalization' to precede a 'structural' one. Durable connections might very well be established and actualized before they are inscribed into the meaning horizon of the global. This phenomenological approach is neither defined by, nor restricted to, a specific discipline or a fixed theoretical frame. Numerous disciplines are capable of adopting a 'second order' perspective and retracing practices of worldmaking in a phenomenological manner. This applies to social science disciplines as well as the domain of cultural theory – for instance the field of literary studies which, as illustrated by Lucy Gasser's contribution to this volume, may comprehend literature as a 'world-making activity' (Cheah 2016: 2).

In this sense, the present volume responds to a research interest that has become particularly pronounced in the field of global history. In this field, conceptual problems such as the micro/macro divide and the global/local distinction are regularly discussed (cf. Conrad 2016: 129ff., 230ff.). In tangible proximity to the sociological discussions outlined above, the advocates of a new global history distance themselves from the universal narratives of historical globalization research, conventionally known as world history. In the course of this reorientation, criticism is also directed at approaches within the field of global history that primarily deal with the reconstruction of transnational networks and the global interconnectedness of structures, goods, ideas, etc. (for a description of this current, see Moyn and Sartori 2013: 9ff.). Global historians like Sebastian Conrad and Duncan Bell challenge this 'diffusionist bias' (Conrad 2018: 824) with a research agenda that explores globalization from the perspective of particular actors, practices and strategies (Conrad 2018: 825; Bell 2013: 257). As part of this 'second order approach' (Moyn and Sartori 2013: 5), categories like 'the global' or 'the West' become the *object* rather than a fixed spatial *frame* of analysis (Bell 2013: 273). The emergence of a global consciousness and its required means of representation and imagination then themselves become a problem of global history (Moyn and Sartori 2013: 16f.).

The perspective on the world and the global suggested here allows the following chapters to take their inspiration from a variety of theoretical backgrounds, such as systems theory, neo-institutionalism and postcolonial theory. Many theoretical traditions possess the heuristic potential to pin wide-scale processes of globalization to concrete practices and processes of communication and observation. This also holds true for systems theory and neo-institutionalism, even though both theoretical traditions, as mentioned above, run the risk of being empirically insensitive and/or giving structural-deterministic accounts of processes of globalization. The notion of 'observation' provides systems theory with a key concept for phenomenologically reconstructing how the global has become a distinct category in particular observational practices (Stichweh 2019: 517). Likewise, by stressing that the diffusion of cultural ideas depends, at least to a certain degree, on their 'theorization', neo-institutionalist scholars have displayed a great deal of sensitivity to the epistemological preconditions that underpin the diffusion of global cultural goods (Strang and Meyer 1993: 492). A common denominator of the conceptual frameworks employed in this volume may be found in their shared constructivist understanding of global social reality. Globalization depends on models, narratives and categories by which the global/the world is observed. The theories drawn upon allow us to investigate empirically how the global is instantiated in particular practices of observation.

The 'second-order' approach pursued here requires the question of whether practices of observation address global matters conceptually as the *world* or as the *global* to be initially left open. In sociology, the notion of *world* serves to establish a phenomenological lens different from the diffusionist grand narratives of globalization. *World* in this sense can be understood as a projective representation of a global horizon created by a social system using its own means and resources (Stichweh 2000: 234). In historical scholarship, by contrast, universal narratives of globalization are ascribed to the field of *world* history while the 'actor's category approach' (Bell 2013: 257) finds its place in *global* history.

The focus on concrete practices follows attempts to apply insights from sociological practice theory to research on globalization (Epple 2018). It is concrete practices that consolidate social structures through routinization. Applied to the theme of this book, the task is to locate small-scale practices that are constitutive of globalization processes (ibid.: 406). Thus, if one concentrates on practices as 'drivers of globalization', the grand narratives typical of globalization research may be fruitfully backed up by diverse empirical accounts. Such an approach holds the potential to combine a phenomenological notion of the global with structural accounts of global social reality, thus also potentially avoiding the seeming reluctance of micro-sociological approaches to engage in theory (building). Global trends, which at first glance may seem to follow a uniform pattern, can thus be analysed with regard to the possible heterogeneity of their constituent practices. As Epple (ibid.: 404) rightly points out, the praxeological perspective sensitizes to the different practical reference problems of certain global developments.

On the basis of case studies, the contributions to this volume thus reconstruct how the global manifests itself in particular practices of observation. Each chapter questions the master narrative of globalization prevalent in the field in question and adds empirical as well as historical depth to it. The individual contributors retrace why, how and in what contexts different sorts of agents and actors position themselves in relation to the global. They attempt to observe how the global is envisioned by different agents and how the specific vision of the global has informed and shaped discourses. This phenomenological stance allows us both to place the spotlight on the driving forces of globalization and to undermine the dichotomy of the micro/macro divide in globalization research. We attempt to comprehend how globalization unfolds in the eyes of the observer. Hence, the focus is on the actors and agents of globalization (Holzer et al. 2015: 5; Epple 2018: 394).

Empirical inspirations

Assuming such a perspective, Werron and Holzer (2009: 13) highlight the field-specific methods of theorizing and modelling that have proven essential for the disembedding of entire social fields from local, regional and national contexts. This angle has the potential to identify the schemes and models that allow field-specific global publics to be addressed. For instance, in order to understand the globalization of economy, attention has to be paid to the field-intrinsic modes of observation which have broadened the scope of economic communication and transaction: 'Economic theorization as a condition of the disembedding of the economic field starts with basic schemes such as prices or product categories that allow for the "commensuration" [...] of formerly unique or incomparable products and lead to increasingly complex and abstract models such as market statistics or neoclassical concepts of the market' (ibid.).

In a similar manner, it has been demonstrated how certain narratives have been pivotal for the emergence of a global mode of observation in the world of sports. Narratives of comparative competition and theoretical models such as tables, records and rankings have been the necessary prerequisites for the idea of simultaneous global competition (ibid.: 14). On the basis of these conditions, modern sport has been driven towards the global. At the turn of the 20th century, the 'projective inclusion' (Stichweh 2000: 234) of the global was palpably present, for instance in the decision to refer to the final competition in the baseball season as the 'World Series' (ibid.; Werron 2005). Certain semantic and media conditions were essential for this turn towards the global. For the development of sport into world sport, the 'local limitation of comparative horizons' (Werron 2008: 105) had to be overcome.

Sebastian Conrad has convincingly illustrated how the field of global history may harness the 'second order' approach sketched above in order to critically engage with the master narratives of globalization research. He examines the practical motives and strategies that led the Japanese to adapt the Western temporal regime in the 1870s. He refutes the assumption that the change in the temporal regime was the product of colonial 'top-down imposition' (Conrad 2018: 840) and the direct 'result of [global] transfers and of connections' (ibid.: 842). As the spread of Western clocks and calendars in Japan well before the 19th century proves, mere cultural transfer cannot satisfactorily explain the Japanese adoption of the modern understanding of time at the end of the 19th century. Rather, as Conrad points out, the 'sweeping societal transformations' (ibid.: 842) within Japan must be closely examined in order to find a plausible explanation for the sudden change of temporal mentality. The overcoming of traditional notions of time through modern temporal representation may then be understood as 'one of the ways historical actors responded to a series of fundamental social changes triggered by technological innovation and large-scale mobility, by projects of state building and empire, by capitalist production and global market integration' (ibid.: 847)

In a similar manner, Angelika Epple has demonstrated how a constructivist perspective on the observation- and communication-based 'making of the global' may be combined with an approach that takes into account questions of social agency. Tracing the process of how *Stollwerck Gold* chocolate has become a global brand, Epple investigates in great detail 'how a global visual language has appeared to be reasonable *from a company-internal perspective*' (Epple 2007: 14, emphasis added). In so doing, she not only shows how the global view in modern marketing and advertising strategies depends on the 'invention' of a universal and spatially decontextualized product brand (a 'world brand'), but also, taking a functionalist perspective, demonstrates that the idea of a product brand emerged as a reaction to new forms of communication in the sale process, notably the fact that the personal relationship between the salesman/producer and the consumer had been rendered obsolete by changing economic dynamics in the 19th century. The preconditions for global marketing strategies may thus be studied at a local level, taking into account the motives that have driven a company to detach a product from its regional and national context (ibid.: 19).

We take these empirical studies as inspirations to further investigate how the global manifests itself in empirical practices of observation. Turning to the fields of social work, literature, philosophy, law, anti-Semitism, foreign politics and international diplomacy, revolutionary politics and migration studies, the contributions to this volume do not simply reiterate broad narratives on how the respective fields and the corresponding agents have turned global. Rather, choosing the 'actor's category approach' (Bell 2013: 257), every contribution empirically retraces how the global has emerged as a specific theme in the respective discourse under investigation and how different agents position themselves in relation to this global horizon.

Overview of chapters

Each of this volume's chapters takes a perspective on envisioning the global in a range of cases and from different disciplinary perspectives, namely IR/political science, sociology, Social Work, literary studies and philosophy.

In her chapter, *Gladys Vásquez* discusses the vision of the 'New World' espoused during the first half of the 19th century in Latin America. She asks how diplomats compared the 'old' to the 'new' world, and demonstrates the contradictions inherent in the intra-regional discussions on the reconfiguration of power after the end of formal colonialism. Her chapter shows how the political representatives of the Americas used visions of the 'old' and 'new' worlds in order to establish a new balance of power. Practices of comparison are used as a theoretical approach in global historical research in order to examine the discourses of the American political elites who attempted to create an American Confederation.

Marc Jacobsen and *Tobias Werron* discuss the emergence of modern nationalism as a worldview both particular and comprehensive. They show how anti-Semitism must not only be understood as hostility towards Jews, but also as a lens for interpreting world affairs and a vision of 'how the world should be'. From a perspective of historical sociology, they outline the connections between globalization, nationalism and anti-Semitism between the late 18th and the mid-19th century. Focusing on examples from German discourse, they show how nationalism is not only a reaction to, but also a product of, globalization. In addition, they trace the historical entanglements between nationalism and anti-Semitism.

Assuming a sociological perspective, *Karlson Preuß'* chapter investigates how the discipline of Comparative Law embraced the notion of world law at the turn of the 20th century. Critically engaging with the cosmopolitan aspirations of comparative legal literature, his contribution historically contextualizes the popular idea that legal practice will induce the global harmonization of different jurisdictions. He detects hidden discursive motives and strategies underlying the ostentatious universalism of early-20th-century comparative lawyers. The chapter demonstrates how many legal scholars invoked the idea of a 'world law' in order to justify a politicized model of judicial decision-making.

Sandra Holtgreve and *Cornelia Giebeler* discuss four dimensions of contemporary Social Work discourse's approaches to 'the global'. They ask which understandings of the concept prevail in discussions of social work practice and theory. Their chapter demonstrates how social workers can be understood as world political actors 'from below', and argues that the global serves firstly as a professional rationale for responding to the effects of globalization, secondly as a perspective from which to respond to heterogeneous lifeworlds, thirdly as a common ethical base for the profession, and fourthly as a global arena for professional action. These four dimensions characterize the particular way in which social work can observe the global from the margins of society, making the profession unavoidably pluralist and critical in relation to universalizing arguments in globalization studies.

Yasin Sunca studies the Kurdish case in order to analyse global politico-social and historical processes in the emergence of revolutions, asking how the revolutionaries' observations of their global environment shaped the events in Rojava. From a perspective of historical sociology, he elaborates on three processes: international relations in the struggle for nation-state formation; the international leftist ideology that underlies radical-democratic social transformation; and global geopolitics during the Syrian war, which opened a space for renegotiating regional hierarchies. These three aspects lead Sunca to the central argument that 'the international' was an integral part of the vision that drove the Rojava revolution from its very beginnings.

Mustafa Aksakal observes how global policies and politics are perceived, and replied to, at local, national and regional level as regards the relation between migration and development. The chapter provides an overview of debates on the migration–development nexus in Latin America. Their inherent focus on structuralism in the 1950s, dependency theory in the 1970–80s, neo-structuralism in the 1990s, and *Buen Vivir* from the 2000s on provided key narratives that promoted a particular way of observing the world. In this context, he is able to develop a counter-narrative to hegemonic discussions on the nexus.

Sergei Akopov analyses practices of mapping the global in contemporary Russian politics. His contribution establishes 'loneliness' as a key factor in reading international relations with regard to Russia. Akopov argues that Vladimir Putin has paved the way for a 'politics of loneliness' that informs Russian claims to sovereignty and the right of intervention, while Russia has reinvented itself as a lonely entity in current world politics in the past decade.

Engaging with Russian politics as well, *Aziz Elmuradov* describes the confrontational dynamics between Russia and the European Union as a conflict of competing visions of the world. Analysing contemporary testimonies from Russian political philosophy and political discourse, Elmuradov demonstrates that the idea of a 'multipolar world' underpins current Russian foreign policy. His contribution retraces the geopolitical, historical and civilizational dimensions of the concept of multipolarity.

The final two chapters draw on literary studies and philosophy in order to develop conceptual alternatives to Eurocentric ways of envisioning the world. *Lucy Gasser* focuses on literature as an imaginative practice of worldmaking. Taking a postcolonial perspective, she explores travel narratives from the Global South that challenge the Eurocentrism of imperialist globalization narratives by recentring the global and creating novel horizons for the world. Her contribution pays tribute to literature from the Global South as a resource for imagining new global centres and pluralistic alternatives to colonial narratives of globalization.

Michael Auer turns to the writings of the philosopher Kostas Axelos in order to propose the notion of 'the planetary' as a conceptual alternative to 'the global'. The chapter reconstructs how Axelos took the planetary paradigm from the philosophical discourse of the Weimar Republic and developed it into a postcolonial alternative to the canonical narratives of European modernity. Opposing the burdened legacy of globalization discourse, Auer honours planetary thinking as an alternative methods of worldmaking that transcends the centrism of Western narratives of modernity.

The present volume in its entirety, and most of its individual chapters, emerged from work carried out within the Research Training Group 'World Politics: The Emergence of Political Arenas and Modes of Observation in World Society' at Bielefeld University. This group's research agenda has two main streams: 'modes of organization' and 'modes of observation'. This distinction reflects the fact that, like all social systems and contexts, modern world politics, like other globalized fields, can and needs to be characterized and analysed in terms of the formation both of distinct structures and of distinct frames of reference. By providing insights into the phenomenological dimension of globalization, the present volume falls squarely into that latter thematic area.

Notes

1   Remarkably, Sassen herself does not seem to fully live up to this call when, for example, she distinguishes between 'the formation of explicitly global institutions and processes', for instance the WTO, on the one hand, and local/national dynamics that involve 'processes that do not necessarily scale at the global level as such yet [...] are part of globalization', on the other hand, thereby suggesting a clear cut between macro-sociological and micro-sociological grasps on globalization (Sassen 2007: 5f.). We argue that the global manifests itself at the same time, yet differently on the micro- and on the macro-level.

2   'The micro/macro distinction reduces the complexity of the description of an object, disregarding reciprocal interdependencies among the levels' (Luhmann 1987: 126).

3   On the relation between this multi-dimensionality and conceptualizations of world society as a social 'whole', see the debate Albert 2007, Robertson 2009 and Albert 2009.

From Region to World, and Back Again
How Latin Americans Envisioned the Global (1810-1840)

Gladys Vásquez

Following the independence of many Spanish colonies in America in the early 19th century, the new American diplomats began seeking to integrate their new states into the international system.[1] To do so, they intensified their diplomacy through congresses and conferences where they created a discourse to integrate with the world as independent states. In 1822 Simón Bolívar summoned the leaders of the former Spanish colonies to the Congress of Panama, the first to initiate the routinization of the American congresses. Bolívar explained that the Congress's objective was to establish an American system that would trace the course of their relations with the world (Bolívar 2010 [1824]: 40ff.). Discussing the American system allowed diplomats to construct a world regional framework that provided a platform to envision the world and to think about global affairs.

How did American diplomats envision the global world through the lens of the regional world? They envisioned it as divided into the New World and the Old. Even though this vision was from a long tradition (Epple 2019: 137ff.), the relationship between the two worlds had changed since American independence. Spain refused to accept the independence of its former American colonies and the other European powers hesitated to accept them as sovereign equals (Petersen and Schultz 2018: 111). Observing this relationship of conflict, diplomats negotiated an American system that conceived international relations as a search for world equilibrium. To understand the world regional framework, it is therefore necessary to examine the comparative practices of the American diplomats, based on their observations of the world. This chapter evaluates the significance of observing and comparing both worlds as these diplomats attempted to construct their system of international relations by examining the communications, essays, acts, and treaties resulting from their interaction. These comparisons supported actors in constructing images and narratives in which conceptualizations like 'the New World', 'the Old World', and 'civilized and uncivilized' were reconstituted.

The focus of this analysis is not on a dichotomy between the New World and the Old but on a triadic relation shaped by diplomats. According to Epple, when people compare 'they always imply a criterion that enables them to place differences and similarities in a comparative relation. This criterion in respect to which entities are compared is the *tertium comparationis*' (Epple 2019: 141). Through their interaction, the diplomats made comparisons between two entities, the New World and the Old, which became the two *comparata*. While these *comparata* were not new, independence made political order an important *tertium*, so actors shaped comparisons between both worlds in relation to it. Leal states that the notion of 'order' became fundamental in Iberoamerica due to the radical political transformations of the early 19th century. It was then that the notion of a 'new order' – understood as 'a new order of things' or 'a new political order' – was developed in contrast to 'the old order' or 'the previous order' (Leal 2017: 16).[2] Leal based these notions of order on the terms used by historical actors. In their discourses, diplomats compared the two worlds in terms of their political order: the 'old order' was represented by the absolute monarchy that had subordinated the New World in a colonial hierarchy, but independence had transformed the Americas into a world region that would institutionalize 'a new political order' opposed to this monarchy and that would reorder the world. The political order became the criterion for distinguishing the New World from the Old.

The chapter is structured as follows: I explain first the context of conflict and negotiation in which the diplomats were situated as well as the perspectives and purposes that conditioned their observations and comparisons of the world; then I consider the reconstruction of the New World based on a world regional discourse.

American diplomats and the post-independence context

The Hispanic American wars of independence were an irregular and violent process that began with the fall of the Spanish monarchy in 1810 and lasted through the first decades of the 19th century (Lynch 1986: 1). It was a conflict that marked the new relationship between the two worlds. While the American colonies were declaring their independence, Spain still claimed ownership over these territories. The conflict that initially arose between Spain and its colonies was reinterpreted by the actors of independence when the Holy Alliance supported the return of the absolute monarchy in Spain. From then on, these actors observed a threat that spread from Spain to a broader Old World. Conversely, in an effort to resolve this conflict, the actors – American diplomats – attempted to negotiate with the Old World to recognize American independence. It should be noted that the professionalization of diplomacy did not occur in most parts of America until later in the 19th century. Early American states often required their representatives to engage in a variety of activities throughout their careers taking on, for example, both military and diplomatic roles. For this reason, when I use the term 'diplomats', I mean those responsible for planning, organizing, and establishing international relations. The negotiation proposals were discussed in the American Congresses of these years. Bernardo de Monteagudo, an independentist from a territory that is now Argentina, constructed a vision of a Hispanic American nation and stressed that a Hispanic American Congress should be held to end the war with Spain, consolidate independence and to confront the threat of the Holy Alliance (Monteagudo 1825: 16f.). It was precisely at the Congress of Panama that the formation of a large American confederation was proposed to enter into negotiations with the Old World on equal terms (Bolívar 2010 [1824]: 40ff.). Proponents of the confederation aimed to institutionalize a new political order in the New World whose authority was based on a General Assembly of American States that was going to create a new order of things in the world.

This section focuses on how American diplomats positioned themselves in relation to the world in the post-independence context of conflict and negotiation. It shows who these diplomats were and why they observed and compared. Diplomats belonged to the *Criollo* elite of lettered men. Anderson describes the *Criollo* as a person of European descent (at least in theory) born in America. *Criollos* shared a common language and ancestry with the Spanish (Anderson 1993: 77). Even so, because they were born in America, *Criollos*, unlike the Spaniards, were not allowed to hold principal civil and ecclesiastical positions in the colonies. This is explained by the fact that America became part of Iberian globalization in the 16th century (Gruzinsky 2010: 51ff.), at which time a hierarchical relationship was built on its political subordination to Europe (Quijano and Wallerstein 1992: 584ff.)

Diplomats participated in a '*Criollo* legal consciousness' that Obregón (2006: 820) defines as a limited set of shared discourses and practices concerning their awareness of regional unity. Obregón explains this consciousness on the basis of two interpretations. First, they assumed that they were part of the metropolitan centre as descendants of Europeans at the same time as they challenged the centre with their regional uniqueness. They defined themselves in opposition to Europeans by claiming a sense of Americanness (ibid.: 815, 818). In his famous *Letter from Jamaica*, Bolívar wrote that Americans were 'neither Indian nor European, but a species midway between' (Bolívar 2015 [1815]: 17). Second, they also assumed that law in the region originated in Spanish law, but believed in the uniqueness of an American interpretation of that law (Obregón 2006: 815). To Bolívar, Americans derived their rights to the New World from Europe; however, they had to assert these rights against those same Europeans (Bolívar 2015 [1815]: 17).

The asymmetrical relationship between the two worlds represented the political hierarchy between America and Europe. After all, 'it was European authors who prescribed what it was to be understood as "old" and what it was to be viewed by comparison as "new" and how the relationship between the two was to be evaluated' (Epple 2019: 144). Feres recalls that the asymmetrical is defined as the condition in which one group names and another is named, but the named group is at the same time unable to react to the act of naming. The named group is almost always excluded from the political community (Feres 2017: 93). Nevertheless, from the 18th century on, it was American scholars who questioned the legitimacy of this asymmetrical relationship and claimed a new comparability assumed by them. Later, wars of independence increased the tendency to make comparisons from observations of the worlds in conflict. Because of American achievements in war, scholars observed a new order in the world where America, according to Feres (2009: 56), received a political identity. That meant the loss of legitimacy of the former power relation between the two worlds. The observation of this political transformation encouraged these scholars to shape a world regional discourse that recreated the old practices of comparison initiated by Europeans.

Hamnett (2013: 40) argues that independence transformed America into 'a new factor in international politics', but the lack of recognition of its independence by Europe became a cause of conflict that continued during the first decades of the 19th century. *Criollos*, who in the new context were already able to hold a government position, appointed their diplomats to negotiate this recognition. The preservation of independence was the maintenance of the new order (Leal 2010: 46). With this aim, they travelled in different delegations to Europe and presented themselves as Americans and no longer as subjects of Spain. They negotiated a shift from the former criterion of comparison that excluded America from the international political community. The break with the monarchical political order transformed the asymmetric relationship and made both worlds equal before the international community – this even though the Old World defended the old order and the New World assumed a political order formed by governments legitimately constituted by the 'will of the peoples' (*la voluntad de los pueblos*) (Monteagudo and Mosquera 2010 [1822]: 14), peoples who 'had broken the chains that cruel Spain had imposed on them from the [Old World]' (Bolívar 2010 [1822]: 3). The will of the peoples replaced the will of the monarch that founded the old order. The term 'people' could be understood at the same time as a set of inhabitants and as the place populated with inhabitants (Melo Ferreira 2009: 1120). This double meaning influenced the use of the term. However, when the diplomats mentioned 'peoples' they were referring mainly to the *Criollo* inhabitants led by their local political elites. During the negotiations, they displayed a vision of the world in which America and Europe no longer had a hierarchical relationship.

The incorporation of Spain into the Holy Alliance in 1816 in support of restoring Spanish absolute monarchy shifted negotiations. Until that time, comparisons regarding the conflict had been based primarily on observations of America and Spain, but when Spain requested the support of the Holy Alliance at the Congress of Aachen in 1818 to regain control of its colonies, Americans began to observe the Old World beyond Spain. Monteagudo reflected that, until then, their struggle had been against 'a nation that was impotent, discredited and sick with anarchy' but from then on 'the danger that threatened them was to enter into conflict with the Holy Alliance' (Monteagudo 1825: 10). For this reason, negotiations by means of delegations were no longer sufficient because, as Monteagudo continued, Americans had to consider 'the probability of a new conflict and the mass of power that (the Holy Alliance) could use against us' (ibid.: 10).

Maintaining the pre-independence balance of power was the goal of the Holy Alliance (ibid.), according to the new leaders of the American governments. Faced with this situation, diplomats discussed new arguments for negotiation that would construct a balance of power where America's independent position would be retained. The importance of establishing a balance of power to keep America from being subjugated again had already been stressed by Bolívar (2012 [1813]: 36):

> The ambition of the nations of Europe carries the yoke of slavery to other parts of the world, and all these parts of the world should seek to establish a balance between them and Europe [...] I call this the equilibrium of the Universe, and it must enter into the forethoughts of American politics.

Following this vision, while representatives of the Holy Alliance relied on old order comparisons to sustain the legitimacy of the former balance of power, American scholars intensified comparative observations to legitimize the position and power they had achieved through independence. I will give more details of these comparative observations in the next section. Power was an important issue in this post-independence context; in particular, American leaders were very aware that their actual capacity to support their claims was limited. According to Robert Burr (1995: 38) the *Criollos* took their cue from observing the European experience which conceived international relations as a search for an equilibrium in power.

Americans analysed their position and considered their opportunities in a conflict between America and the Holy Alliance. This way they sustained the formation of an American alliance that would create a new international balance of power. Considering the European experience, Americans found the Congress of Vienna a successful diplomatic event but 'for the monarchies of the Old World' (Monteagudo 1825: 19), setting down laws of alliance and union through which they obtained successful results against France (Belis et al. 2010 [1826]: 159). For this reason, Bolívar summoned the American leaders to the Congress of Panama to create a great American confederation. He wrote that the congress was destined to establish 'a truly new order of things' through the formation of an extraordinary league against which the Holy Alliance could be inferior in power (Bolívar 2010 [1826]: 51f.). According to Leal (2017: 16), the first elaborations of a new order were shaped in debates that highlighted the struggle between constituted power (the old order) and a power in the process of being constituted (a new order). In contrast to the aims of the Congress of Vienna, stated Pedro Gual, Colombian Foreign Minister and author of the constitution of the Republic of Florida:

> this confederation should not be formed simply on the principles of an ordinary alliance for offence and defence: it should be much narrower than the one that has been formed recently in Europe against the freedoms of peoples. Ours must be a Society of sister nations... (Gual 2010 [1821]: 8)

When diplomats discussed the construction of a confederation, they intended to distinguish their confederation from the characteristics observed in the European experience. To begin with, unlike the Congress of Vienna, the American gathering would create a permanent assembly. Then, the Congress of Panama would be the first of many congresses that would establish the routinization of diplomatic interaction. Thanks to this confederation, the nations of the New World would be linked by a common law that would fix their international relations (Bolívar 2010 [1826]: 52). Under this common law, the diplomats would resume their negotiations, representing not a single nation but a whole world region. The attendees at this first congress were the Republics of La Gran Colombia (currently Colombia, Ecuador, Venezuela and Panama), Mexico, Peru, Bolivia and the Central American Federation (currently Guatemala, Honduras, Costa Rica, Nicaragua and El Salvador).

To the American diplomats, the Congress of Vienna defended the legitimacy of the order of the *ancien régime* by which Spain claimed possession of its former colonies, whereas the Congress of Panama defended a new order of the world based on the legitimacy of American independence. At the same time, this *truly new order* would establish a *perfect balance* (Bolívar 2010 [1826]: 52). Bolívar understood this perfect balance as resulting from actions taken by the Confederation to prevent any power from dominating the American states and altering both their internal and external order; in the first case the confederation would be the arbiter that would prevent any American state from accumulating more power with respect to the other American states, and in the second the Confederation would combine the efforts of the American states to prevent any European power from seeking to return America to the old order. For Monteagudo, the Congress was a necessity, a view that he sustained in his essay 'On the Necessity of a General Federation among the Spanish-American States' when he was Minister of Government and Foreign Affairs for Peru. He explained the two purposes of the confederation: to unite the resources of the American peoples against the common enemy and secondly, to gather the representatives, who until then had problems communicating, in one place to organize an American system directed by a permanent assembly (Monteagudo 1825: 5ff.).

As a result, when considering their own system of international relations, the diplomats created a world regional framework. Excluded for centuries from public positions, this framework allowed *Criollos* to justify their position as leaders of the New World and a new order of the world. To construct the American system, they assumed comparability from a political point of view.

In this sense, to demonstrate that America and Europe were equal political actors in the world order, the diplomats placed similarities and differences in a comparative relation by focusing on the political order and their relation with morality, history and the standard of civilization.

The reconstruction of the New World

The vision of the New World before independence was built on comparisons whose most 'prominent topics were comparisons of climate, of nature, of the role of European antiquity, religion and customs, of the level of art culture and sciences; and of physique, disease and sexuality or the relationship between sexes' (Epple 2019: 153). While these comparisons may have recognized some advantages for the New World, they were not meant to break the hierarchical relationship. However, independence changed the topics of the comparisons. Leaders of the new republics that emerged, like Monteagudo, presented independence as an event that changed their 'way of being and existing in the universe', that is to say, it canceled all the colonial obligations and indicated their new relationships with the world (Monteagudo 1825: 5). As Epple and colleagues understand it, 'the one who claims comparability and detects or determines the perspective, the tertium comparationis, holds the power to confront and to evaluate the comparata' (Epple et al. 2020: 16). American diplomats then set their standard for comparing the world, discouraging comparisons that legitimized the colonial relationship and encouraging those that provided the New World with a political identity in the new order. It should be stressed, as Feres (2009: 54) argues, that during the first decades of the 19th century there was a period of high politicization and conceptual change. This section focuses on the work of diplomats to reconstruct the world order and the image of the New World – more specifically, on how they put America in a new relationship with Europe when the legitimacy of independence was both a cause of conflict and a motive for negotiation with the Old World.

Before continuing, I should mention the geographical vision of both worlds generated by the diplomats. The Old World was not clearly defined. On some occasions it represented only Spain, but then this vision was extended to the members of the Holy Alliance. The position of Great Britain as part of Europe was also not fixed. However, they made a distinction for Southern Europe (*Mediodía de Europa*) even though they did not clearly define it. The European South was seen as a victim of the principles of the Holy

Alliance. The New World, meanwhile, was better defined, mostly understood as the America that had been colonized by Spain (*la America antes Españo*), but they also had a more extended vision of the continent that generated controversy. Some argued about including the United States, Haiti or Brazil, while others, for political and cultural reasons, thought that these republics should not be included.

Once independence was obtained, America was assumed to be similar to Europe because it became a 'subject of international law' (Chiaramonte 2016). Both worlds were equal (or almost equal): 'We are constituted in states with rights equal to those of the Europeans' (Vidaurre 2010 [1826]: 189), was a statement constantly reproduced by the diplomats. Even though the two world regions pursued different political orders, their political orders made them both legitimate subjects of international law, having the same rights before the international system. It should be stressed that 'comparing begins with an assumption that the two comparata are in some way similar' (Epple 2019: 142). As actors assumed this new comparability, they began to relate similarities and differences between the New World and the Old, based on two levels of observation: the act of observation and the act of self-observation. In the first case, they emphasized similarities between the two worlds for the purposes of negotiation while in the second case they emphasized their differences in view of the conflict between them.

For the Americans, the threat of the Holy Alliance, the presence of the Spanish army in their territory and its confrontations with the liberating armies, the sending of military reinforcements from Spain and the Spanish resistance to recognizing independence, confirmed the continuing conflict between both worlds. The conflict increased reflexive comparisons in which diplomats distanced America from Europe creating an insight that made them politically superior to the Old World. This distance was created from self-observation, from observing what was specific to them through which they shaped their image of America. It was then that the criterion of political order was used to distinguish forms of government and their political system. In this sense, diplomats identified two forms of government: monarchical government situated in the Old World and republican government situated in the New. On the other hand, both worlds sustained the legitimacy of their governments by the formation of international systems, one created at the Congress of Vienna and the other at the Congress of Panama. When diplomats discussed the institutionalization of the American international system, they created a self-image of a unique New World. Obregón states that American regionalism in international law is a consequence of a *Criollo* legal consciousness that assumed a belief in American uniqueness (Obregón 2006: 815, 817), since it was a big nation that became independent and a subject of international law by *the will of the people* and not by will of a monarch. For them, Europe defended the return of absolutism while America defended the institutionalization of liberalism. In his analysis of liberalism in the Ibero-American Atlantic, Fernandez (2009: 706) affirms that in those years *liberal* had a political-moral sense associated with freedom and equality and opposed to tyranny and despotisms. Diplomats transformed the perception of the New World through images of a world ideally placed to develop liberal principles through a system that would balance the world, namely the American Confederation. During their interaction, the main differences reflected were based on two topics: the political system and its relation to history.

According to the *Criollo* legal consciousness, differences were self-interpreted as advantages vis-à-vis a monolithic European view of the world (Obregón 2006: 817). In this interpretation, European order was reconstructed as the political system of the *ancien régime* but American order was constructed as a liberal system made up of nations that had fought together for freedom, and eventually transformed themselves into a single nation, the *American nation*. These qualities made America the ideal place to establish a successful confederate system. The Colombian scholar Miguel Pombo described European forms of government as monarchies characterized by 'tyranny and despotism' (Pombo 2010 [1811]: 32f.). Pombo was executed in 1816 during the Spanish reconquest of New Granada for his publications defending a federal system in America, like *'Principles and Advantages of the Federative System'* of 1811. He argued that America was a place that secured freedom for the people in opposition to Europe that preserved the privileges of a few (ibid.: 43). His negative description of the political features of Europe comes out when he (ibid.: 32f.) asks himself if America will follow any particular European people's system:

> Will it be that of the indolent Spaniard, perpetual slave of his aged habits, eternal victim of his kings and of a ministry necessarily corrupted? Will it be that of the Portuguese, ignorant and always degraded under the tutelage of England? Will it be that of the Prussian in his military slavery? Will it be that of the German with his numerous masters? To the Pole under the despotism of the nobles? To the Muscovite with his still barbaric luxury and his slavery? To Italy with its misery and its palaces? To France with its despotic emperor

on the ruins of the Republic, or to England in short that with its Magna Carta, its constitution and its liberties, still has the vices of feudal tyranny?

In addition, the American system would be superior because it was formed by *a family of nations*. Since they were a family, they had stronger ties than the European nations united only by vicious institutions (ibid.: 43). It should be noted that diplomats sustained America's new image by reappropriating concepts such as legitimacy, freedom, and nation (Fernandez 2009: 43). During these years, political concepts were transformed into singular collectives (Fernandez 2007:169), for example 'freedoms' became 'freedom', 'the American nations' became 'the American nation'. Diplomats also referred to the American system as 'the great American family united in a federal pact' (*pacto de la grande familia americana*) (Guadalupe Victoria 2010 [1827]: LX). On the other hand, the New World had as an advantage its knowledge of the European confederal experience. Manuel Lorenzo Vidaurre – who wrote *American Letters*, and *Plan of America* with a dedication to Bolívar – affirmed that diplomats sent to the Congress of Panama had analysed Europe's 'errors and sciences, virtues and vices of sixty-two centuries' (Vidaurre 2010 [1826]: 185f.). Other analyses established, for example, that the association of the 13 cantons of Switzerland was a union that did not defend the new rights but preserved the old ones (Pombo 2010 [1811]: 43), while the bases of the American confederation were liberal principles (Alamán 2010 [1831]: 262). Likewise, there was no routinization of the Swiss conferences (Pombo 2010 [1811]: 43). Conversely, however, America would have a permanent assembly that would promote constant conferences in established places (Gual 2010 [1821]: 9). The Belgian confederation had the vice of very dispersed sovereignty among its provinces (Pombo 2010 [1811]: 44), while the American confederation would form an assembly that would function as an intermediary among the provinces (Pando 2010 [1826]: 68).

When diplomats observed their history, they looked for reasons that made the New World a unique place to establish a successful confederation; for this reason, they wanted to present the history of the political evolution of the New World. Guillermo Zermeño (2017 [2009]: 575) explains that history became a set of new experiences after independence because, according to Javier Fernandez (2009: 13), the experience of time changed and people became aware of the historicity of societies. Carole Leal (2017: 23) also states that the acceleration of historical time was defined by the actors as a revolution that divided the waters between the past (*the old order*) and expectations of the future (*a new order* to be created). Thus, the results of two important historical moments described modern American politics: the civilizations before the Spanish conquest and independence. As far as the colonial past was concerned, it was seen as an interruption in their historical evolution. Reflecting on their past, diplomats observed that confederalism had existed in America before the conquest. Bolívar wrote that independence restored the old confederalism (Bolívar 2010 [1824]: 41). Similarly, Pombo stated that this system was not foreign to the New World, he affirmed that 'the Swiss, the Dutch in the old continent had the idea of federal government, but we also established it among the different nations of the America at the time of their invasion' (Pombo 2010 [1811]: 39), like the federation of the Tlaxcaltecas and the barbarian and federative state of the heroic Araucanos (ibid.: 40). During independence a 'concept of history emerged and it was marked by the consciousness of a historical actor who is making history (for) posterity' (Almarza 2009: 685); in this way, diplomats were making history in their present by organizing the Confederation that would defend the future of independence which, according to Vidaurre (2010 [1826]: 185), was an incomparable moral and political revolution. When they reconstructed their history, it was the combination of a glorious past, a liberal present and a hopeful future that reshaped the image of the New World.

Being accepted into the family of civilized nations was the best way for diplomats to guarantee their new political order. They wanted to continue to negotiate political equality with their European peers, so they focused on the similarities between the Old and New World, which made them both subject to international law. When American diplomats compared both political orders, they observed that both worlds were constituted by states (monarchical and republican) who created principles and norms that regulated their international relations. That made them subjects to international law. Also, both worlds had formed international systems (Concert of Europe and American Confederation) that relied on the continuation of their congresses. Both organized congresses (Congress of Vienna and Congress of Panama) that encouraged the interaction of their diplomats to create regulations. Both international systems aimed to preserve their internal orders because the international order depended on internal order. However, the Old World's system defended the principle of intervention to maintain internal order in the event of a threat to its monarchical legitimacy. For American diplomats, the principle of intervention was a threat to the legitimacy of their independence before the civilized world. By considering these similarities, they sought to demonstrate that American order was created not by barbarians, but rather by peoples who had gained their freedom and deserved acceptance with full rights in this civilized world (Vanegas 2009: 1044). They found in the notion of civilization an argument to support their discourse of political equality. According to Obregón (2006: 823f.), civilization was also part of the *Criollo* legal consciousness and a power discourse that assigned political, cultural and moral virtues. There were already differences between the Old and New Worlds with regard to the first two virtues; however, morality was a virtue that could enable greater comparability. Consequently, they highlighted two aspects of their political similarities: their standards of civilization and of morality.

Independence reopened a dispute over the New World's place in the history of civilization (Gerbi 1955). During the colonial era, Spain was 'quoted as example of civilization in relation to its colonies in America' (Feres 2017: 97). However, as Monteagudo (1825: 19) put it, America acquired, through the war of independence, indisputable rights in accordance with the forms of civilized countries. As the diplomats claimed, America was in an advanced stage of civilization inspired by the 'republican spirit that is the soul and the invisible agent of the civilized world, that manifests itself and sprouts above all' (Roldán 2017 [1831]: 2120). American uniqueness fostered the spirit used to reshape the image of the New World; nevertheless, to legitimize this image before the Old World, they must establish their own institutions to present themselves to the world as civilized (*Actas del Congreso de Cucuta* 1821). During these years, the concept of civilization was understood as a model to imitate: civilized families were contrasted with the barbaric peoples of the world (Feres 2017: 96f.). It was then that the civilized served to 'make comparisons between nations and peoples', and 'to produce a dualistic geography of the world, divided between civilized and uncivilized' (ibid.: 97). In this sense, the advanced state of civilization of the New World allowed diplomatic negotiations as equals.

To prove that the New World was at a high stage of civilization, the abolition of slavery throughout the confederate territory was one of the first points to be discussed on the Congress of Panama's moral agenda. The agenda's main points, in fact, were the will to avoid war (Monteagudo and Mosquera 2010 [1822]: 11) and the end of slavery (Revenga 2010 [1825]: 76). In his speech for the inauguration of the Congress of Panama, Manuel Vidaurre expressed the sentiment that the Confederation must be based on 'peace with the universe, respecting the governments established in European countries, even when they are diametrically opposed to the general one that is adopted in our America' (Vidaurre 2010 [1826]: 186). Likewise, slavery could not be part of the civilized world. José R. Revenga (2010 [1825]: 76f.), Colombian minister of foreign affairs, was very clear in his instructions to Congress of Panama diplomats, Pedro Gual and Pedro Briceño, when he specified that

> the interest shown by the civilized world in the abolition and suppression of the slave trade in Africa also demands that the Assembly of American States deal with it. This matter presents our Republics with a beautiful opportunity to give a splendid example of the liberality and philanthropy of its principles.

Many members of the *Criollo* elite owned slaves and found the proposal to abolish slavery a threat to their economic interests. Although diplomats were highly interested in proving that they followed the customs of the civilized world, the original idea of abolishing slavery was replaced by the idea of banning the slave trade, also established at the Congress of Vienna.

Conclusions

This chapter has highlighted the impact of the reconstruction of the New World by observing and comparing. Diplomatic interaction created a vision of the world based on a new relation between the New and Old Worlds in light of the independence process. In this context, diplomats desired to legitimize America's independence, so their comparisons were used as a strategy to negotiate their vision of being integrated into international society. Their main interest was the establishment of a new global order, in that sense, they were determined to negotiate the *tertium* that would move the *comparata* to a new political order and change the relationship between the two worlds. Diplomats encouraged a new comparability on the basis of a political perspective, their own political perspective, since the New World was conceived of as a unique political entity that had created a new symmetrical power relation that regulated interaction between the two worlds. In this way, the global world was developed within world regional discourse.

By creating an American Confederation, they sought to generate a new balance in the world. Consequently, comparative practices became politicized in discussions about the distribution of power. It was through regional global discourse that the Americans diplomats tried to assert their arguments about the distribution of power in the world. Having carried out this analysis, I would like to highlight some of the issues raised by the process of reconstruction of the New World and the world order among American diplomats. The first thing to be noted is the development of a new space for discussion as a result of the diplomatic interaction that began with the process of independence. This process was characterized by an intense politicization of the semantics inherited from colonial times. Thus, these discussions encouraged a reappropriation of the concept and image of the New World. These transformations have previously been studied above all from a conceptual point of view. This chapter was intended to be a contribution to understanding this reappropriation of the New World and its impact on the world regional framework not only as a conceptual transformation, but also as a transformation of its image, one that, in Anderson's words, lives in the mind of every member of a nation (Anderson 1993: 23).

Notes

1 The term Latin America was not created until the second half of the 19th century. As this chapter considers how the regional framework provided a platform for thinking about global affairs, I have stayed true to the terminology of the historical actors I am studying. I use 'America' to designate what is now commonly known as 'Latin America'.
2 All translations in this chapter are my own.

The World of Anti-Semitism
A Historical-Sociological Analysis of the Global Element of Hostility Against Jews in Germany (1780-1925)

Marc Jacobsen and Tobias Werron

Introduction

This chapter analyses an important change in the history of modern anti-Semitism that dates back to the mid to late 19th century. Our argument is predicated on the observation that modern anti-Semitism is more than hostility to and prejudice against Jews. It is a comprehensive worldview that offers an interpretation of world affairs and a vision of how the world should be. This affords anti-Semites the ability to re-evaluate everything that is going on in the world from an anti-Semitic point of view. On this basis, we show that certain *observations and interpretations of the global* manifest themselves in the image of the Jew as the 'universal other'. Anti-Semitism therefore represents a specific *practice of observing the global*. While we cannot discuss the global diffusion of anti-Semitism here, we agree with the introduction to this volume in suspecting that this *phenomenological dimension* of the global is an important factor underlying the spread of modern anti-Semitism throughout the 19th and 20th centuries and is still relevant today. In other words, we need to understand 'the world' of anti-Semitism in order to understand the globalization of anti-Semitism.

The global dimension of the anti-Semitic worldview is often neglected or studied in limited, largely ahistorical ways. Modern anti-Semitism is commonly understood as an expression of aggressive nationalism that arises when national homogeneity and sovereignty are challenged by globalization (e.g. Bonefeld 2005; Jacobs 2011; Weitzman 2017). While such descriptions rightly emphasize historical relationships between nationalism and globalization, they are problematic in that they conceive of nationalism and anti-Semitism as fundamental opposites of globalization. In so doing, they underestimate the degree to which nationalism and anti-Semitism are global phenomena in and of themselves, connected not just through their ideological content but also as modern ways of *envisioning the world*.

While research on globalization has already shown that nationalism and globalization are mutually reinforcing phenomena (Mann 1997; Bayly 2004; Pryke 2009; Werron 2012, 2021), research on anti-Semitism has only just started to recognize that enmity towards Jews is a multifaceted global phenomenon (e.g. Braun and Ziege 2004; Rabinovici et al. 2004; Salzborn 2020). With few exceptions, however, the empirical focus is on developments after 1945, while processes of globalization and their consequences before that are hardly considered. The theory of 'national anti-Semitism' stands out, because it emphasizes both the nationalist foundation of anti-Semitism and its international implications by describing modern anti-Semitism as having invented 'the Jew' as a fundamental threat to a national world order in the 19th century (Holz 2001; Weyand 2016).

This chapter draws on, connects and complements these discussions and insights. We argue that there was a connection between anti-Semitism, nationalism and globalization as early as the 19th century, when Jews were already described as rootless and cosmopolitan. But the main problem relating to the so-called Jewish question back then was the supposed seclusion of Jews as 'a state within the state'; the stereotype of a 'Jewish world conspiracy' became more popular only at the end of the 19th century. Its increasing popularity at that point in history reflects intensifying global connections, relations and structures that became manifest, among other things, in the emergence of a globalizing system of nation-states. We therefore propose to distinguish between two phases in the development of national anti-Semitism: first, the phase of *emergent national anti-Semitism* between the late 18th and mid-19th century; second, the phase of *universalizing national anti-Semitism* starting in the 1870s. It is against the background of this distinction, then, that we should re-evaluate the formation and global diffusion of anti-Semitism in the 20th and early 21st centuries.

The chapter is structured as follows: We will first present the idea of nationalism and globalization as mutually reinforcing phenomena, highlighting the universal element of modern nationalism itself. We subsequently introduce the concept of national anti-Semitism, arguing that the formation of its universal element has not been studied yet as a historical phenomenon in its own right. Our chapter aims to fill this gap. Drawing on examples from German anti-Semitic discourse between 1780 and 1925, we show that the worldview of anti-Semitism 'globalized' from the 1870s and how it did so. We focus on the German discourse of anti-Semitism as the emergence and universalization of national anti-Semitism was particularly evident in Germany, often preceding similar developments in other world regions. In this way we hope to contribute to a better understanding of anti-Semitism as a *specific practice of observing and envisioning the world* that reflects historical connections between the histories of nationalism and globalization. The conclusion draws attention to some general insights and research questions that follow from this analysis, arguing that our view adds urgently needed historical perspective to the current discussion on global anti-Semitism.

Nationalism and globalization

Globalization scholars tend to assume that nationalism will lose its significance because of globalization (e.g. Albrow 1996; Beck 2002), leading them to repeatedly declare the 'end of the nation-state', only to be surprised by the persistence and resurgence of nationalism over and over again. In contrast to this 'presentist' view, historical research on globalization and nationalism has pointed out that the relationship between the two phenomena is by no means a zero-sum game: more globalization does not necessarily mean less nationalism and vice versa. Nationalism over the last two centuries has become established throughout the world as the primary legitimizing basis of political organization. In other words, the history of nationalism is a globalization story in its own right. From this perspective, it is no surprise to learn that there is no significant evidence that globalization profoundly weakens the nation-state (Mann 1997). Nationalist ideas of collective identity and political sovereignty have been woven into the basic structures of global modernity, in often 'banal' (Billig 1995) ways that let them appear as natural.

Sociologically, then, nationalism can be described as a global institution (Werron 2021). Some scholars locate its origins in revolutionary France, others in the anti-colonial Americas. Irrespective of such differences, in the early to mid-19th century two basic models for the construction of national identities and their political ambitions were ready for copying: a primarily political model that aimed at legitimizing and stabilizing a given state structure, and a primarily cultural model that aimed at the founding and legitimizing of new states. Based on these models, nationalism spread around the world in the 19th and 20th centuries, almost completely dividing the globe into nation-states (Wimmer and Feinstein 2010).

The global character of nationalism, however, results not only from globalist worldwide diffusion but also from *the universalist imaginary built into it*. Modern nationalism can be interpreted as a discursive model that comprises a cultural, a political and a universal or global element (Werron 2021; Calhoun 1997; Özkirimli 2010). Nationalism entails the construction of collective identities to legitimize claims of political sovereignty over a territory; however, it also includes the idea that all 'nations' of the world may pursue their own claims to political sovereignty. This, in turn, implies the idea of a *world order* consisting of, and based on, a multitude of nation-states.[1]

The universal element in nationalism points to the historical process by which nationalism contributed to transforming the early modern state system into a global nation-state system. By anchoring the principle of national legitimacy in a universalistic worldview, nationalism has helped extend the borders of the initially European 'international society' so that the external borders of the state system have indeed become congruent with the entire world (Mayall 1990). Building on the institutions of the early modern state system ('international society') such as sovereignty, diplomacy and international law, nationalism introduced a *universal* source of legitimacy for them. For this reason, it soon attracted all kinds of social groups looking to legitimize their state-building projects in an increasingly globalized environment – including, most notably, anti-colonial movements outside Europe.

The success of nationalism is also a result of its in-built universalism as a model of political organization. Nationalism not only constructs collective identities and legitimizes their claims of independent statehood. It is also an idea of a global order which implies a multitude of national collective identities. Nationalism is, therefore, also a form of observing the world: the whole world is observed and interpreted through the lenses of nationalism. This worldview also informs what we associate with society in everyday language today: a culturally and politically integrated unit that shares the surface of the earth with numerous other units of this type. From any nationalist's perspective, there is a German society, French society, Argentine society, Haitian society, etc.

The combination of particularism and universalism within the nationalist worldview is a defining element of both modern nationalism and modern world society. The epochal achievement of nationalism lies in having developed and enforced a universalist notion of a world ordered by national particularisms. Thus, all forms of nationalism are both inclusive and exclusive at the same time. Nationalism is exclusive because it must always draw a line between the in-group and various out-groups. It is also inclusive in that it affords, at least in principle, all nations a right to claim their own state. This does not preclude hierarchies, discrimination, competition or conflicts between nation-states (Werron 2012; 2015). But, fundamentally, all these phenomena are based on the perception of social groups as nations and on the perception that all of these nations have an *equal* right to rule their own nation-states.

There are, however, exceptions to this rule of equality between nations. Anti-Semitism points to one of them. In the worldview of anti-Semitism, which developed from the late 19th century and is still with us today, Jews are both related to and excluded from the world of nations. Modern anti-Semitism is based on nationalism. It adopts nationalism's view of the world but adds to it the antithesis of 'the Jew' as the 'ultimate enemy' of the national principle. On this basis, it radically excludes Jews from the world of nations, denying them both the right to be part of an existing nation and the right of national self-determination.

Nationalism and anti-Semitism

Modern anti-Semitism is not merely a kind of prejudice, but also a comprehensive worldview (Salzborn 2012). Anti-Jewish stereotypes condense into an overarching 'explanation' for numerous social phenomena and processes (Rürup 1975). For anti-Semites, all the ills of the world are caused by the machinations of malicious Jews. This implies a clear, profound and binary distinction between good and evil (Haury 2002: 105ff.). The alleged group of (Jewish) perpetrators is always related to an alleged group of (non-Jewish) victims. The construction of collective identities is, therefore, also an essential part of anti-Semitic ideology (Holz 2001).

With the emergence of nationalism, collective identities were increasingly constructed and contrasted on the basis of national identities, so that medieval anti-Judaism was 'transformed' into modern anti-Semitism (Weyand 2016). Religious discrimination was replaced by an ethnic distinction and the Jews were re-invented as a threat to the nation. This historical link between modern anti-Semitism and nationalism quickly became a research consensus among scholars (Stögner and Schmidinger 2010: 387). For this reason, researchers often tended to view anti-Semitism as an expression of extreme and aggressive nationalism that excludes Jews.

In line with the latest trends in the study of nationalism, however, research into anti-Semitism has also begun to focus on the relationship between nationalism, internationalism and anti-Jewish hostility (e.g. Braun and Ziege 2004; Goldhagen 2013; Aly 2017; König and Schulz 2019). A notable contribution is the systematic analysis of the relationship between anti-Semitism and nationalism by Holz (2001), who also highlights the international and universal implications of this interconnection. A key insight here is that Jews are not only regarded as enemies of one's own nation but are more generally perceived as enemies of all nations. Thus, anti-Semitism, like nationalism, contains both particularistic and universal elements. The anti-Jewish concept of the enemy is related to a national self-image, but this national self-image implies that there are many other national collectives that are also threatened by the Jews. For this reason, Jews are not regarded as a nation like others, but as something fundamentally different: *a threat to the very idea of a national world order*. Modern anti-Semitism is therefore based on two main distinctions: the first distinguishes one's own nation from others, the second distinguishes all nations from the Jews (Holz 2000).

On these grounds, then, it appears that anti-Semitism solves a fundamental problem of nationalism. As many scholars have argued, national identities are constructed in contradistinction to other national identities. Usually, historical and genealogical narratives assert (fundamental) historical, political, cultural, ethnic and even biological differences between individual nations and their populations, from which friendships, enmities and hierarchies may be derived and on the basis of which conflicting interests and conflicts can be legitimized (Weyand 2016: 137ff.). But, despite all these differences, nations share the fact that they are nations. National images of oneself and others are, therefore, symmetrical pairs of opposites (Richter 1996). The same category, 'nation', is used to describe both sides of the distinction. Any assertion of asymmetries and hierarchies between nations has to accept this fundamental symmetry. However, distinctions between nations presuppose, rather than explain, what 'nations' are. To determine the shared characteristics of all nations, therefore, nationalists of all colours might be inclined to look for *opposites to the very idea of the nation*, thus specifying what nations are *not* in order to specify what all nations have in common.

Modern anti-Semitism provides a specific solution to this problem by inventing 'the Jew' as a counter-concept to the nation. It is not by coincidence, then, that most characteristics ascribed to Jews are the exact opposite of what constitutes legitimate nationality and nationhood (as conceived by certain nationalists): Jews are described as international, rootless, cosmopolitan, exploitative, impure, artificial, selfish and so on (Haury 2002: 84ff.). On this basis, Jews are regarded by anti-Semites as being incapable of integrating themselves into any existing nation or of forming a nation on and of their own. The 'wandering Jew' is portrayed as a parasitic entity that by its very nature contradicts and threatens the fundamental principles of nationalism. The paradox that Jews are nevertheless often described as a 'peculiar people' or a 'scattered nation' is based on the universal logic of nationalism, according to which non-national elements of any kind are not compatible with the national world order (Holz 2000: 283ff.).

By imagining 'the Jew' as an evil third party, anti-Semitism serves another important function for certain variants of nationalism: Everything that questions the validity of the nation can be personified in 'the Jew'. Anti-Semitism conceals the manifold ambivalences and conflicts of nationalism by means of externalization. All dangers and uncertainties can be transformed into an external threat. In this respect, anti-Semitism expresses implicit doubts, uncertainties and crises in the (global) reproduction of nationalism (Haury 2002: 48ff.). While anti-Semitic descriptions of Jews may serve to stabilize nationalism, they are also a constant reminder of the contradictions and fragility of nationalism. As non-national elements, they personify the possibility of a world without nations, which in turn makes them appear as *the ultimate enemy*. They need to be combated, expelled and/or eliminated not only to save one's own nation, but to save the national world order as such. Thus, both in the description of the enemy and the self, and in the possible strategies against the omnipresent threat of the Jews, the problem is by no means limited to the national sphere. Rather, it reflects the fact that the distinction on which anti-Semitism is based is not only that between Jews and Germans (or other nations), but between Jews and *all* nations (Holz 2000: 270). The so-called Jewish question is, therefore, always an international question. The perspective of anti-Semitism is global.

These considerations are based on a formal analysis of anti-Semitic semantics that appears plausible on a theoretical level but, in its original formulation, has been relatively insensitive to the history of anti-Semitism and to historical changes in anti-Semitism's ideological content. Only recently has the emergence of national anti-Semitism been evidenced in detail as a result of the socio-historical process of secularization and nation-building in the late 18th and 19th centuries (Weyand 2016). The establishment of the modern state with a centralized monopoly on the use of force and a secular self-understanding led to the erosion of religious self-images. Discrimination against Jews solely on religious grounds was therefore no longer plausible. While Jews, at first, experienced more legal equality, anti-Jewish animosity did not disappear. Instead, anti-Jewish hostility slowly adapted to the new social context and transformed itself. Throughout the 19th century, the basis of anti-Semitic images of Jews shifted from religion to nation.

Weyand (ibid.: 189) argues that the figure of 'the Jew' as the enemy of all nations plays a central role in modern anti-Semitism from the late 18th century to the present day. Descriptions of Jews as an international collective that is fundamentally different from other nations are particularly relevant here. He also claims that notions of Jewish 'internationality' and 'world conspiracy' had been present since the late 18th century but became more prominent in the late 19th century. This suggests that the universal dimension of anti-Semitism is not static but is transformed from an implicit to an explicit dimension of national anti-Semitism over time.

However, the universal and global character of anti-Semitism has never been studied as an object of analysis in its own right. The question therefore remains when, how, to what extent and to what effect anti-Semitism has incorporated ideas and meanings of *the international* and *the global*. By reconsidering previous research findings and re-examining important examples of modern anti-Semitism in light of this question, we aim to show that the significance of the universal dimension did indeed increase in the course of the 19th century and how it did so.

National and universal elements in German anti-Semitic discourse (1780-1925)

In this section, we look at how the nationalist and universal dimensions of anti-Semitic ideology developed in Germany from 1870 to 1925. We do not aim at a comprehensive overview of the history of anti-Semitism. Our focus is on when and how anti-Semitic stereotypes played a role in the construction, description and observation of *the national* and *the global*. We find that the imagined 'internationality' of Jews was described early on. However, in the late 18th to mid-19th century the focus of anti-Semites was on the internal affairs of the (emerging) nation. Only later in the course of the 19th century, did the observation of the global (from a nationalistic perspective) become increasingly relevant, slowly developing into a full-blown element of modern anti-Semitism.

The national locus of the Jewish question: a 'state within a state'

Since the late 18th century, when religion in Europe was slowly losing its significance as an ordering principle and as secularization and liberalization were fundamentally altering social relations in society, the religiously legitimized exclusion of the Jewish minority became increasingly difficult to maintain. The transformation from a static societal system of status to a dynamic class society, whose contradictions were quasi-suspended in the emergent idea of a shared nationality, formed the basis of Jewish emancipation (Grab 1991: 13). With the demand for legal equality for Jews, first advocated by Christian Konrad Wilhelm von Dohm in 1781, discussions about the conditions, possibilities and limits of the integration of the Jewish minority started all over Europe (Hettling et al. 2013). The changing social environment did not lead seamlessly to a change in attitudes towards Jews. Rather, the latter's (gradual) emancipation formed a new field of conflict in which anti-Jewish resentments were re-articulated (Erb and Bergmann 1989). With secularization and the emergence of nationalism, religious images of Jews were successively recrafted to bring them in line with nationalist ideas of ethnicity, descent and identity (Weyand 2016). But in the context of early nation building, the debate on Jewish emancipation was not only about the Jews. It was also about the identity of one's own nation and who legitimately belonged to it (Schulin 1999).

The so-called Jewish question was not a specific German phenomenon. However, the German debate on the Jewish question not only had a great external impact, but was also of enormous intensity, expressed in public campaigns and petitions, numerous pamphlets and even street violence (Hettling et al. 2013: 11; Bergmann et al. 2002: 19; Pfahl-Traughber 2002: 50ff.).

Although the rejection of the emancipation of Jews was advocated by different political groups from various social backgrounds and is therefore characterized by a variety of motives, anti-Jewish agitation and accusations converged in the allegation that Jews posed an internal threat to the emerging German state. At the heart of this was the idea that Jews would form 'a state within the state' because they either could not or were not willing to assimilate (Katz 1980: 88ff.). The animosity towards Jews was further based on the belief that Jews formed the antithesis to 'Germanism', which became an important topic in the process of nation building and the construction of a collective identity (Harket 2019: 183).

A closer look at influential texts of this early phase of modernizing anti-Semitism reveals that universal elements and conspiracy accusations already existed.[2] Immediately following Dohm's demand, the ability of Jews to integrate and thus their right to emancipation was questioned. As early as 1784, the philosopher Johann H. Schulz formulated the accusation that Jews form a 'state within a state' in his response to Dohm (Katz 1971). Schulz accused the Jews of not being able to form a loyal relationship to the state in which they lived. Rather, they remained an exclusive community with their own customs, religious and cultural traditions, which they did not want to give up (Schulz 1784: 218ff.). The accusation that Jews formed a 'state within the state' was initially based on their religiousness but became increasingly 'ethnicized' in the course of the 19th century (Weyand 2016: 182ff.). Central to this assumption was a concern for Jewish disloyalty, but also for Jewish influence and power within the state – a concern that distinguished anti-Semitic prejudices from the majority of racist prejudices in that Jews were not considered inferior but superior.[3]

In the period immediately after the Congress of Vienna there was a new wave of chauvinist writings in which hostility towards Jews was embedded in nationalist rhetoric. The rejection of Jewish equality escalated for the first time around 1819 in the violent Hep-Hep riots. In the years between 1830 and 1870 the debate on the Jewish question intensified, as manifested in an increase of pamphlets and violence (Purschewitz 2013). In these years, the phantasmagoria of Jewish national seclusion posing an inner threat to the developing German nation became a central topic of anti-Semitic discourse.

In 1814, the influential historian and writer Ernst Moritz Arndt positioned himself as an opponent of the emancipation of the Jews: 'The Jews as Jews do not fit into this world and into these states, and for this reason I do not want them to procreate unproperly in Germany. I also do not want this because they are alien people and because I wish to keep the German stock as free from foreign elements as possible' (Arndt 1814: 188f.).[4] Arndt also agitated against Napoleon and the French. But he regarded them as external enemies. The Jews, in contrast, were the inner enemy. In 1831 the theologian Heinrich Paulus even published a book explicitly dedicated to the alleged problem of Jewish 'national seclusion' (*Nationalabsonderung*), which triggered a big controversy (Sterling 1969: 81). Paulus argued that Jews could not obtain citizenship rights because Jewry itself wanted to stay 'an isolated nation, which believes that it is its religious duty to remain a nation separated from all other nations' (Paulus 1831: 2f.).

Similar characterizations can be found in other works by known opponents of Jewish emancipation during that time (Hortzitz 1988: 255ff.). Especially in the first half of the 19th century, it is striking that religious attributions were by no means obsolete. However, they were successively being woven into a nationalistic semantic in which they gradually became a secondary element. Religious affiliation no longer stood for itself but specified affiliation to a nation (Weyand 2016: 205ff.).

The examples from the early period of modern anti-Semitism make it clear that the intersection of particularistic and universal elements was evident early on. The idea that Jews had not integrated themselves into the German nation, which, according to some authors, the Jews simply did not want, or were even unable, to do, was usually accompanied by the assumption that Jews did not integrate into other nations either. Everywhere in the world, they kept themselves to themselves and were only committed to themselves. This was considered a problem because Jews were assumed to have numerous negative characteristics that were contrasted with one's own national character. Central accusations were moral vice, claims to superiority and the ruthless assertion of their own interests at the expense of others, on the basis of which conspiracy myths were formed.

There are several examples of pamphlets in the early 19th century accusing Jews of striving for power and even of international machinations, especially in the context of the economy. As early as 1819, the notorious anti-Semite Hartwig von Hundt-Radowsky wrote in his much-noticed '*Judenspiegel*' of ruthless enrichment as the 'collective national goal' (*gemeinschaftliches Volksziel*) of the Jews, whom he described as being characterized by a 'hostile, malicious isolation, by which, after the destruction of Jerusalem, all Jews separated themselves from all the people among whom they lived' (Hundt-Radowsky 1821: 12f.). Furthermore, he even describes how Jews exert power in the world due to their economic capabilities:

> With their immense wealth, Jews [...] can unhinge the world. Emperors, kings and princes are deep in debt to them, they have lent money to whole nations at high interest, money which they did not earn in a righteous, charitable manner but with lies and deception, sleight of hand, robbery and theft. (ibid.: 13)

What is striking, however, is that in the early to mid-19th century the Jewish question was usually presented as being solvable at the national or state level. Jews should integrate or would have to be discriminated against and excluded. Proposals for an international solution to the Jewish question seem not to have played an explicit role yet.

Parallel to the peak of Jewish emancipation in the 1870s, the German Empire saw a rise of political mobilization and organization of anti-Semites (Pulzer 2004). Many scholars consider this politicization of Jew hatred a new phase in the history of anti-Semitism (e.g. Levy 1975; Massing 1949). Some point to the full-blown secularization and racialization of the Jewish question as a new stage in the radicalization of Jew hatred (Benz 2015: 42ff.). Others argue that anti-Semitism was changing because, after legal equality for the Jews had been achieved, it was moving away from a (to some degree) real conflict. Consequently, anti-Semitism was no longer only directed solely at Jews but became a general model for explaining the world (Rürup 1975).

Still, in this period the Jews continued to be regarded primarily as an enemy who was damaging the nation from within. Thus, anti-Semitism in the German Empire showed clear parallels to previous manifestations of Jew hatred. According to anti-Semites, legal equality should have been revoked, since, for various reasons, Jews basically could not be part of the German nation. Even if they seemed to have been assimilated and to have given up their peculiar rites, in reality they would still undermine and destroy German culture from within, endangering the homogeneity and sovereignty of the nation.

The Berlin anti-Semitism controversy from 1879 to 1881, for example, was sparked when Heinrich von Treitschke expressed sympathy with the idea of revoking Jewish emancipation as he identified Jewish seclusion within Germany as a cause of several domestic problems (Stoetzler 2008: 3ff.). Treitschke demanded the Jews become Germans, because he did not want 'thousands of years of Germanic civilization to be followed by an era of German-Jewish mixed culture' (Treitschke 1879: 573). He feared the 'flock of ambitious young men selling trousers' that crossed 'over our eastern border, year after year, from the inexhaustible Polish cradle' and 'whose children and grandchildren would in time dominate Germany's stock exchanges and newspapers'(ibid.: 572f.). Although the dispute was among educated elites and is therefore not representative of the anti-Semitic movement (and its opponents), Treitschke's remarks were a crucial instance in the development of anti-Semitism after the legal emancipation of Jews (Stoetzler 2008: 4).

The universal dimension of the Jewish Question: 'International Jewry'

The problem of the Jews within Germany remained a central concern of anti-Semites, but the period after 1870 was also characterized by the rising importance of the idea of an internationally operating Jewry. With the notion of a 'Jewish International' gradually gaining importance in the second half of the 19th century, the universal dimension of anti-Semitism became more explicit. While the activities of Jews in other countries were already being addressed at the beginning of the 19th century, these ideas were now elaborated more concretely. Concepts of an international conspiracy became more elaborate and the phantasmagoria that Jews were also an external enemy of all other nations was postulated more explicitly. Connected with this was the view that Judaism was striving for world domination, that a secret organization existed which directed the fate of the Jews and the world, and that it was attempting to subjugate all non-Jews (Weil 1924: 15). Even though there were numerous forerunners of this idea, it was not until the 1870s that it was condensed and popularized into the assumption of a conspiracy with international reach. Accordingly, the battlefield for the fight against anti-Semitism was no longer primarily national but international. And indeed, anti-Semitic texts after the 1870s show a heightened awareness of the globalizing relations of an emerging world society.

An example is the term 'Golden international', which became established in the 1870s as a description of Jews and their activities in finance (Lange 2011: 112). The term was apparently first used by Ottomar Beta in his work on 'Darwin, Germany and the Jews or Jew-Jesuitism' [*Darwin, Deutschland und die Juden oder der Juda-Jesuitismus*] (1875), but it was Karl Wilmanns, a lawyer and member of the German Conservative Party, who popularized the term in his book on 'The Golden International and the Necessity of a Social Reform Party' [*Die 'goldene' Internationale und die Notwendigkeit einer socialen Reformpartei*] (1876), in which he connected Judaism with financial capitalism and thereby explained Jewish dominance in society. In the second half of the 19th century, the term 'golden international' became frequently used to describe Jewish activities on the (financial) world market.[5] In 1881, orientalist Paul de Lagarde (1920: 388ff.) not only uses the notion of a 'Golden International' for Jews but also the more explicit term 'Jewish International' to describe the 'Alliance Israélite Universelle' which he characterizes as 'an international conspiracy, similar to freemasonry, aiming at Jewish world domination' (ibid.: 278).

While at the beginning of the 19th century anti-Semitic literature was still directed essentially against Jews as internal enemies and a state minority, from the 1870s there was an increasing emphasis on Jews being both an internal *and* an external threat. Pamphlets dealing with 'Jewish cosmopolitanism' and 'internationalism' became popular. Hermann Ahlwardt's (1890) books about the 'Desperate Struggle of the Aryan peoples with Judaism' [*Verzweiflungskampf der arischen Völker mit dem Judentum*], or Carl Paasch's book on 'Secret Judaism, Secondary Governments and Jewish World Domination' [*Geheimes Judenthum, Nebenregierungen und jüdische Weltherrschaft*] (1892) are characteristic examples of this formative era of an increasingly globally oriented anti-Semitic discourse.

With the increasing emphasis on the 'international Jewish threat' also came a heightened awareness of a common struggle of Western culture, (European) nations and/or the Aryan race against the Jews. As early as the 1880s, attempts were being made to organize internationally against the alleged Jewish peril. The character of these meetings was by no means as international as intended since it was mostly Germans, with some Austro-Hungarians and Russians, who attended them (Wyrwa 2009).[6] Still, the goal of a common international struggle against the Jews declared at these meetings is remarkable. In the 'Manifesto to the Governments and Peoples of the Christian World Threatened by Judaism' [*Manifest an die Regierungen und Völker der durch das Judenthum gefährdeten christlichen Staaten*], issued at the first anti-Jewish international congress in 1882, Jews were described as striving for world domination and wanting to bind the European Christian peoples in chains. The purpose of the congress was said to be the confidential consultation 'regarding the next objectives of the anti-Jewish movement and the means needed in the battle against the Jewish position in high finance and trade, in agriculture and craft, in politics and local relations, in the press and in the arts and sciences' (Istóczy 1882: 10).

After the failure of the first attempts at a European anti-Jewish organization, Otto Böckel's short-lived political rise began. Among the anti-Semites of the 19th century, Böckel was probably the one with the strongest focus on the European dimensions of the fight against the Jews. Although other anti-Semites were already referring to the worldwide or European dimension of the Jewish question, it was Böckel who gave the European vision of doom a programmatic character (Wyrwa 2009). Under the pseudonym 'Capistrano', he published a work that explicitly dealt with the 'Jewish Danger to Europe' [*Die europäische Judengefahr*] (Capistrano 1886) in the late 1880s. This explicit international orientation remained characteristic of anti-Semitism in the following decades. The comprehensive presentation of Jewish influence in all areas of society on an international level became a central topic. However, despite myths about a Jewish world conspiracy, the focus here was clearly on Europe.

During the Weimar Republic, anti-Semitism increased once again (Benz 2015: 86ff.). The tendency, already apparent at the end of the 19th century, to regard Jews as both an internal and external enemy, continued to grow in the aftermath of World War I. Besides allegations that Jews were unpatriotic traitors or profiteers (Pfahl-Traughber 2002: 83ff.), descriptions of the international machinations of Jews and their alleged secret plans became even more popular and were specified in numerous anti-Semitic writings.

Of great importance was the publication of the infamous 'Protocols of the Elders of Zion', which first appeared in Russia in 1902 and subsequently spread throughout the world. The 'Protocols' allegedly contained evidence of a Jewish world conspiracy. They were represented as being an authentic source documenting the main features of Jewish world politics and the strategies to be applied in order to achieve world domination. The 'Protocols' became an international success, thereby popularizing the phantasmagoria of a Jewish world conspiracy on a global scale (Webman 2011).

From the 1920s on, Alfred Rosenberg, who was to become Hitler's 'chief ideologist' (Piper 2005), also spread the legend of a Jewish–Masonic world conspiracy in countless writings. His essay on 'Jewish World Politics' [*Jüdische Weltpolitik*] (1924), published in the journal *Der Weltkampf*, which was devoted to the 'Jewish question of all countries', gives a concise summary of his anti-Semitic worldview. The fundamental problem for Rosenberg was the 'international idea' that manifested itself especially in socialism and social democracy but also in international finance, all products of Jewish machinations. According to Rosenberg, the aim of 'the Jews' is to establish an international all-Jewish private syndicate by promoting socialism, Marxism and social democracy. Jews tried to create a Jewish World Bank or a World Syndicate, which at its core was 'a financial system that was united above all states' (Rosenberg 1924: 8). The process of establishing this supranational organization had been accompanied by wars and crises, which Rosenberg described as a means of 'economic enslavement of all peoples' (ibid.: 5). Jews, he warns, 'long since constituted themselves everywhere as a state within the state and at the same time as a state above the state' (ibid.: 8). He is therefore certain 'that we all have a common enemy which is first and foremost: the Jewish Red-

Golden International and its political pimps, as embodied in professional parliamentarians and professional journalists' (ibid.: 11). Rosenberg argues that international Jewish machinations prevented other nations from interacting harmoniously, or at least naturally, with each other. They were all victims of a supranational organization that must be fought together in order to restore a natural and peaceful world order of race and nationalism: 'But one thing should become clear to all: that peoples can and should fight for their freedom and their right to exist, but that the long-standing situation must finally be eliminated, whereby they murder each other for the benefit of one and the same laughing foreign-bred third party' (ibid.: 11).

Rosenberg's remarks summarize quite well how the anti-Jewish discourse in Germany had changed since the early 19th century. Whereas, in the rejection of Jewish emancipation, Jews had been denounced for being disloyal, unpatriotic, foreign, they were now characterized as a supranational conspiracy as well. They were still accused of being a threat from within because they did not want to assimilate, but their international connections, especially in economics and politics, were emphasized much more forcefully after the turn of the century. The explicit notion of 'Jewish world politics' used by Rosenberg was another indication of this. Its use pointed to the necessity of a common effort by all nations against the Jews. This makes it particularly clear how much anti-Semitism was based not only on particularistic assumptions about one's own nation, but also on a universal idea of a national world order, which must be actively and collectively restored by fighting the Jews on a global scale. The arena of this (imagined) conflict had shifted from a primarily national to an international level. That this belief – that the solution to the Jewish question required an international approach and could not be solved simply at the national level – would become a cornerstone of anti-Semitism was by no means obvious at the beginning of the 19th century. Although the universal dimension of anti-Semitism was there from the very beginning, it became much more pronounced in the course of the 19th and early 20th centuries.

Conclusion: Towards a historical perspective on the globalization of anti-Semitism

In this chapter we have argued that modern anti-Semitism should be seen not just as a reaction to, but also as a genuine *product* of, globalization. We have also tried to show that nationalism and anti-Semitism are closely connected *through* processes of globalization. Let us conclude by highlighting the main conceptual implications of our analysis, concerning, firstly, the history of anti-Semitism itself and, secondly, the relationship between nationalism and anti-Semitism.

Analysis of anti-Semitic discourse in Germany in the 19th and early 20th centuries suggests that two periods should be distinguished in the history of modern anti-Semitism. In the first, taking shape in the late 18th and largely dominant during the 19th century, anti-Semites perceived the Jews (only) as a rootless, parasitic people who formed a state within the state. This could be called *the period of emergent national anti-Semitism*. In the second, developing in the late 19th to early 20th century, Jews were increasingly (also) seen as a supranational quasi-organization and international conspiracy. In this period anti-Semitism redefined its world as one where international Jewry posed a threat to all nations alike. In such a world, hatred of Jews became much more than a local reaction to alleged parasitic behaviour; it became a fundamental way of sense-making shared by anti-Semites around the world. With this thinking, then, we enter what could be called the *period of universalized national anti-Semitism*.

This view also implied a new perspective on the relationship between modern nationalism and modern anti-Semitism. In both periods, anti-Semitism was closely connected to nationalism. Only in the second period, however, did anti-Semitism and nationalism become connected *through* processes of globalization and a common endeavour to make sense of the globalizing world. Both found common ground in reimagining themselves as worldviews that defined the world as a space that should consist of nations. Anti-Semitism, however, added to this the depiction of Jews as a 'rootless' people that did not fit into the world of nations as defined by nationalism.

Our analysis is, of course, only a first step towards an understanding of this 'self-universalization' of nationalism and anti-Semitism and the ways in which both are connected through processes of globalization. Beyond the examples from the German discourse used here, we need empirical studies of anti-Semitic discourses in various languages and countries to understand how, when and in which varieties 'universalized national anti-Semitism' actually came into being in the late 19th and early 20th century. We also need empirical studies of how both nationalists and anti-Semites used the emerging global infrastructure of communication in the 19th and 20th century to connect with each other and work on their ideologies. Most notably, on this basis, we need studies investigating the *longue durée* of universalized national anti-Semitism, including the global diffusion of this worldview from the late 19th century to today. We need such studies not just to make new sense of the history of modern anti-Semitism but also to understand its current forms. Our aim was to outline a starting point for such studies by showing that the global character of anti-Semitism is not just a reaction to recent globalization dynamics but a product of long-term globalization processes that can be traced back to the late 19th century.

Notes

1. Since the universal dimension refers to a global order of nation-states, we use the terms 'global' and 'universal' as well as 'international'. However, we do not use these terms interchangeably. Rather, the addition 'global' denotes a spatial limitation of the universal dimension: at least for the time being, the universality of nationalism refers only to our planet as a place differentiated into territorial and sovereign nation-states. The term 'international' refers to how *the global* is spatially and politically ordered according to the universal principle of nationalism.
2. This is not surprising in so far as already in the Middle Ages numerous conspiracy theories about Jews were in circulation (Heil 2006). Within research, however, insufficient emphasis is placed on a more precise analysis of what is meant by 'world' and what geographical scope the assumed conspiracy has. An analysis of the changing meanings and semantics of the world within the anti-Semitic discourse is still missing. For a short history of conspiracy myths in the 19th century, see also Gregory (2012).
3. For a more detailed description of the (ideal-typical) differences between racism and anti-Semitism, see Haury (2002: 116ff.). For a critical discussion of connections and disconnections in the study of racism and anti-Semitism within sociological inquiry, see Cousin and Fine (2012).
4. All translations in this chapter are our own.
5. In a speech in 1882, anti-Semitic preacher Adolf Stoecker warned that Jews 'remain […] exclusive, in the international context they build the great golden international which covers the world with its networks' ['sie bleiben […] exklusiv, in internationalem Zusammenhang miteinander in der großen goldenen Internationale, welche mit ihren Netzen die Welt umspannen'] (quoted in Mumm 1914: 213). Wilhelm Marr, co-founder of

the 'Antisemitenliga', also uses the image of the 'golden International' which according to him 'knows no fatherland' (Marr 1879: 43).
6   Since the 1920s, however, international congresses by anti-Semites were held on a regular basis and became an important meeting point for European demagogues (Hagemeister 2017: 59ff.).

Envisioning a World Law
Reflections on the *Congrès international de droit comparé* (1900) and the Latent Underpinnings of Comparative Legal Practice

Karlson Preuß

Constructing a world law through legal practice?

This chapter discusses the jurisprudential vision of world law. Since the end of the 19th century, jurisprudence has been advocating its own thesis on the globalization of law. According to popular belief, legal practice drives the harmonization of national legal systems. By quoting and borrowing from foreign courts and legislations, judges introduce foreign law into domestic jurisdiction and thus pave the way for harmonizing different legal systems. In what follows, the cosmopolitan dreams of Comparative Law will be dampened. Responding to the scepticism towards universalistic globalization narratives underlying the contributions to this volume, this chapter challenges the narrative popular among legal scholars according to which legal practice possesses the normative potential to unify the different national legal systems. To this end, the idea that legal practice gradually realizes a world law will be historically contextualized. Current debates on the legal borrowing of foreign law, which are mainly conducted in the field of Constitutional Law, are examined against the background of the first International Conference on Comparative Law, which took place in Paris in 1900. Similar to contemporary debates in constitutional law, prominent participants in this conference, which was mostly dominated by issues of private law, placed great hopes in legal practice for the gradual realization of a uniform world law. Around 1900, the figure of the judge already embodied the cosmopolitan projections of eminent comparative lawyers. These projections will be dissected as part of the 'second order approach' described in the Introduction to this volume. Instead of taking the legal idea of a world law for granted, I will scrutinize the discursive context in which the world became the analytical scope of comparative law. The field-specific dynamics underlying the discursive 'construction' of a global legal space will come under the spotlight. The following sections will examine the visible and latent motives and strategies behind current and early-20th-century Comparative Law's preoccupation with world law. Taking up the research question of this volume, I will pursue the field-immanent motives and problems that historically brought about the 'projective inclusion' (Stichweh 2000: 234) of the world in comparative law literature.

Two conflicting hypotheses on law's contribution to globalization

The belief in law's potential to normatively integrate world society continues unabated among a great many legal scholars. This belief is often underpinned by an activist tonality and an ostentatious commitment to normative universalism. Particularly in the field of Constitutional Law, there are visible efforts to promote the harmonization of different national legal systems. Remarkably, the hopes of many cosmopolitically oriented lawyers are directed towards legal *practice*. As often stressed by progressive constitutional lawyers, national courts assume a crucial role in gradually implementing a transnational legal sphere by quoting from foreign legal systems, thus enriching domestic law by external legal experiences. The (progressive) judge enjoys the utmost trust in these intellectual circles. Anne-Marie Slaughter (2004: 65, 69), for instance, charges constitutional judges with the task of constructing a 'global legal system' through 'constitutional cross-fertilization'. The globalization of law is envisioned as a process taking place in domestic court rooms, cutting across national parliaments and international or global institutions.

Current developments seem to support such hopes and predictions as today there is indeed a 'growing horizontal communication between constitutional systems' (Halmai 2012: 1346). In many jurisdictions, judges quote foreign law to decide domestic legal issues, especially in the realm of constitutional adjudication. Judicial 'legal borrowing' or 'legal transplants' are no longer a taboo, if they ever were one.[1] This legal trend seems to refute an older thesis of globalization research. Niklas Luhmann (1991 [1971]: 63) suggested that worldwide interaction is primarily established in areas of society that maintain a style of *cognitive* as opposed to *normative* expectation. Cognitive expectations are characterized by a willingness to adapt in the event of disappointment. This style of expectation prevails, for example, in the fields of science and economy where involved actors are prepared to modify their expectations in response to economic market fluctuations or scientific progress. By contrast, normative expectations are sustained in the event of disappointment. In the domain of law, for instance, the violation of a statute usually does not lead to its amendment, but to its implementation. Now, the suggestion that law as a field based on a normative style of expectation is less susceptible to globalized modes of interaction seems to be refuted by the continuously growing entanglement of constitutional and ordinary courts. Legal practice appears to be a driving force of globalization.

In order to take sides in this controversy on law's contribution to globalization, I will take a step back and examine the function that comparative law fulfils in cosmopolitical legal literature. To this end, the next section outlines the current debate on legal borrowing in Comparative Constitutional Law. This debate will then be linked to the First International Conference on Comparative Law (1900). Three contributions to this conference, which are strongly committed to the cosmopolitan cause, will be examined in more detail. As I will argue, there are two motives which led these early legal cosmopolitans to the field of Comparative Law. First, the method of comparative law is openly praised as a necessary means for the realization of world law. Behind this ostensible motive, however, hides a second function of comparative law, which the presenters at the conference mostly kept latent but which can, nonetheless, be distilled from their contributions. According to this, comparative law provides assistance for teleological decision-making in court. At the turn of the 20th century, reform-oriented lawyers of Western jurisdictions established the view that, in the event of legal gaps, the judge should first and foremost consider the consequences of the decision when reaching a verdict. In the context of this teleological conception of judicial decision-making, comparisons to experiences in other jurisdictions may provide a welcome orientation to better assessing the consequences of certain decisions. Remarkably, many legal scholars who preach a normative universalism simultaneously advocate a teleological model of judicial interpretation; this is the case both for Comparative Law around 1900 and for today's literature. This impulse to engage with comparative law undermines the cosmopolitan pleas for world law voiced at the international conference.

The current constitutional debate on legal borrowing in court

Among many constitutional courts, it is a widespread practice to turn to foreign jurisprudence and foreign law in order to resolve domestic legal issues. Since the 2000s, this practice has attracted a lot of attention within the discipline of (Comparative) Constitutional Law. Particularly in the US, triggered by two Supreme Court decisions in which the Court's majority partly relied on foreign legal sources to settle delicate human rights issues, a fierce debate over the legitimacy of turning to foreign law to resolve domestic legal disputes has evolved. Some courts and judges have been fiercely attacked for relying on foreign legal material.[2] Among constitutional scholars, there is an intense debate over the epistemic status these foreign sources assume in domestic courts.

Next to the case *Lawrence v. Texas* (2003), the decision rendered by the US Supreme Court in *Roper vs. Simmons* (2005) has fuelled this debate. In *Roper*, the Court declared it unconstitutional to impose the death penalty on offenders who were under the age of eighteen when their crimes were committed. Justice Kennedy, who delivered the majority opinion, drew criticism from countless constitutional lawyers for backing the ruling with international treaties that the American government had explicitly declined to adopt.[3] The majority's strategy of building on treaties that had not been ratified by the US constituted the main point of contention. In a dissenting opinion, Justice Scalia attacked the majority's line of reasoning from a separation of powers perspective by pointing to the legally non-binding nature of the legal sources invoked by Justice Kennedy: 'Unless the Court has added to its arsenal the power to join and ratify treaties on behalf of the United States, I cannot see how this evidence favours, rather than refutes, its position' (*Roper v. Simmons*, 2005).

Even though constitutional scholars had already encountered the issue of comparative constitutional interpretation on an earlier occasion (Choudhry 1999), the *Roper* case spurred on the controversy over the legitimacy of legal borrowing in court. What is interesting here, is the fact that in legal scholarship this issue has been construed as a debate between normative universalism and normative particularism. For instance, it is customary to distinguish *particularist* constitutional cultures such, as that in the US whose courts traditionally are rather reluctant to turn to foreign case law and literature, from those pursuing an open-minded or *universalist* approach, such as the highest courts in Canada, Israel and South Africa, which seek judicial guidance from foreign legal experiences on a regular basis (Choudhry 1999; Markesinis and Fedtke 2006). Similarly, the normative question of the *legitimacy* of legal borrowing in court is raised in identical terms. Among proponents of practised legal comparison, universalism is invoked as a normative argument. Defending the Supreme Court's outreach to foreign legal material, constitutional scholar Vicky Jackson (2005: 118) claims that 'foreign or international legal sources may illuminate "suprapositive" dimensions of constitutional rights', thus highlighting their universal nature. She argues that the resistance to drawing on foreign law in constitutional adjudication cannot be justified in light of the 'universalist components' (ibid.: 122) of the US Constitution. In a similar spirit, Sujit Choudhry identifies a judicial style of 'universalist interpretation' and stresses that 'the constant use of foreign jurisprudence will serve to remind not only courts, but other actors in the legal system as well – governments, legal counsel, and private litigants – that a nation's particular constitutional guarantees are shared with other countries' (Choudhry 1999: 888).

Conversely, legal scholars taking a critical stance towards transnational legal borrowing pursue the same conceptual approach. Richard Posner (2005: 85) resents the normative universalism on which Justice Kennedy's judgments were allegedly based:

> I do not think the citation of these foreign decisions is an accident, or that it is unrelated to moral vanguardism. It marks Justice Kennedy [...] as a natural lawyer. The basic idea of natural law is that there are universal principles of law that inform – and constrain – positive law. If they are indeed universal, they should be visible in foreign legal systems and so it is 'natural' to look to the decisions of foreign courts for evidence of universality.

This is an attitude that Posner describes as unacceptable. Normative universalism is rejected as the theoretical manifestation of a bygone era, that is, the era of natural law. The debate thus amounts to a dispute over normative convictions. Both opponents and supporters of using comparative law as a source in court conceive of this debate in identical terms, namely as an argument between universalism and particularism. Likewise, neutral observers like Mark Tushnet or Jeremy Waldron construe this debate as the fight of constitutional patriotism against normative universalism (Tushnet 2006) or as the alternative of 'law as will' and 'law as reason' (Waldron 2005: 146).

It is perfectly understandable to present this issue in these terms. However, universalist lawyers must have noticed by now that judicial borrowing is not just a cosmopolitical success story. The Hungarian Constitutional Court, which played an inglorious role in underpinning Orban's path to illiberal democracy, invoked, whether justifiably or not, a ruling by the German Federal Constitutional Court when defending the 'constitutional identity' of Hungary against European impositions (Halmai 2017). Some critics of this legal borrowing in court have recognized that the cosmopolitan promises of many constitutional lawyers and judges may conceal other motives, most importantly personal 'political preferences' (Posner 2005: 85). In a conversation with Justice Stephen Breyer, Justice Antonin Scalia dispelled the universalistic claim of his opponents. Mockingly, Scalia put himself in the shoes of a judge who looks for legal sources all over the world to solve a domestic legal dispute:

> I as a judge am not looking for the original meaning of the Constitution, nor for the current standards of decency of American society; I'm looking for what is the best answer to this social question in my judgment as an intelligent person. And for that purpose I take into account the views of other judges, throughout the world. (Dorsen et al. 2005: 526)

According to Scalia, the political inclination of the judge rather than a normative interest in a globally shared legal framework forms the basis of practised legal borrowing. Scalia recognizes that another dimension is hidden behind the displayed universalism. The constitutional judge applying comparative law does not try to *interpret* the domestic constitutional framework, but to find an answer to a particular social question. According to Scalia, the different approaches to legal borrowing stem from different conceptions of the judge. Behind the dispute between constitutional particularism and universalism – this is also recognized by the progressive side – lie different images of judicial decision-making.

This two-dimensionality has accompanied Comparative Law since its institutional foundation. The following sections historically retrace the current constitutional debate by analysing key contributions to the first International Conference on Comparative Law in 1900. The historical comparison will reveal that today's advocates of world law reproduce commonplaces that were already firmly anchored in Comparative Law around 1900. During that time, prominent legal scholars used similar arguments in their pursuit of a world law realized through legal practice. As will be demonstrated, the pioneers of modern comparative law have not only excelled in normative universalism. Rather, these authors stand for a general change of mentality within legal methodology, which has been decisive for the emergence of practices of legal borrowing. Contextualizing current debates on practised comparative law in historical terms will reinforce the suspicion of some critics that today's partisans of legal borrowing are driven by more than cosmopolitan motives.

Visible and latent motives of early Comparative Law: The *Congrès international de droit comparé* (1900)

Throughout the 19th century, jurists of the Western legal sphere were on the lookout for legal developments in other countries. The departure from natural law towards the end of the 18th century created the necessary epistemic leeway for the discipline of Comparative Law. While in the pre-modern period the problem of legal comparison in the narrower sense did not arise because of the absolute claims of religiously or rationalistically grounded natural law, the early 19th century experienced the complete implementation of a voluntarist understanding of law, which made the comparison of different legal systems of equal status possible in the first place. As early as the first half of the 19th century, the first journals dealing with foreign and comparative law were founded (Gordley 2006: 760; Zweigert and Kötz 1998: 55). In the greater part of the 19th century, during which national jurisprudences established themselves as scientific disciplines in the modern sense, perspectives on foreign law were typically taken in order to foster the systematization and autonomization of a *national* jurisprudence rather than to promote the assimilation of different legal orders (Steinmetz 2005: 38). Even though from the early 19th century jurists were inspired by the legal trends of other countries, the national legal sciences maintained the idea of a national legal system tied to conceptual entities such as the *Volksgeist*, the *Code Napoléon* or the *American Common Law*.

In the second half of the 19th century, the discipline of Comparative Law became increasingly institutionalized through the founding of learned societies, professorial chairs and further journals, particularly in France (Zweigert et al. 1998: 58). The discipline took a decisive step forward in 1900, when the *Congrès international de droit comparé* was organized on the occasion of the World Exhibition, thus assembling jurists from all over the (Western) world in Paris (Frankenberg 2018: 44). The great interest in comparative law originated primarily from the field of private law, owing to intensified trade and the ensuing problem of international legal harmonization. As can be seen from the 1888 treatise *Die Anfänge eines Weltverkehrsrechts* by Georg Cohn – an important author for early comparative law – international trade relations established the need for global unification of railway law, maritime law, copyright law and many other legal domains. In the context of this diagnosis, Cohn advocated the idea of a 'world law' [*Weltrecht*] for the domain of traffic law (Cohn 1888: 137). At the turn of the 20th century, legal scholarship distanced itself from the national conceptual foundations of 19th-century jurisprudence. The great projects of the classical era of modern jurisprudence – for instance James Kent's *Commentaries on American Law* (since 1830), Savigny's *System des heutigen römischen Rechts* (since 1840) and Charles Aubry and Charles Rau's *Cours de droit civil français* (1839) – had been written with the intention of giving a solid jurisprudential basis to national legal systems. Towards the end of the 19th century, new talking points emerged.

Visible function of comparative law: Realizing a common law of mankind

This conceptual reorientation is also noticeable at the Paris Conference. Some of the lectures given at this conference will now be examined in more detail. A glance at these contributions reveals that it is not a new strategy to rely on comparative law in order to drive forward the project of normative universalism. The main protagonists at the conference, not least the organizers Édouard Lambert and Raymond Saleilles, opted for exactly this strategy. The participants were aware that the conference was a milestone for their discipline. Therefore, many speakers used their lectures to elaborate on the function of comparative law for jurisprudence and society in a programmatic fashion. The vision of a global legal system plays a special role in this context. As demanded by Saleilles, the discipline of Comparative Law must ultimately contribute 'to the formation of a common law of civilized humanity' (Saleilles 1905 [1900]: 181).[4] Similarly, Lambert embarked on an activist agenda. He distanced himself from a purely scientific way of treating comparative law, which he labels as the sociological path and proposes a legal approach which construes 'comparative law as an instrument of action on the progress of law' (Lambert 1905 [1900]: 46). Lambert charged this variant of comparative law with nothing less than the approximation of different legal systems by 'gradually eliminating the differences between legislations governing peoples of the same civilization' (ibid.: 38). According to Lambert, who evokes Cohn's notion of *Weltrecht* (ibid.: 34), comparative law fulfils the same function as the ancient *jus commune*, for instance the *Deutsche Gemeinrecht*, did in the premodern period by transcending the legal patchwork stemming from the plurality of sovereign political powers (ibid.: 39). Comparative law may thus assist in creating a new kind of transnational 'common legislative law' [*droit commun législatif*] (ibid.: 39) that is capable of aligning the different legal systems of similarly developed nations. The contributions of both Saleilles and Lambert at the Conference conjure up the cosmopolitan utopia of 'a common law of mankind' (Zweigert and Kötz 1998: 3).

Similarly, Ernst Zitelmann and Josef Kohler, two important representatives of German civil law, appealed to the goal of global legal unification in their contributions to the conference. Mirroring the stance taken by Lambert, Zitelmann (1905 [1900]: 194) considered the discipline of Comparative Law as the most powerful means of preparing for the unification of different national systems of private law. Kohler's speech (1905 [1900]: 227) takes a similar direction while not lacking a peculiar universalist pathos:

> The science of comparative law is a product of modern legal science; it goes beyond the fields of local law and is at the forefront of world law, the law of all peoples. Each jurist, while maintaining a sense of his or her own nationality, at the same time feels as a citizen of humanity and perceives in his or her heart the pulsations common to all peoples.

It is thus a proven strategy to emphasize the cosmopolitan underpinnings of comparative law. In contrast to classical foundations of legal provisions in nationalist concepts such as the *Volksgeist* or the *Code Civil*, comparative private law in the late 19th century takes an angle towards the global. Among the above-mentioned participants in the conference, comparative law is regarded as the most promising instrument for the realization of a globally shared legal space.

But on what assumptions is this universalism based? As will now be shown, the contributions made by the above-mentioned participants at the International Conference evince very specific ideas about the nature of judicial decision-making. The next section produces evidence that late-19th-century discourse in comparative law is partly sustained by a latent motive that may undermine its universalist aspirations.

Latent function of comparative law: Assisting teleological decision-making in court

The authors previously considered draw on comparative law for another purpose besides its claimed contribution to realizing world law. This purpose is not apparent but remains latent. There are two conspicuous aspects which lead me to the assumption that the pursuit of a world law is not the only driving force for the comparative lawyers under investigation. First, it is striking that major protagonists of the International Conference were affiliated to a very similar movement of reform in late-19th-century jurisprudence. This movement was transnational in nature, but operated domestically in the critiques of jurists targeting their respective national legal traditions. From the late 19th century on, Lambert, Saleilles, Kohler and Zitelmann, among other participants at the conference excelled in criticizing the legal methodologies of their domestic legal traditions.

At the turn of the century, the French and German legal discourses cultivated the derogatory terms 'conceptual jurisprudence' [*Begriffsjurisprudenz*] and 'exegetic school' [*école de l'exégèse*] in order to disparage the classical period of 19th-century jurisprudence. First and foremost, the transnational uprising revolved around the theory of judicial interpretation. The central question is how the judge should act in cases of legal lacunae (Gängel and Mollnau 1992: 299). In essence, reform-oriented jurists campaigned for the teleological nature of judicial decision-making to be acknowledged. According to this spirit of reform, the evaluation of the possible consequences of a verdict must become an explicit and determining factor in the process of judicial interpretation. In reformed legal methodology, teleological concepts such as the *purpose* of the law or individual and social *interest* assume a prominent status. Legal reformers from the late 19th century were the first to elaborate the notion of functional or teleological judicial decision-making (Schelsky 1980: 173; Zweigert 1970: 244). As mentioned above, many of the participants of the Conference on Comparative Law in Paris embraced this reformist mindset too.

The second striking feature, related to the first one, is that none of the above-mentioned participants involved in the conference advocated an understanding of comparative law dedicated exclusively to the comparison of different national *statutory* frameworks. It is important to realize that there are different ways of practising comparative law. One very obvious way is to compare the laws of different jurisdictions. A cosmopolitan legal vision could then be expressed through proposals for legislative reform. In the lectures that were given, the comparison of different domestic legislation and the possible influence exerted by comparative lawyers on parliaments is only recognized as a minor task of comparative law. This task is accompanied and completely outshone by another. As contended by eminent participants at the Conference, *comparative law must be practised in court by providing assistance in the process of judicial decision-making*. Not the legislature, but the judge was in the foreground of the contributions to the conference.

The fact that the lecturers advocated the reform of judicial interpretation in similar fashion and dedicated their contributions mainly to the judge indicates, in my opinion, an interest in comparative law which was not primarily based on the objective of realizing a world law. Subliminally, but nevertheless visibly, the authors defended the stance that comparative law mainly assists in findings answers to certain domestic problems. According to this view, comparative law is an effective instrument for filling legal gaps, not a cosmopolitan end in itself. The understanding of comparative law as a useful element for judicial interpretation was the product of the legal reform movement of the late 19th century. Zweigert and Siehr (1971: 220) credit Rudolf von Jhering with the insight that comparative law and renewed judicial methodology were interconnected:

> his idea that the judge, in his law-applying functions, does not always act like a machine but plays an actively creative role, opened the way for comparative law to aid in interpreting statutes, and even more in finding the law in areas which are void of established legal rules.

Comparative law may provide support in a judicial judgement which is explicitly oriented towards criteria of usefulness. It was particularly reform-oriented legal scholars around 1900 who turned against the stereotypical image of the judge as a mere subsumption machine. Comparative law, among other tools, is then seen as a valuable instrument for solving certain social problems that arise due to gaps in the legal system. In this way of addressing comparative law, the idea of a world law has no conceptual place. This latent aspect of comparative law can be extracted from the lectures given by Kohler, Lambert and Saleilles.[5]

As Kohler (1905 [1900]: 234) emphasized, current developments in the field of international law evoke new duties for the legal profession:

> We recognize that we contribute to the improvement of civilization [...]; moreover, we know that we can hold ourselves, by our intelligence and thoughtful action, the flag of progress; we also know that we can find in foreign law important materials that can benefit our people and render considerable services to the development of law. We now recognize that the jurist is not only a researcher of law, but also a politician of law, that his

experiences can be put to good use for the advancement of law; in particular, the jurist who practises comparative law is able to refer to foreign law, and thereby indicate the most appropriate means to benefit our own law and the nation to which we belong.

This passage is interesting for two reasons. First, Kohler takes up central topoi of the movement to reform judicial interpretation. This is particularly evident in his conception of the jurist as a legal politician. In this context, he distances himself from traditional jurisprudence which 'denied the jurist the competence to engage in legal politics and considered that his only business was to honour and worship positive law without taking into account its value or merit' (ibid.: 234). Hereby, Kohler reproduces a widely disseminated preconception of legal reformists regarding traditional 19th-century jurisprudence. At the International Conference, Kohler did not explicitly refer to the tasks of the *judge*, but elaborated on the general duties of jurisprudence. However, reading these statements against the backdrop of his own doctrine of judicial interpretation, in which he defends the notion of judge-made law (Kohler 1886: 60), we may assume that his general expectations of the jurist announced at the conference were addressed mainly to the judge. Echoing a general sentiment around 1900, Kohler resisted a rigid notion of separation of powers by highlighting the political responsibility of judicial decision-making. The value of comparative law is connected to a new understanding of the judge. If the judge is released from his role as a legal scientist and recognized as a politician, comparative law assumes major importance. As described by Kohler, comparative law becomes a powerful tool in the context of such political considerations of expediency, which ought also to be practised by judges.

Second, Kohler's speech reveals that comparative law is first and foremost an instrument for solving national problems. It is true that human civilization as a whole is said to benefit from it, but comparative law is meant to directly promote the advancement of 'our people' and 'our own law'. Kohler thus sets a new focus: comparative law is not, as pretended, conceived in terms of the goal of a world law, but rather serves as a means of progressing domestic law and society. A look abroad may help the jurist, or the judge, to implement better legal solutions in his own legal system.

In the lecture by Lambert, the conceptual linking of comparative law and reformed judicial methodology becomes more obvious. As described above, Lambert considers the approximation and gradual unification of different legal systems to be the main task of comparative law. How is this 'common legislative law' [*droit commun législatif*] (Lambert 1905 [1900]: 39) to be realized? Lambert puts all his hopes in the judge. As argued, the harmonization of different legal systems must be achieved by means of judicial interpretation.

> Just as common customary law and the *Deutsches Privatrecht* were applied by the courts in the silence of local customs and particular laws, common legislative law may be introduced in each country through the gaps of domestic case law. It will not only be used by the courts as evidence of written reason, but as an expression of the common understanding of domestic and parental law. The work of interpretation continually brought the provisions of our old customs closer to those of customary common law, which seemed to better reflect the present spirit of the whole of these customs; at the same time, it slowly brought the provisions of the Landrechte closer to the rules of *Deutsches Privatrecht* (ibid.: 45).

Lambert connects the general theme of comparative law with the issue of legal lacunae, the linchpin of legal reform literature. Against this background, it is instructive to compare Lambert's lecture with an article he published in the same year. In this article, he approaches comparative law starting from the problem of judicial interpretation rather than from the perspective of world law. Reform-oriented legal scholars around 1900 pursued different methodological agendas to solve the problem of legal gaps. Francois Gény, for example, countered the 'traditional method', which he attributed to 19th-century jurisprudence, with '*libre recherche scientifique*', by which the judge further advances the legal system in a socially and morally beneficial way. Lambert, by contrast, draws on comparative law as an methodological alternative for Gény's *libre recherche scientifique* (Jamin 2010: 382), proclaiming: 'Where will we find the directions, the indispensable points of support to guide the course of case law in this way? In the science of comparative civil law' (Lambert 1900: 240). Within the conceptual framework of teleological decision-making, comparative law provides the orientation that many of Lambert's contemporaries (for instance, Roscoe Pound, Raymond Saleilles, Eugen Ehrlich and Ernst Fuchs) saw in sociology. The consequences of a legal decision, as assumed by Lambert, can be better assessed through the experience that other jurisdictions have had in dealing with similar problems. Thus, in this article, the line of argumentation is reversed compared to his lecture at the International Conference. Comparative law does not primarily serve to establish a world law. Rather, it is intended to assist in interpreting an incomplete body of laws and thus to provide illustrative material for the resolution of certain social problems.

Nevertheless, Lambert's contribution to the International Conference was also marked by features that run counter to his ostentatious cosmopolitanism. The great importance Lambert attached to the dimension of legal practice in this lecture reflects his idea that comparative law provides an answer to the problem of legal lacunae. The relevance of *this* motive is also expressed in the fact that Lambert instructs the comparative lawyer to consult foreign law in order to find the best 'solution' to certain social 'problems' (Lambert 1905 [1900]: 50ff.). This functionalist language is indicative of his actual concern. The main function of comparative law is to provide the judge with instructive templates for solving certain problems. In this context, world law forfeits its absolute claim: 'When, with the help of these instruments, the comparatist sees the definite superiority of one of these solutions – and only then – will he lend it the character of a provision of common legislative law' (ibid.: 52). Approaching comparative law in functionalist terms, common legislative law, Lambert's expression for world law, is simply defined as the *best* possible solution to a particular problem. In his lecture at the conference, world law is not pursued as an end in itself. The cosmopolitan charisma vanishes in this instrumental definition of world law. By defining the function of comparative law as a means of providing illustrative material for the solution of certain (domestic) problems, the discipline as a whole is placed in the hands of domestic factors.

Saleilles's contribution to the International Conference pursues a similar line of reasoning. By analogy with Lambert, he sets an activist tone stating that comparative law must not be limited to a purely historical and sociological role, it ought rather to pave the way for 'legal politics' (*politique juridique*) (Saleilles 1905 [1900]: 177). While the diversity of legal cultures is to be respected, the objective of the political initiative advocated by Saleilles is to propel the unification of different legal systems (ibid.: 178). Comparative law is supposed to assume a pioneering role in this process: 'Jurisprudence [*droit*] studies the existing law, comparative law seeks to deduce the law that ought to be [*la loi qui doit être*]' (ibid.: 179).

Saleilles's idea of *politique juridique*, as described above, envisages the ideal of a common law of mankind (ibid.: 181). Even though he distinguishes three mechanisms by which this ideal state may be accomplished, namely legislation, scientific doctrine and judicial interpretation (ibid.: 182), his greatest interest by far is in the mechanism of legal interpretation. Here too, the project of comparative law is linked to the issue of legal gaps. Comparative law, he contends, assumes a crucial function in supplementing the gaps in the legal system. Most importantly, foreign law thus becomes a significant tool in *teleological* interpretatory practice:

> The idea that must prevail in this case, where the law no longer applies formally, is that the interpretation must be made in the sense of the practical, economic and social purpose of the law, in accordance with all the legal principles on which it is based. Now, the practical, economic and social purpose of a law becomes increasingly apparent to the extent that it concerns institutions responding to general and permanent needs, thus moving away from the narrowness of locally applied law in order to draw inspiration from the progress achieved throughout the civilized world. This is particularly true when it comes to remedying ills or inconveniences of a public nature, or to satisfying needs that meet a principle of superior morality (ibid.: 183f.).

The teleological language betrays that comparative law is not simply placed in the service of a world law, the judge must be concerned with finding answers to certain 'needs' and realizing the 'purposes' of certain laws. As with Lambert, looking at the legal experiences of other jurisdictions is not an end in itself. Comparative law is a source of 'inspiration' for the domestic legal system. Legal comparison thus provides valuable assistance to the process of outcome-oriented judicial decision-making. Like many conference participants, Saleilles set himself apart from the traditional methodological notion of judicial interpretation and propagated the ideal of a policy-driven judiciary. Comparative law thus turns into an instrument to judicially 'loosen the law' (ibid.: 187). The variety of foreign legal sources provides the judge with a wide range of material that allows him to take the 'organic initiative' (ibid.: 187) for the further development of the legal system.

Like Lambert and Kohler, Saleilles represents a model of purposive judicial interpretation. Judicial decision-making must be guided and founded upon considerations of social expediency. In Saleilles's lecture, too, this understanding is echoed by functionalist terminology. Discussing the mechanism of judicial interpretation, he does not instruct the judge to transcend the national legal horizon in order to access an area of transnationally shared legal norms, but to find *solutions* to certain social *problems*:

> The question is [...] whether the interpretation of national law must and can be carried out in accordance with the guidance provided by comparative law,

and therefore in line with the solutions which, at a given moment in history, constitute the ideal type of legal progress. (ibid.: 182)

Taking up a fundamental trope of the late-19th-century legal reform movement, it is a general trait of the conference lectures examined here to embed law and judicial interpretation in a functionalist conceptual framework (next to Lambert, see also Zitelmann 1905 [1900]: 193). It is crucial to note that this functional/teleological understanding of law is not limited to the sphere of the legislature, but refers to the process of judicial decision-making. The proliferation of functionalist terminology at the Conference on Comparative Law may be read as the manifestation of a newly established mentality in judicial methodology. Comparative Law then becomes a crucial factor in the context of a theory of interpretation according to which the judge may or must openly profess a policy-oriented attitude in the process of applying the law.

Deceptive universalism

In the three lectures, two distinct problems are blended together. Firstly, the authors claim to pursue the normative goal of a universalist world law. Secondly, this goal is repeatedly flanked by the completely different issue of judicial interpretation. This second question puts the cosmopolitan vision of a universal world law into perspective. It is one thing to pursue the goal of a common law of mankind as an end in itself; another to consult comparative law as part of an attractive teleological mechanism for filling legal gaps. In the latter case, comparative law and with it the idea of a world law are harnessed as resources for policy-oriented modes of judicial decision-making in the absence of a clear legislative basis. *The utopia of a common law of mankind, to which the comparative lawyers of the International Conference seem to be committed, is at odds with an understanding of comparative jurisprudence that serves to provide illustrative material for resolving certain social problems.* The great attention paid to legal practice as opposed to statutory law, especially in the case of Saleilles and Lambert, is self-exposing in this regard. If the normative goal of a world law were driving these authors, then we would not be witnessing a one-sided fixation on the judge. This feeds the suspicion that the normative universalism often propagated in comparative law at the turn of the 20th century was oblique. At the conference, the authors discussed above advocated a certain idea of judicial decision-making that had not primarily evolved out of a jurisprudential interest in comparative or world law. Their contributions indirectly served another jurisprudential cause, which, in turn, had an impact on their cosmopolitan aspirations.

In order to understand the peculiarity of combining these two motives, one should be aware of alternative approaches to comparative law. As described above, modern jurisprudence had already encountered the idea of comparative law before the late 19th century. Rudolf von Jhering, for example, in his early period of writing during which he had not yet polemicized against the classical methodology of so-called 'conceptual jurisprudence' [*Begriffsjurisprudenz*], had already called for lawyers to look abroad to solve domestic legal issues. His motto, announced in 1866, has become a frequently quoted topos in the field of Comparative Law:

> The question of the reception of foreign legal institutions is not a question of nationality, but simply one of expediency, of need. No one will fetch a thing from abroad when he has as good or better at home; but only a fool will reject the bark of the cinchona because it did not grow in his vegetable garden. (Jhering 1866: 8f.)[6]

In contrast to the legal discourse around 1900, however, the young Jhering did not understand comparative legal research as a mandate for the judge. Jhering's remarks may be read as an appeal to the legislature to look abroad before passing a law. Although this approach to legal comparison reveals a utilitarian understanding of law it is not a plea to base judicial decision-making on teleological considerations. There is a crucial difference between conceptualizing law in general in teleological terms and doing the same for judicial decision-making, a difference usually neglected in historical research on legal thought (for instance Kennedy 2006: 22). Only the late 19th century saw a teleological theory of interpretation emerging which, as described in the last section, was strongly represented at the International Conference in Paris.

Strikingly, the discipline of Comparative Law was institutionalized at a historical juncture in which jurisprudence established a new image of the judge and judicial decision-making. Traditional legal theory conceived judicial interpretation as a process in which legal norms were either directly applied or, in the case of legal lacunae, in which the legal system was further developed from within on the basis of existing legal principles and in accordance with scientific standards. From the late 19th century, by contrast, the *political* dimension of judicial decision-making came to the fore. The judge was increasingly perceived as a figure responsible for solving certain social problems and who, for this purpose, ought to take appropriate policy considerations into account. The scope of applying comparative law thus noticeably widened for reform-minded legal scholars of late 19th century. Legal comparison appears to be of particular interest for jurisprudence in the context of a legal theory that grants judges the opportunity to build on foreign legal experiences in order to pursue certain policies. This does not imply that consulting comparative law as a source of inspiration for the domestic *legislature* disappeared at the end of the 19th century. Christophe Jamin claims that most French legal scholars of the early 20th century continued to practise comparative law along these conventional lines, Lambert and Saleilles being the exception (Jamin 2010).

Undisputedly, the global emerges as a central category in the discourse of comparative law around 1900, for instance in the shape of a *Weltrecht* or the *droit commun de l'humanité*. Central actors at the *Congrès international de droit comparé*, which in 1900 brought renowned jurists from all over the world together in Paris, transcended classical national legal conceptions by placing comparative law at the service of envisioning a global horizon of law. However, the normative universalism frequently displayed among comparative lawyers disintegrated due to their idea of teleological interpretation, as the cosmopolitan potential of the underlying theory of judicial interpretation is limited. The spirit of legal reform takes as its starting point the alleged inability of classical legal methodology to meet social problems, for instance in the field of labour law, in a satisfactory manner. The dispute between traditional and reformed jurisprudence was conducted within a national frame of reference despite the international entanglements of the involved jurists. In response to the problem of legal lacunae, legal reformers have developed different agendas to achieve specific social objectives through the courts. The world or the global did not play a role here. The evocation of a world law occurring at the International Conference is thus accompanied by a concept that was fashioned for unrelated purposes. This unrelatedness is reflected in the twofold recourse to comparative law in the lectures. On the one hand, comparative law is used as a path to world law. On the other, it is drawn upon as a useful tool for judicial decision-making.

In the conference lectures examined above, the notion of world law is built on unstable ground. The globalist vision of a world law degenerates into a normative appeal addressed to the judge. As stipulated, it is incumbent upon the judiciary to gradually enforce universal world law. Even leaving aside questions of *global* law, there is already enough reason to doubt whether the high level of trust placed in the socio-political capacity of the judiciary by reform-oriented jurists around 1900 was justified. The cult of the judge, however, was completely exaggerated when comparative lawyers around 1900 placed their hopes in the judicature to ensure the harmonization of different national legal frameworks. Empirically, confidence in a cosmopolitan cause pursued by the judiciary was refuted. National Socialist jurisprudence demonstrated how the achievements of the legal reform movement could be harnessed for its own purposes. Instead of paving the way for a world law, German jurisprudence of the 1930s took advantage of the insight into the political nature of judicial decision-making to exempt domestic courts from the formal pressure exerted by the legal system and let them openly pursue fascist policies (Schröder 1985: 114ff.). The comparative lawyers of the late 19th century tied the project of a global law to prerequisites that potentially led astray from their universalistic inclinations.

World law: The bad conscience of the progressive lawyer?

Putting the constitutional debate on comparative legal practice into a historical context, we may register that the current issues dealt with in the field of Comparative *Constitutional* Law are basically repetitions of issues that have been present in Comparative Law since the late 19th century, particularly in the field of Civil Law. The differences between civil and constitutional law can be neglected here. For the purposes of this chapter, it is irrelevant whether the comparative lawyer turns to foreign legal sources in order to examine problems of copyright law or to verify the constitutionality of criminal law in dealing with minor offenders. Both at the International Conference around 1900, which took place under the auspices of private law, and in the constitutional debate on legal borrowing carried on since the 2000s universalist and teleological motives have run side by side. In my estimation, for both time periods it can be stated that especially advocates of a teleological interpretation preach a normative universalism.[7] It is certainly no coincidence that the constitutional lawyer Aharon Barak, who drives forward the agenda of practised legal comparison as few others do, at the same time stands out as a central author of reference for a contemporary model of a 'Purposive Interpretation in Law' (Barak 2005).

If this speculation holds up, how could the connection between the two motives be explained? Why do jurists who support a teleological model of judicial interpretation in particular tend to solemnly declare their commitment to world law? To give a speculative answer to this question, let us resume Luhmann's above-mentioned thesis that globalization is particularly prevalent in fields with cognitive as opposed to normative styles of expectation. Judging by the self-description of numerous comparative lawyers, this thesis is untenable, since their discipline holds the potential to normatively integrate world society. Rephrasing their stance in Luhmannian terms, one could say that comparative law practitioners implement normative expectations on a global scale by horizontally connecting the legal systems of different countries and opening up a global legal space.

However, the evidence gathered in this chapter supports rather than undermines the thesis advanced by Luhmann. The preceding analysis dispels the claim of comparative law to establish a universal, disappointment-proof style of expectation. Many advocates of a world law are associated with a reformist agenda that has vehemently challenged the dominance of normative expectation structures in the judiciary. At the turn of the 20th century, countless reformist legal scholars campaigned for an open and adaptive judicial methodology or, in Luhmann's terms, for opening up the process of judicial interpretation in favour of a style of *cognitive* expectation. In its most radical manifestations, for example among some representatives of the living law doctrine [*Freirechtsdoktrin*], a doctrine of interpretation is being propagated by legal reformists in which the normative expectation stipulated by law must be occasionally ignored or virtually rewritten so that the judge can reach a socially desired goal (Fuchs 1970 [1910]: 464). But even the less radical representatives of the reform movement are making selective efforts to change the style of expectation prevalent in law. Legal scholars who, like the participants in the Parisian Conference discussed above, instruct the judge to look abroad for legal solutions to certain problems, are not advocating a normative but a cognitive style of expectation.

In my view, it is no coincidence that Comparative Law embraced the idea of a universal law of mankind at a historical juncture when an influential reform movement tried to establish a cognitive expectation style in jurisprudence alongside the traditional structure of normative expectation. Such demands represent a departure from the traditional promise of law in general, namely to ensure reliability of expectations. Policy-oriented decision-making in court transcends the normative style of expectation by which law as a field is generally characterized. The emphatic advocacy of world law is the normative compensation for this rupture. The concept of world law then serves to legitimize the contestable model of purposive legal interpretation. Breaking with the expectation structure peculiar to law is cushioned by the metaphysical assumption that the teleological orientation of the judge is normatively secured by an existing world law. The normative universalism proclaimed by many comparative lawyers is a proven discursive strategy to semantically stabilize the newly developed political understanding of judicial decision-making. The fact that the model of teleological interpretation is concealed by an ostentatious commitment to a common law of mankind may explain the intensity of the reactions to the transnational expeditions of the American Supreme Court. Against this backdrop, the concerns of Scalia and other critical judges and legal scholars cannot be dismissed. Behind the promise of a world law hides the bad conscience of the politicized judge.

Notes

1. In comparative law literature, there are numerous metaphors and terminologies to describe the process of transferring foreign law into a domestic legal system. I am aware of the weaknesses of the term 'legal borrowing' and I realize that it carries other connotations compared to the term 'legal transplants'. Terminological debates of this kind will not be resumed or addressed here. The following analysis takes some terminological liberties by providing an external perspective on current debates in comparative (constitutional) law. For an informative overview of the diverse terminologies, see Perju (2012: 1306ff.).
2. The majority's reliance on foreign legal sources has been heavily criticized going so far that conservative politicians proposed a bill in Congress which would prohibit the use of foreign law in American Courts. In this context, even calls for impeaching the liberal Justices have been issued.
3. Justice Kennedy invoked the *Convention on the Rights of the Child* which has never been ratified by the US and the *International Covenant on Civil and Political Rights* which has been ratified by the US, *however* under the condition that the US may reserve the right to impose capital punishment on minors.
4. The translations of all passages taken from contributions to the *Congrès* are provided by the author.

5   Unfortunately, Zitelmann's contribution is too short to dare a substantial analysis.
6   For the translation, see Zweigert and Siehr (1971: 215).
7   This presumption needs to be examined more closely, for example by analysing contributions to the international conference that do not subscribe to the teleological method of interpretation.

Determining *the Global* from a Social Work Perspective

Sandra Holtgreve and Cornelia Giebeler

Introduction

The present chapter envisions perceptions of the global in Social Work debates.[1] It answers the question as to which understandings of the global prevail in discussions of the practice and theory of social work. It also addresses significant lacunae in globalization research, where the unique views of social workers as world political actors from below receive almost no attention. Furthermore, it responds to the lack of systematic endeavours in Social Work debates to classify existing literature and propose conceptual work on positions adopted in Social Work with regard to globalization. How do authors in the field observe the global? How do actors in the field make sense of such a framework and what conclusions can be drawn to determine imaginaries of the global within the discipline?

Our questions align with the other contributions to the present volume, all of which engage with the inquiry into how different groups of people such as lawyers, travellers or revolutionaries make sense of the world. The perspectives of Social Work are particularly valuable in this regard, because they occupy a unique position in the global arena – at the margins of societal exclusion, which connect the global and the local. Professional social workers exist in almost every country of the world, where they deal with the negative consequences of globalization. They advocate for its 'losers' and use the global arena to (re)negotiate their sphere of influence and pursue social transformations. However, social workers cope with different conditions (and constraints) than the other groups mentioned at the beginning of the paragraph. They not only defend the interests of their clients; they also have to respond to the objectives of their employers. This is not without conflict and makes it highly interesting to analyse how perceptions of the global relate to the in-between position of social work and the purpose of its mediating this professional double role.

This chapter shares the overall objective of the volume: to look at practices of observation. We pay attention not only to what Social Work scholars observe, but also to *how* they observe, including the subtle meanings that underlie their observations. This systematic focus on practices of observing the global challenges a debate that too often presupposes a clear and commonly held understanding of the subject matter and therefore underestimates the conceptual variety characterizing the field. For example, discussions on the effects of globalization are often framed in terms of 'international social work'. Sometimes texts juxtapose or interchange ideas on the 'international', 'transnational', 'intercultural' or 'global' elements in social work, failing to differentiate the nuances and to determine more precisely the epistemological starting point(s) for carrying out 'global social work'. Like doctors who first study human anatomy in order to define the treatment, we conceptualize the latent understandings of the global first in order to substantiate the strategic planning, coordination and execution of social actions in response to global phenomena. This gives a more differentiated view of global social work. Against this background, the chapter encourages its diverse readership to engage further with the basic characteristics of the profession and discipline of Social Work, the challenges that are faced in this field and the underpinnings of the global that prevail in the contemporary debate.

To address the conceptual frames of the global in Social Work literature, we distinguish four subtle functions: (a) positing globalization as the root of social inequalities grants legitimacy to the profession; (b) the global methodological paradigm responds to the heterogeneity and multidimensionality of social reality from global to local in social work research and practice; (c) the global frame of reference enables social workers to defend common interests as a community, and (d) the global arena as a working field demands particular skills of them and poses new challenges for social work. The remainder of the chapter is divided into three parts. In the first, we give an introductory overview of the main literature and lines of argumentation in current debates in the field of Social Work. We then review contemporary literature to scrutinize the four above-mentioned dimensions. Whereas the first two have to do with ways in which social workers observe the world, the last two indicate the ways in which social workers react to the world based on their perceptions and organize themselves within it. We conclude that the position of social work at the margins of exclusion makes its view on the global unavoidably critical and plural.

The nexus of global and local in the emergence of social work

Social work can be described as a profession that develops interventions on a scientific basis serving to support and assist people, groups and communities in different life contexts in various areas. These include psychiatry, education, impairment, the penal system, social counselling and families. The professionalization of social work and social pedagogy in different nations evolved as a consequence of crisis-ridden eruptions of social conditions in which humanitarian aid or domestic – usually female – obligations to provide support were no longer sufficient. These eruptions were, in particular, the wars in Europe in the 19th and early 20th centuries, but also dramatic economic events such as the abolition of nitrate extraction in northern Chile, which caused the rapid impoverishment of thousands of working families. Historically, social work evolved constantly as a result of the mutually dependent interface between welfare state developments and social upheavals embodied by the emergence or rise of mass poverty and infirmity as well as the neglect of children and young people (the classic target group of social education).

The emergence of the profession can be explained, on the one hand, as a reaction to the atrocities resulting from capitalist modes of production. On the other hand, its evolution was based on an increasing understanding of the social rights of all individuals to a barrier-free life with all its consequences. Striving for equality, for practices of recognition, for the abolition of oppression, exclusion and incapacitation and – at the same time – for competent help with the implementation of needs, support of all kinds is at the heart of the profession. Nevertheless, implementation differs in different national contexts, significantly depending on the legal situation. In consequence, fields of intervention vary depending on national decisions, but the aims, theoretical approaches and methods adopted in the teaching of social work are widely similar. Thus, the profession is characterized by a holistic approach to supporting people in a globalized range of fields, only embedded in the national conditions of welfare states and in international organizations.

One of the internationally recognized ethical premises is that social work is fundamentally rooted in its so-called triple mandate. Firstly, professionals must act on behalf of their public or private employers. Secondly, they represent their addressees and defend their interests. Thirdly, they commit themselves to unique, internationally shared agreements on what constitutes professional working competence. Even if the legal context varies nationally, certain professional principles remain internationally binding – for example, the orientation towards human rights principles, which the international organizations of social work have erected as central pillars. At the same time, the profession reacts sensitively to global developments such as the consequences of the financial crisis in 2008, migration flows in Europe in 2015 or in Mexico since 2006 and the Coronavirus crisis in 2020. It responds to natural disasters resulting from climate change and to demographic changes such as the disintegration of intergenerational family care systems and the associated emergence of poverty and disability in elderly people. It is also reacting to the release of labour through the relocation of production, to the flexibilization of the world of work and to women's movements all over the world promulgating female care-work as the basis of society.

Against this background, three approaches to social work come to the fore in relation to its emergence within the global. Social work first emerged in response to the international processes of war, migration, the release of wage labour and the associated injuries to individuals, groups and communities. Then, the internationalization of human rights became a matter of fundamental agreement between peoples after the Second World War, associated with the conviction that cultural, social and economic human rights must be implemented. Finally, the local practice of social work encountered ever new challenges from destructive international markets, a diverging social gap between wealth and poverty, and an unresolved colonial history. The victims of this colonial history on one hand aim for recognition and reparations and on the other are part of migration processes into the former colonizing regions provoking decolonizing processes and asking for social work support as refugees or migrants.

Reliant on these historical roots, Social Work is inextricably linked to the global. But scholars and professionals in Germany, in contrast to those in other countries, have lagged behind in incorporating this link into their discussions. Until the end of the 20th century, scholars considered social work as predominantly a locally acting profession. This perception has only recently been questioned (Wagner and Lutz 2018; Giebeler 2003) and contested by a more transverse understanding of how social workers act in concrete local settings, use the possibilities and limits of national law and respond to global problems, adapting to the broader context of publications in other countries (Friesenhahn and Thimmel 2012; Bähr et al. 2014).

Beyond the German setting, links to global research are a particularly salient feature in current debates covering professional practice and education in Social Work to a similar extent. Scholars emphasize the need to take indigenous knowledges into account (Mafile´o and Vakalahi 2016), point to linguistic imperialism and further power differentials (Midgley 2016; Dominelli and Lorenz 2017), highlight regionalization, provincialization and decolonization efforts (Sałustowicz 2009; Gómez-Hernández 2018), or discuss the Sustainable Development Goals, and the Global Agenda 2030 as professional frameworks. Given the increasing number of articles, journals, book series, handbooks and conferences with an explicit international focus (Bunk et al. 2019), concepts in the discourse such as the transcultural, international, postcolonial etc. diversify and get blurred. Despite their manifold meanings, these terms for describing the global in Social Work are sometimes used interchangeably by scholars without further differentiation or concretization of the underlying understandings of the world that they embody.

The practices of observation of the global in the field of Social Work, meaning the way that the profession uses the global to define its standards, visions, objectives, mandate and frame of actions, can take different forms. Social workers, as a rule, act as agents of the state (or its subsidiary agencies) or on behalf of private organizations with specific support objectives, for example in development cooperation, international migration or globally networked anti-racist, feminist or ecologically based endeavours. In contrast to the other mentioned professional groups and political actors, social workers contribute to the regulation and execution of politics. To understand the political function of social work, it is important to recognize that it arose as a response to the context of the social question. The group became an important force of political control for states that was originally intended for the regulation and cleaning up of the massive, devastating social transformations that accompanied the installation of the capitalist social system. Thus, social work is highly politicized as a practice for implementing political decisions.

In all fields of social work, the global is visible and invisible at the same time. Global trends in film, theatre or music such as hip hop, treated as an expression of youth culture, may become the basis for concepts of youth work. New Zealand, for example, constructs and runs differentiated services for different ethnic groups, the separate refuges for battered Maori women being a case in point (cf. Watson 2019). Social workers elsewhere, for example in

Germany, assume concepts based on difference theory to be a form of gendered culturalization. Here scholars consider that practices of differentiation promote racism and so they criticize separate women's refuges for migrants. Thus, these concepts can be applied globally, but must always be viewed critically in light of local conditions. Sometimes, the global in social work is not directly visible, but can be approached through concepts of the unknown and of frightening strangeness (*Konzeptualisierung beängstigender Fremdheit*, cf. Giebeler 2019). Both can latently underlie the phenotypical perception of individuals, groups, communities and polities, favelas and barrios. Thus, the global is invisible, but accessible through experiences of strangeness in the unknown lifeworlds of clients.[2] The same applies to institutional assistance given to victims of violence, as well as work with children and youth, psychiatry and penitentiary work. Such insecurity and fear of strangeness brings professional social workers to the limits of their capabilities and forces them to learn about the appearance of the global in all cases of social work (Giebeler 1998). Finally, what do these examples from professional practice tell us about the global?

Four perceptions of the global in Social Work

Globalization's effects: focusing on inequalities as a professional rationale

The first way to address the global is as a way of *explaining the need for social work*. Thus, the world appears as the root cause of problems. In academic debates, the main concern remains the ways in which social workers deal with the negative consequences of economic, political, and cultural interactions worldwide. On the one hand, social workers discuss the effects which globalization has on the lives of their clients with the intention of developing appropriate ways of dealing with individuals, groups or local communities and mitigating the negative impacts of globalization. On the other hand, they look at the consequences of globalization for the system of professional aid itself. As a result of this development, social workers increasingly take on a double role: they find themselves acting not only as representatives of their clients but also as members of a professional group which itself is affected by the transnationalization of the care and social service sector.

Through the lens of inequalities, the first perspective emphasizes how globalization (re)produces or aggravates social problems at the levels below. Staub-Bernasconi (2003: 2) shows by means of the emblematic case of a disabled woman from Kosovo, how social workers address social problems resulting from chains of exclusion across borders, which start as globalization phenomena (in this case migration) and end up affecting the lifeworlds of their target groups. Excluded from the job market, security and an appropriate level of public safety (being subject to repeated rapes), without the right to public healthcare and hidden from society because her family was ashamed of her disability, the woman fled alone to Switzerland. She was told that the country was 'rich' with promising job prospects, the opportunity for financial security for her and her family back home, with access to health assistance and insurance, and where she could live 'safely' without discrimination due to her disability. But in Switzerland she was also excluded, although for different reasons, namely, her residence status. Apart from international migration, other factors such as the uncontrollability of global risks, climate change and its consequences, the supremacy of neoliberal ideologies, social spaces and contested identities, refugee movements, urbanization and rural poverty, the systematic violation of human rights and political violence, animals being used as objects of mass production and global water scarcity produce similar dynamics and effects and are challenges that social workers have to cope with (Spitzer 2019).

A second perspective surveys the influence of globalization on the social support system. Here, the focus shifts from target groups/recipients to the organization of aid itself. It is noticeable that discussions are less diverse, primarily criticizing neoliberal changes. Authors describe not only how global competition produces scarcity of resources for social programmes and the erosion of welfare state structures, but also the way in which structural changes influence working dynamics in social organizations such as increased work pressure in reaction to global economization (Bartley and Beddoe 2018; Lyons 2016; Lutz 2007). The latter especially has a significant impact on legal conflicts between national and supranational social policies regulating social work and care work. Contributions from these authors further focus on the question of how social services structures transnationalize through programmes of civic engagement in, for example, au-pair schemes, voluntary services abroad, the recruitment of foreign staff, and transnational service concepts, which diversify the landscape of social support services and challenge the understanding of professionalism in the field. These studies critically discuss the quality of professional services under pressure to economize or the social effects of an increasingly transnationalized care system on the wellbeing of clients (Lyons 2016; Schröer and Schweppe 2013; Winker 2018).

Analyses of the effects of globalization on both people's living conditions and the aid system have a common basis: the global appears as a threatening space and a motor of multiple inequalities which take on different shapes and are fraught with numerous challenges. Destructive effects must at the same time be decisively countered (Bartley and Beddoe 2018; Schirilla 2018) – a perception that equips social work to advocate for the 'losers of globalization, the excluded of modernity, the new precarious proletariat' (see Spitzer 2019). During the World Social Work Conference in 2012, Friesenhahn and Thimmel (2012) shed light on the consequences of this recognition. They highlight an ambivalence between normatively charged idealism and hopeless overburdening that leads to resignation. Globalization as a challenge exacerbates social work's task of engaging in damage control, but at the same time underlines the need for action.

Global perspectives: addressing heterogeneous living realities in research

The recognition of the need to counteract the effects of globalization goes along with the need to *develop appropriate tools for research and intervention* in globalized social realities. Scholars do not take an active but an indirect position vis-à-vis the global, which acknowledges that national and even international frames of observation are insufficient for research and intervention. Thus, this section does not address a direct way of envisioning the global, but a way to see it through the abstract idea of delimitation of spaces of intervention. By delimitation we mean that the spaces in which social workers are active are less and less defined by clear boundaries. Instead, they take on more and more dynamic forms (e.g. through transnational family structures).

> Following an overall trend in the social sciences since the 2000s, scholars are seeking to reframe social problems and overcome methodological nationalism. In this sense, shedding light on the global through an analytical view of inter- and transnationality and inter- and transculturality appears a safe strategy for scholars in Social Work. They widely agree that national frameworks are limiting in light of constant cross-border flows of goods, informa-

tion and people. At the same time, they hesitate to apply a holistic, global perspective in the sense of a 'global social work' to design and try to implement approaches with the goal of a theory-driven homogenization and a 'global profession'. Rather it [social work] should perceive and make differences among diverse groups' ethnicities, interests and forms of social support in its local, regional and (trans)local contexts. (Gray and Coates 2010: 23 cit. from Bähr et al. 2014: 19f.; authors' translation)

At the same time, the popularity of cross-national and cultural comparisons remains large (see Bartley and Beddoe 2018; Feize and Gonzalez 2018). These studies have contributed to the global understanding of social work since its beginnings. But both strategies are contested by critical scepticism. Critics argue that terms such as inter- or transnationality re-emphasize the category of the nation-state instead of overcoming it. Furthermore, those critical voices point to the centrality of legal frameworks which underline the importance of constitutional and national social laws, a line of argumentation which aims to foreground the limitations of transnational analysis. There are also scholars who have explored border identities and border spaces before debates on transnationalism in Social Work even gained prominence. Concrete alternative approaches to Social Work research are often marginalized in current debates, whereas the nation-state remains a crucial axis in research perspectives on the global.

A different type of research and different methods of intervention are central to the understanding of lifeworlds. In these analyses, which entail a strong focus on interpersonal relations, culturalist, power-critical views, which are sensitive to diversity, prevail. They critically review the construction of otherness. Contributions here cover a broad range of issues. They range from macrolevel conceptions to microlevel concerns and practical implementation. Some review underlying conceptions of being human, room and space and foreignness (Gómez-Hernández 2018) or include discussions on terminology and discriminatory language (Harrison 2006; Dominelli and Lorenz 2017). Others provide case studies of social organizations (Muy 2018; Duscha 2016), conceptualize practical forms of intervention (Midgley 2016), apply them to social problems (Fereidooni 2017), or produce didactic material and templates for social pedagogical workshops. Reflecting on ascriptions of the self, one's own professional role, and the other in heterogeneous working fields is considered a key competence. This implies an understanding of and self-reflection in unfamiliar contexts (cf. Giebeler 2008 and 2009; Pawar 2017).[3]

Preparing students for these realities appears a particular concern of scholars in Social Work. Many publications on the impacts of globalization already discuss how to prepare future social workers to work in highly complex, multicultural and entangled environments. Discussing the role of internships in the so-called Global South is therefore not new (Midgley 2016; Nagy et al. 2019). The educational aspects of Social Work often address the strangeness experience of aspects of the global that we mentioned in the beginning. By learning a combination of skills that can become important in heterogeneous working environments, students are equipped with the ability to gain increasing confidence by dealing repeatedly with different forms of unknown settings during their training. For example, they discuss topics such as anti-racism, expand their language skills by learning a local/foreign language, develop pedagogical methods for dealing with diversity, practice communication in transcultural settings again and again, and self-reflect on their own experience of foreignness in an unknown environment (Giebeler 2003 and 2019). This should reduce reservations and counteract prejudices through students developing their professional attitude towards intercultural settings.

Nowadays, students often gain experiences abroad as volunteers or interns before starting their studies. This is a more recent trend that has developed over the past decade. But it raises new challenges for lecturers as to how to enhance students' intercultural competencies, how to guide them in reflecting on their experiences in order to develop professional skills out of them, and how to speak with authority on issues of globalization, interculturality and strangeness. Studies range across regional settings, highlight the importance of self-reflexive competences and the capacity to establish contact, and mainly explore formats of internship projects or specialization programmes that increase students' cultural awareness and sensitivity for other people's lifeworlds (Feize and Gonzalez 2018; Pawar 2017; Giebeler 2009; Rehklau and Lutz 2009; Nagy et al. 2019).

The global appears as an abstract space, which is less threatening from a scientific point of view but remains highly complex. It comprises social complexity in its entirety but is hard to grasp due to its elusiveness, which is based on the strong subject-oriented lifeworld orientation of social work. All social interaction, every dynamic, is a part of this global totality, which is also referred to as world society. At the same time, the global becomes accessible through the particularity of social cases. In this sense, the social workers' view of the global acquired through research and action is comparable with the view through a prism where the light is refracted again and again, depending on the angle of blink, position and time. Each case produces a unique image that may be similar to others in some or even all aspects but is at the same time never the same. Thus, plurality becomes the central principle of social workers' global social reality.

Global frame of reference: building a common ethical base for the profession

So far, we have discussed how the perception of the global as an inequality-producing space gives legitimacy to the profession of social work as such. We have further shown that a desire to find adequate responses to this complex space nurtured the ambition to reframe methods. In contradistinction to both, where observation is the protagonist, the third perspective addresses the global as an arena. Here, social workers *actively position themselves as a professional group through a shared frame of reference* for the benefit of the community – a reference frame that forms part of the debates on colonialism (Salustowicz 2009) and is based upon the latest Global Definition of Social Work, established in 2014[4], which conveys the core mandate, principles, and understanding of knowledge and practice, a code of ethics (IASSW 2018), educational guidelines and a decennial Global Agenda (Jones 2018). Written down in official documents, this shared code and guidelines relies on values that the profession acknowledges as universally valid. In addition, the profession gives voice and life to this normative frame through common position papers on current political decisions, thus further increasing the visibility and recognition of the social work community as a globally operating actor and unit (IFSW 2014).

Scholars agree that the global reference frame is beneficial inasmuch as it represents the social work community and strengthens its standpoint as an external advisor for international aid organizations such as the United Nations Economic and Social Council (ECOSOC), the United Nations Children's Fund (UNICEF), the World Health Organization (WHO), the Office of the High Commissioner for Human Rights (OHCHR) and the United Nations High Commissioner for Refugees (UNHCR) (Staub-Bernasconi 2008; Lyons 2016; Healy and Hall 2009). Silvia Staub-Bernasconi (2008: 11) highlights the special relevance of the documents for future social work. In her eyes, above all, they are a response to the fact that the framework conditions for social work are influenced not only by national (socio-political) legislation, but also by the structure and dynamics of world society and its laws as embodied in UN conventions, directives of the WTO, IMF and the World Bank, the Geneva Convention, EU legislation, GATS, TRIPS etc. For this reason, national self-sufficiency and ignorance cannot be good advisors in matters concerning international developments in the future. (authors' translation)

The discussion has significant overlaps with debates on colonialism, where 'the worldwide spread of social work [is considered] a consequence of the colonialization process in two senses of the word' (Sałustowicz 2009: 62). Besides being a direct consequence of the colonization process, it is also an indirect consequence in that European curricula have been transferred to countries outside the region. These – as well as further power-sensitive approaches – regard the diffusion of a global normative set of rules critically. The International Federation of Social Workers (IFSW), the International Association of Schools of Social Work (IASSW) and the International Council on Social Welfare (ICSW) state clear ambitions to play an active role in global social policies.

However, internal opinions on how to carry out the world political mandate are controversial. Numerous regional and national supplementary comments on the global definition and position papers (IFSW 2014) depict the global as a space for negotiations. The power distribution within the professional community and in collaboration with external actors has to be balanced. Members discuss this discrepancy between public perception and power divisions within the associations extensively. They weigh the opportunities for making political impacts against the costs of homogenization. The latter simplifies the plurality of different regions and reproduces hegemonic relations within social work.

Next to institutional frameworks, social workers use theoretical frameworks which rely on shared values and principles. The idea of human rights is the most striking and prevalent example of such a framework (see Staub-Bernasconi 2008; Kandylaki and Kallinikaki 2018).[5] Others argue that these global frameworks help social workers enact their indignation and resistance against global inequalities (Prasad 2019) and strive for more professional autonomy. By relying upon global ethical standards or principles of human rights, professional social workers allow themselves to intervene, where employers or authorities do not (sufficiently) assume their duties or where intervention would even oppose the interests of these authorities. The significance of self-responsibility in social work increases to the degree that social security systems, principles of the rule of law and separation of powers decrease. This happens when transnational corporations prefer policies of compensation for damage claims to respecting acts or law governing working conditions or preventing forced relocation, or when the state cannot or does not want to guarantee minorities protection against persecution and aggression. But self-responsible intervention applies also to comparably 'trivial offences'. Sebastian Muy exemplifies this point and refers to the situation in collective housing offered to applicants for asylum. A specific case, where the required skills and demands have become 'to "somehow deal" with the contradictory demands and appear as "perfect problem-solving experts" [... whereas] under the general conditions of deprivation of rights acting "justly" has become impossible for employees [...].' (Muy 2018: 157; authors' translation).

The shared institutional and the theoretical frame of reference together determine capacities to practically engage with, negotiate and solve conflicts of power. This double bind is typical of social work. Unlike former approximations to the global, this view emphasizes it as a resource for professional empowerment. Social workers can play it off against institutional and governmental demands and empower themselves in the reconfiguration of injustices. The distinguishing feature of the institutional frame rests in the expansion of the possibilities to experience the global space and the interplay of power in the organizational field. Social workers collectively participate actively and experience their role as world political actors who take part in negotiations on social exclusion. The theoretical frame facilitates a political act of empowerment, where social workers can individually instrumentalize global principles of human rights or global social justice. In settings where the question arises of how to deal with the mandates of clients that oppose the missions of employers, social workers freely use and interpret their mandate to justify resistance, strengthening themselves against external actors who act (grossly) negligently.

Global arena: potential working fields

Social workers not only establish their own representative associations and organizations, they *form an integral part of the multi-professional teams of international organizations*. For example, they assist and support migrants worldwide, nowadays especially in the context of initiatives launched by countries of the 'North'. These involvements cover operations in Lampedusa, Lesbos, Israel, Lebanon, Suruc, Dar-es-Salaam, the US border zone, Chile and Peru, to name only a few. In sum, social workers take jobs in the European Union or United Nations and in the realm of transnationally operating welfare organizations such as Caritas International or the Red Cross, but also in foundations and consultancy services. Moreover, they are actively involved in transnational social movement associations. The organizational structure of helping institutions differs. Services may be financed by public or private funds, supported by governmental, non-governmental or private, ecclesiastical or human rights organizations. Institutions of the same social agency operate in worldwide networks, but communication between those agencies may often be complicated. Regional and international conferences take place and fulfil the function of coordination platforms. Depending on the operational field of social work in question, they also foster exchanges on concrete policies and different options for handling border regimes and determining the needs of the addressees and occupational groups involved.

Discussions centred on the participation of social workers in these organizations, or which explicitly examine their role in detail, are few and far between. The involvement of social workers in suborganizations of the United Nations, International Organization of Migration or International Criminal Court is not always present and/or comprehensively reflected in scientific work, despite (or explicitly because of) the long history of involvement by social workers in international organizations (Groterath 2011; Wagner 2009). There are several reasonable explanations for this dearth of information on the role of social workers in international organizations. Firstly, social workers are normally embedded in the organizational structures and operational fields of nation-states even though the national and international departments of the same organization may be involved (in the German case, this is true of most of the large welfare organizations, i.e. Caritas and Caritas International). Secondly, writings on issues of social development and international cooperation rarely address the intersection with social work explicitly. Instead, they describe or name it by using other terms and stick to a more predominant discourse. The same goes for international organizations that devote themselves to humanitarian help or human rights approaches. They all too often do not recognize the special competencies of social workers in these fields.

Social work in international organizations is driven by, or reduced to, two predominant narratives: developmental aid-assistance-cooperation on the one hand and the field of migration and mobility on the other (Blank et al. 2018; Lutz 2018). Almost no other area in Social Work has received so much attention in recent years. To subsume the work of international organizations to the two paradigms of 'development' and 'migration/mobility' simplifies the diversity of the landscape and, in particular, the skills and knowledge necessary to provide high-quality social services. International adoption processes, for example, are not the only field that receives little attention. Here, social workers offer expert assessments of the

> interdependencies of double parenthood, cultural affiliations of the adopted child and adopting parents on the micro-level, which means the individual or family level of identity and family construction, the macro-level of institutional structures (verification, brokerage, follow-up support), and the level of societal representation, which means stereotyping and discrimination. (Sauer and Wießmeier 2016: 23; authors' translation).

International adoptions are a controversial and highly political issue. A Social Work approach evaluates social mobilities, opportunity structures, complex identity formation under double parenthood as well as the dangers of dubious private adoption organizations, child trafficking and abuse.

The global appears here as a border space in which social workers enact their professional practice. A narrower understanding would refer to intervention near the geographic border, for example in refugee camps, human trafficking, and institutions of first admittance at national borders. A broader conceptualization allows for the incorporation of a variety of institutions – a pathway that leads to the inclusion of Aliens Departments, consultancy services and residential groups for migrants, school social work (i.e. with integrative classes) or street work in the context of sex work and human trafficking. Border spaces cause tensions between transnationality and heterogeneous lifeworlds in a concentrated form, because in them transnationality, transculturality, and transreligiosity are institutionally enforced. Border spaces are different from the political and economic spaces of enterprises or state summits, where the transnational encounters of politicians and entrepreneurs are more interest-driven. The emergence of border spaces like refugee camps or favelas is less politically intended (and maybe not at all), nor is it desired but it has to be managed anyway. These spaces are volatile and persistent in their plurality at the same time, due to the fluctuation of clients. This is how you come to appreciate the particular position of social workers and their power to explain global political dynamics from the perspective of their discipline, which provides a perception of the global from below, meaning from the precarious, exclusory, unintended side of globalization.

Conclusions

The four areas presented in this contribution cover different perspectives of Social Work on the global. They show the global as: (a) the overall context of globalization dynamics, being the principal source of contemporary social inequalities. This understanding grants legitimacy to contemporary intervention by social workers and deals with the core of analysis in social science; (b) a complex space, which requires corresponding Social Work research and practices to encompass the heterogeneity and multidimensionality of social reality from global to local; (c) a contested politicized space, where social workers not only observe but also experience and actively relate to the global. On the one hand, this space opens opportunities through umbrella organizations like IFSW, IASSW, and ICSW to intervene through international cooperation. However, professionals' influence on the space of global social policy is still only sparse. On the other hand, global theoretical concepts such as human rights, dignity and global social justice facilitate social workers' agency to decide more autonomously and self-responsibly how they enact professional principles against diverging interests; and finally (d) a potential work field for social workers, especially in the shape of international networks, institutions welfare organizations and NGOs. This work requires specific competences and skills such as personal, political and research training in analysing foreign life worlds, developing personal competencies in working with the poor of the Global South and political standing to challenge power structures liable to marginalize subaltern people. The social work profession plays an important role beyond national frameworks and in border spaces.

The perspectives reveal an inclination in Social Work towards the global. Social workers possess broad means to observe, analyse and evaluate the global. But they are confronted by limited organizational capacities and structures that inhibit their capacity to intervene properly. The latter covers the fact that social work has not only reacted, and still reacts, to the global social question but that it has further fomented the former by stabilizing global political dynamics that uphold a centralization of power and global structures of exclusion. In contemporary world society, such an externalization of social problems has become impossible. Thus, acknowledging the social question as a global social question from the start brings great potential. Social work may conduct explorations in the role of an observer of world politics from the margins, but also as an actor who regulates and stabilizes the dynamics of the global political stage outlined at the margins of exclusion. This text argues for a deeper understanding of this role and recommends actions that strengthen its capacity to act.

The present volume does not seek to describe structural world ordering principles or dynamics. Instead it envisions views of globalization and a global world phenomenologically. It interrogates what different groups perceive as global, how and why they do it and how similar or different these perceptions appear. We took this question literally for the field of Social Work. We have found that, in the emergence of this globally connected world, Social Work takes the position of a counterweight and a response with the aim of mitigating its disastrous effects. We have also elaborated on Social Work´s view of the relationship between the global and the local, arguing that they are closely intertwined through the chains of exclusion.

The four dimensions that compose a Social Work perspective on the global can never be uniform nor generalizable. Although we have provided a conceptual systematization of the nexus between social work and globalization, we do not want this work to be understood as a simplification of the social complexity that social workers confront. We conclude that the global appears as an extremely exclusive space from the point of view of Social Work. Its task of regulating the margins of societal exclusion makes a social work perspective highly sensitive to the limits of the (supposedly) 'global world'. The analysis of global dynamics in social work is conditioned by the diversity of practical experiences in direct contact with people, groups and communities, their daily lives and localities. This position enables Social Work to critically question global world ordering approaches such as the world system, world culture or world society approaches by unravelling the arbitrariness of these approaches when it comes to their empirical micro-foundations.

Notes

1   In the following text, the use of the term 'Social Work' as an academic subject and discipline is marked by capitalization.

2   Hans Thiersch and Klaus Grundwald did several efforts to conceptualize lifeworlds (*Lebenswelten*) as a central element of Social Work. For an introduction, see: Grunwald and Thiersch 2014.
3   At this point we want to refer to the numerous efforts of Cornelia Giebeler to conceptualise experiencing strangeness and transcultural contacts in establishing professional relationships. The cited works are a selection of this work.
4   The first Global Definition of Social Work was established in 2000 by the International Federation of Social Workers. Since then, the community proves and (re-) ratifies it in regular intervals. Over time the definition of Social Work enjoyed growing popularity. Especially since 2014 publications of Social Work have often cited it.
5   Although the idea of human rights is the most prevalent approach, other concepts such as dignity, global social justice, socio-ecological sustainability and development determine the horizon of the profession (Neuser and Chacon 2003; Rolfes 2003; Giebeler 2003).

The Revolution in Rojava and the International

Yasin Sunca

Introduction

This chapter engages with the embeddedness of global politico-social and historical processes in the emergence of revolutions from the perspective of international historical sociology.[1] There are three overall processes in the unfolding of revolutions: revolutionary situations, trajectories and outcomes. Parallel to this, the constitution of revolutionary agency is based on the local conditions and constraints working against naturalized hegemonic structures and semantics on a global level. Thus, a revolution does not take place only against the power holders of a given state; more importantly, it challenges the entirety of the political and social structures that, in one way or another, made the contested regime possible. Following one of the primary premises of this volume – that the actualization of *the global* takes place through particular local acts – I put forward the idea that a revolution is co-constituted by global-level hegemonic structures and the organized resistance to them. This, in other words, means that *the global* unfolds in *the local* through processes of interaction. Ultimately, the 'envisioned global', in the case of revolutions, is a combination of hegemonic structures and semantics that are co-constitutive of revolutionary agency. The case of the Rojava revolution is particularly instructive in understanding the unfolding of the global given the statelessness of the Kurds in a world of nation-states and countless Kurdish attempts at emancipatory political/military activities. The chapter draws theoretically on the international historical sociology of hegemony and resistance; empirically, it focuses on the case of Rojava (West Kurdistan, Syria) to illustrate the argument.

On 19 July 2012 regime troops withdrew from the northern and northeastern regions of Syria and the control was taken over by the People's Protection Units (YPG – *Yekîniyên Parasitna Gel*) and Women's Protection Units (YPJ

– *Yekîniyên Parasitna Jin*), the Kurdish forces being led politically by the Democratic Union Party (PYD – *Partiya Yekîtiya Demokrat*). A region-wide Kurdish national question that had been in existence for at least a century and had shaped, and been shaped by, the historico-social conditions of state formation in the region, thus reached yet another turning point: for the first time, Kurdish forces with a left-leaning ideological position found a practical ground on which to put a radical-democratic social transformation into action. Immediately after the take-over of power, however, the revolution came under attack from the geopolitically backed and socially grounded genocidal masculinity of jihadi Islam. In Kobanê in 2014, as a result of its globally televised resistance to ISIS (also known as *Daesh* or 'Islamic State in Iraq and Al-Sham'), the revolution was stabilized and legitimized internationally. Serious geopolitical and geosocial problems, however, still lay ahead.

The Rojava revolution, not, admittedly, a power transition of the customary kind, became a topical issue as much within the study of revolutions and international relations as in mainstream media. The global historical sociological lineages of this revolution, however, were covered in a haphazard way, if not totally ignored. The greater part of the literature focuses on the geopolitical conditions of the revolution (see, for example: Kaya and Whiting 2017; Charountaki 2015; Gunes and Lowe 2015). A considerable proportion of it offers nothing more than popular geopolitics, which is journalism rather than a serious investigation into the causalities (Hevian 2013). There were, nonetheless, a number of authors who handled the Rojava case as a politico-social phenomenon (see, for example: Küçük and Özselçuk 2016). But among them two main currents seem to exist: one integrating the revolution into an internationalist revolutionary discourse to inspire and exemplify emancipatory practices (see, for example: saed 2017; Stanchev 2015); the other, its antagonist, mainly informed by a linear-modernist determinism and naturalized liberal-representative democracy, trying to demonstrate how undemocratic the Rojava experience was by decontextualizing it spatiotemporally (see, for example: Tejel 2014; Paasche 2015). These perspectives deploy either a revolutionary romanticism or hegemonic Eurocentrism. In contrast to this scholarship on Rojava, I shall attempt to give an 'international historical sociological' account here, building on the co-constitutive role of global hegemonic structures and the dynamics of resistance in the emergence of revolutions. In this sense, the question guiding the present chapter is how the continuous interaction between global structures and local reactions to them shapes revolutionary agency.

In the following, I illustrate the ways in which the actors – in this case the revolutionaries of Rojava – reacted to their historically evolved global environment in materializing their political project. Instead of attributional – and therefore fixed – categorizations of causality in understanding revolutions, this work carries out processual analyses of the Rojava case since revolutions are assemblages of historically specific processes (for a discussion on attributional versus processual ontology, see Lawson 2016). Based on a theoretical reading of the international historical sociology of revolutions, my analysis of the Rojava event explores three entangled processes in which the revolutionaries engaged with the global: (a) the international historical sociology of state formation in West Asia, which rendered stateless entities defenceless; (b) the ideological and organizational upheaval of the anti-systemic movements, particularly in the post-Soviet era, which conditioned a search for other solutions; (c) the geopolitical constraints of the Syrian war as a result of hegemony-seeking interventions, which victimized those with less geopolitical capacity for bargaining. Needless to say, while these processes can and should be separated for analytical purposes, in practice they are intertwined in many respects.

In each of these processes, I argue, the revolutionaries of Rojava mobilized the dynamics of resistance to the perceived or actually existing hegemonic structures. In other words, both the hegemonic structures and resistance practices emerged through a historical interaction and were informed by their global lineages. In this sense, I argue that the emergence of the revolution in Rojava was international all the way down, through the interactions that were constitutive of its agency. Again, this analysis can helpfully draw on the distinction between the historical, ideological, and geopolitical dimensions: the historical dimension pertains to the formulation of resistance dynamics based on a historical understanding of regional power relations; the ideological dimension to a radical-democratic reassessment of the ideological and organizational structures hegemonic in national-liberationist pathways; and the geopolitical dimension to an instrumentalization of the geopolitical vacuum emerging as a result of hegemonic confrontations.

Whereas international historical sociology serves as the theoretical framework, I rely on interviews with and public statements from relevant actors to illustrate the international lineages of the Rojava revolution.[2] In what follows, I first undertake a brief theoretical domiciliation of revolutions in *the international*. In this, I attempt to include the dynamics of hegemony and resistance in the nexus of revolutions and world politics. I then go into the details of the three analytical categories of the Rojava revolution's international lineages in order to illustrate the dynamics of hegemony and resistance in concrete historical and contemporary processes.

Revolutions and the international

One structuralist definition of a revolution would be that it is a world historical event: Theda Skocpol (1979) argues that it is a power shift as a result of social transformations that come after structurally entangled processes. Alternatively, with Fred Halliday (1999: 21), revolutions could be seen as 'major political and social transformations in the context of a contradictory modernity involving mass participation and aspiration to establish a radically different society'. In the former definition, the revolution *comes*, it is not *made*, whereas in the latter agency is in play. A reconciliation between these two definitions can probably be achieved by referring to Marx, who features prominently in both Skocpol's and Halliday's work: 'Man makes his own history, but he does not make it out of the whole cloth; he does not make it out of conditions chosen by himself, but out of such as he finds close at hand' (Marx 2008 [1852]: 1). Despite the structuralist determinism of broader Marxian scholarship, this well-known quotation from Marx clearly points to its constructivist dimension involving the agential will or power of those who can work towards making a revolution, whether successfully or not. This contention forms the basis upon which revolutionary agency can be related to the international.

The meaning of the international can vary in different schools of International Relations (IR). The present chapter, however, engages with historical sociological premises beyond the narrow (neo-)realist and (neo-)liberal conceptualizations. The question at hand is about politico-social phenomena that can be understood only through their spatiotemporal embeddedness, without caging them in states or dehistoricizing the unfolding of their constitutive events. Accordingly, one can conceive of the international as hegemonic power relations (Cox 1987), a systemic totality (Frank and Gills 1993; Wallerstein 2004), a communication-based social whole (Albert 2016), a combined totality of unevenness (Rosenberg 2006), or as one world constituted by many worlds (Blaney and Tickner 2017; Law 2011). Regardless of their motivational contention, in each of these explanations the external (of any political formation) is constitutive of, and constituted by, the internal. More precisely, the international is integral to any social phenomenon. What is at stake here, accordingly, is a particular presence of the international pertaining to agency formation in political processes. If the desire behind a revolution is for a radically different life and hence a transformation, then the existing hegemonic structures, against which a revolution is mobilized, are also constitutive of agency. So, without any exclusion of different conceptions of the international, one can contend that the spatiotemporally grown hegemonic structures and the interactive dynamics of resistance are constitutive of it.

The embeddedness of the international in the revolutionary processes has long been a matter of debate. But the fourth-generation theory of the study of revolution has taken a firm step in incorporating the international into revolutionary situations, revolutionary trajectories and revolutionary outcomes (Lawson 2016, 2019). The international matters as much when there is a social or political upheaval as when it is relatively calmer (Halliday 1999: 7). However, if the processual interaction between the agents of revolutionary change and their global environment is constitutive of a revolutionary situation, then this accumulation and gradual radicalization of revolutionary claims happens well before the situation comes to be. In other words, hegemonic structures are resisted both in an organized and unorganized fashion, until resistance melts into a revolutionary moment. The terms and structures of this resistance also emerge from within a global ideological context; it learns from, and speaks back to, the global environment of anti-systemic movements. International historical and sociological accumulation, in combination with the processual transformation of ideology, then, determines the revolutionary agency within the immediate geopolitics of revolutionary trajectories. These interactions ultimately shape the ways and processes whereby the global unfolds in the local.

The Kurdish experience of joining the world of nation-states as a stateless nation conditioned the Kurdish interaction with global processes from below. This experience of modernity was formed through an understanding of resistance built on three dimensions of the interaction between the global and the local: the historical-sociological, ideological-organizational and geopolitical.

The historical sociology of the revolution in Rojava

The Rojava revolution was the outcome of the face-off between a century-long status quo and a great upheaval in the region. Inter-social turmoil forms the ground for an international political upheaval which eventually renders certain political formations (in our case, states) vulnerable to bottom-up processes (Lawson 2019: 74ff.). One century later we seem to be going through such a period of destructive turmoil in the region (Bozarslan 2011). Global historical processes and resultant power constellations reconfigured the region in such a way that doomed-to-fail nation-states were formed arbitrarily in the 20th century.

The historical origins of the Rojava revolution nest in the resistance to the hegemonic state system in the region that continuously conditioned Kurdish deprivation. More precisely, Kurdish political agency in the 20th century was transformed through interaction with the hegemonic nation-states system, the intergroup dynamics in Syria, and the windows of opportunity resulting from inter-state contradictions. The processual unfolding of these interactions shaped the historicity of the Rojava revolution.

The late 19th and early 20th century was a historical moment of inter-social reconfiguration for West Asia and North Africa: empires were either replaced by nation-states as a result of successful nationalist mobilizations, or weakened by eventually unsuccessful ones. The regional state system had been consolidated by the first half of the 20th century. The Ottoman Empire, which had once expanded territorially over three continents, faced nationalist uprisings by different ethnic and religious groups in the territories under its domination. A weakening economy and transforming power relations under the impact of the French and English revolutions, combined with French and English imperialism, forced the empire to take some pre-emptive measures which eventually embodied its centralization policies. Parallel to this, two broadly defined power constellations were trying to control the Ottoman state: Westernizers led by the Young Turks movement and the *ancien régime* (Bozarslan 2013: 305ff.).

The regional state system and the characters of these states stabilized as a result of the fatal damage inflicted on central mechanisms of the empire by the First World War. The intense conflict by quickly shifting geopolitics among different ethnic groups, imperialist forces and the power constellations in the empire forged the new power relations in the region. The centralized, hegemonic and homogenizing nation-state model was alien to the historical conditions of coexistence and inter-social relations in the region where it was applied in the absence of a 'nation' (Bozarslan 1997: 61ff.; Halliday 2005: 88ff.). This process is central to the historical domination over the Kurds in the form of assimilation, the division of Kurdish-inhabited land, and conflicts lasting decades. With such an understanding of the historical relations of hegemonic structures and resistance dynamics, the PYD co-leader Saleh Muslim stated that 'with the development of the nation-state in Europe the Arabs began to see things differently' adding, with the emphasis on the hegemonic nation-states, 'the land of the Kurds was divided into four parts and there was repression and massacres took place' (Ekurd Daily 2014).[3]

Like the other ethnic groups living under the Ottoman rule, the Kurds were also seeking some kind of emancipation. Yet the Kurdish political forces could not manage to unite and mobilize Kurdish nationalism, mainly due to the interest-based divisions of the co-opted Kurdish elites. The divisions were manifold, on a spectrum from the Kurdish notables who were aware of the nationalist turn in the world history and pursued a Kurdish nationalist agenda to the traditional elites who insisted on staying part of the unity of the *Ummah* under the Ottoman roof. Exacerbated by the struggles for local tribal interests, this incompatibility in imagining a future Kurdistan radically shaped the mutually nullifying relations between, on the one hand, Kurdish tribalism/Ottomanism, and, on the other, Kurdish nationalism/modernism (cf. Hitchins 2000; Özoğlu 2001). Different forms of the same dynamic are in place even today.

Kurdish political actors were either collaborating with or fighting three forces: the Ottoman Empire (and later republican Turkey), the British Empire and the French Empire. The confrontation within this triangle was caused by the division of the Ottoman territory in Iraq, the Levant and South-East Anatolia into zones of influence for France and Britain. With Turkey's war of independence, its borders were more or less drawn. The Kurds in Turkey, for various reasons, largely supported the independence war. From the 1920s onwards, the Kurds sought the help of Britain in Iraqi Kurdistan, but British imperial rule did not recognize the Kurdish endeavour for independence for strategic geopolitical reasons (McDowall 1996: 121ff.). The French, on the other hand, signed the Ankara agreement defining the Turkey–Syria border, to avoid further loss of territory in Anatolia (ibid.: 139f.). In this way the Kurdish-inhabited land fell under the control of four different states. Although the political and social dynamics of Kurdish resistance to oppression differed in each country, the very presence of oppression originates from the homogenizing enforcement of the nation-state model (Bozarslan 1997: 61ff.; Vali 1998). The resistance-to-oppression dynamics in Syria diverge from other Kurdish experiences in some geopolitical details, although originating from the same core.

The main determinants of Kurdish policy in Syria emerge from inter-group dynamics and their interaction with the central state institutions. The representative of the PYD (Democratic Union Party) in France made their understanding of historical hegemonic structures clear:

> the current organization and borders went back to the period of the French mandate which, after having envisaged it, had finally given up granting autonomy to minorities, like the Alawites or the Druze, to favour the construction of a centralized state, [an] over-centralized [state] which could only hold by force. (Groupe France-Syrie 2016; author's translation)

Within this context, there were probably two main determinants of Syrian policy towards the Kurds, especially after full independence from France: (a) the exclusion of the Kurds and deprivation of their fundamental rights; (b) the implementation of an Arabization policy under the geopolitical premises of pan-Arabism and hence the assimilation of the Kurds. The regime did not accept one third of the Kurds as 'true Syrians' after the 1962 census (Tejel 2009: 51f.). The 1962 census laid the foundations for a more coercive policy by the Syrian state against the Kurds as an *alien group*. This brought about the repression of Kurdish political mobilization by the regime to the extent that any political demand for greater Kurdish rights or demonstrations in any form faced relentless punishment.

Kurdish political resistance in Syria has historically been dependent on the Kurdish movements in neighbouring states. Kurdish parties with relative social support among the Syrian Kurds have almost exclusively been offshoots of the Kurdish parties in Turkey or Iraq. A central (geo-)political reason for this is to be found in the dynamics of early nation-state formation: as part of its regional policy for dealing with more powerful neighbours, the Syrian regime provided sanctuary to Kurdish movements fighting against a neighbouring country. This made the Syrian regime's hand stronger in other issues such as the dispute over water with Turkey. This was the case with the *Xoybûn*, a region-wide Kurdish nationalist organization with its political base in Damascus in the late 1920s; the Iraqi Kurdish leaders, most notably Jalal Talabani, in the 1970s; and the PKK from the 1980s onwards (Tejel 2009): 'Whenever the [Kurdish] parties had difficulties' said a YPG commander 'they ended up in Rojava, and the Rojavans have always fought in other parts of Kurdistan.' (YPG commander, interview, 22 September 2019; author's translation).

Because of the convergence of interests between the PKK and the regime of Hafez al-Assad – the PKK used Syrian soil and the Beqaa Valley from 1979 to 1998 as a space for political and military training while the regime benefitted from the regional impacts of the PKK's presence in Syria – it did not target the Syrian state.

> Taner Akçam, (the leader of DEV-YOL [Revolutionary Path], the largest leftist political organization before the 1980 coup in Turkey) told Öcalan that al-Mukhabarat (the Syrian secret service) will use you and throw you away. In response Öcalan said "Yes, I know. But when they want to throw me away it will be too late". That was precisely how it was. (Former YPG fighter, interview, 21 July 2019; author's translation).

Besides making use of safe camps there for military and political training for the fight in Turkey, the PKK always lived among the Rojava Kurds, recruited cadres, trained and organized people, and eventually managed to strike root in the region (Akkaya 2015). It was these recruits that would lead the politico-social transformation in Rojava from 2012 on.

In the early 2000s, the regional impact of the developments in Iraqi Kurdistan and Öcalan's being handed over to Turkey by the US were the main sources of increased involvement by the PKK-led Kurdish movement[4] in anti-Ba'ath mobilization. The US intervention in 2003 in Iraq, which led to the independence-like-autonomy of Iraqi Kurdistan, pushed the other Kurdish political actors to become more proactive. Under this regional impact, the Kurdish organizations in Syria intensified their demonstrations and protests. Encouraged by the US, Turkey forced the Syrian regime to expel Öcalan and the US-administration eventually delivered him to Turkey (Yetkin 2004). This ended the PKK's tacit deal with the Syrian regime. As a result, the PKK-led movement reshaped its policies against the Syrian regime. In 2004, an uprising erupted after a game of football in Qamishlo, which was followed by a series of demonstrations throughout Rojava that were eventually violently extinguished by the regime, leaving 50 dead, many injured and around 2000 imprisoned. Liberated from its geopolitically constraining ties with the regime, the PYD-led movement also mobilized the Kurdish population in its strongholds. Despite its high cost, this revolt in Qamishlo and the spreading of demonstrations across the northern regions further raised a consciousness in Rojava of the area as a separate political entity (Gauthier 2005; Tejel 2017). Since then the Kurdish parties have been active to further mobilize the people for their eventual emancipation.

The arbitrary formation of nation-states in the post-Ottoman era left the Kurds to undergo assimilation policies in four states and a constant resistance-to-oppression dynamic. This also locked the states in a constant struggle, firstly against some sections of their own population and secondly against each other as a result of historical social, economic and (geo-)political dynamics. While Kurdish resistance was generated by the former dynamic in the first place, the later inter-state dynamic facilitated its continuity. The Rojava revolution is primarily an outcome of, and a response to, a particular configuration of the global transition from empires to nation-states. The historicity of the revolutionary agency, in this respect, lies at the intersection of the historical and social dynamics of regional state formation and various engagements between the Kurds and these hegemonic structures.

The ideological reconstitution of revolutionary agency in Rojava

One of the main insights resulting from the study of failed uprisings is that while these uprisings are often successful in ousting a regime, this often happens at the expense of having a plan ready for what happens after (see Lawson 2019: 222). How to reconstruct society after a revolution is a matter of having a vision for the aftertime that is directly connected to the ideology of the revolutionaries. The particular challenge to the Rojava revolutionaries was not to take down the existing power holders, but to make good on their claim to reconstruct and maintain social relations based on non-exclusionary, non-hierarchical and gender-libertarian principles. The ideological vision in question was present among the revolutionaries of Rojava, yet had not come into existence out of a void. This vision can be detected in the PKK's problematization and gradual transformation of the hegemonic national liberation ideology and organizational structure throughout the 1990s and 2000s. The processual-interactive relationship between the ideological-organizational line hegemonic within global anti-systemic movements and its problematization by the revolutionaries of Rojava shaped their revolutionary agency. In the analytical tradition of world-system theory, the term 'anti-systemic movements' refers to globally interconnected mobilizations against structural exploitation and domination by the capitalist world-system, as in class- or national-liberation-based movements, feminist or ecologist movements and so on (Wallerstein 2014). Anti-systemic movements join global processes from a standpoint of challenging them; yet, they also create the hegemonic ideology and structures of this challenge. The ideological lineages of the Rojava revolution are embedded in the locally based problematization of the hegemonic national liberation ideology.

What was strikingly different in the Rojava revolution compared to the other movements in 2011 in West Asia and North Africa was its radical reimagining of power relations. I do not intend to give a detailed account of this radical process here, but rather want to focus on the international historical and sociological process of its unfolding. It is important, however, to mention that the transformation was made from an independence-seeking national liberation movement to a radical politico-social assemblage by means of three interdependent struggles: (1) a struggle for direct and radical democracy, formulated as *democratic autonomy*, serving as a way of solving the problems in the locality concerned; (2) a struggle for the transformation of the state into a *democratic republic*, in order to render it permissive to the rights and demands of dissident political groups and different identities, including its Kurdish population; (3) a struggle to connect different social and political formations that were separated by nation-state borders by means of *democratic confederalism* as opposed to the idea of forming an independent Kurdistan (Öcalan 2013a, 2013b). Playing a central role in the Rojava revolution, this re-imagination of revolutionary transformation was profoundly related to the confrontation between the hegemonic ideological and organizational structures in anti-systemic movements and the historical patterns of West Asian dynamics of resistance.

The PKK was one of the leftist organizations in Turkey in the second half of the 1970s that rapidly grew in the 1980s. The contemporaneous movements in Turkey, in line with the global 68 movement and national liberation movements (e.g. in Vietnam, Cuba and Angola), shared certain characteristics such as, most notably, a Leninist party model, a national-liberation ideology and (as an aim) a guerrilla campaign (Akkaya 2013). Two factors were determinant throughout the emergence of the PKK. On the one hand, they established non-hierarchical relations with the local Kurds.[5] On the other, they made strategic use of violence against the state, tribal structures, and other Kurdish organizations.[6] The guerrilla warfare from 1984 onwards followed the example of other guerrilla struggles for national liberation (Gunes 2013; Tezcür 2015) and continued until the early 1990s.[7] However, the collapse of the Soviet Union would compel the PKK to engage with its organizational structure and ideological positioning.

In the early 1990s, the PKK was under heavy pressure to transform itself ideologically and structurally for three central reasons: (a) the transformations in the anti-systemic movements, (b) the structural need to transcend orthodox Marxism and the Leninist party model, and (c) the post-Cold-War social and (geo-)political conditions in West Asia. The world system theorists' problematization of socialist states, social democracy and national liberation movements is illustrative of the PKK's understanding of the ideological crisis that the left was going through:

> Have social democrats achieved anything more than some redistribution to middle strata? Have communist parties achieved anything more than some economic development? And even so, has this not been primarily to benefit the so-called new class of bureaucratic elite? Have nationalist movements achieved anything more than allowing the so-called comprador class a slightly larger slice of the world pie? (Arrighi et al. 1989: 34; author's translation)

Although asynchronously, these questions underlay the ideological-political determinants of a globally observable crisis.[8] The PKK was engaging with the orthodox national liberationist path and real socialism in order to trigger a transformation. Two decades later, in his assessments of the early 1990s, Öcalan (2013b: 287ff.) said that they were trying to build a Kurdistan without knowing what socialism and nation-statism really were and how these ideologies were impacting on personalities: 'We managed to be in authority [in the 1990s]. But we either did not know what to achieve with authority or many of us started to think we were "special"' (ibid.: 290).[9] This diagnosis of the degeneration of the PKK cadre conditioned an ideological intervention in the party's organizational structures by Öcalan. He aimed at addressing the combined effect of nation-statism and real socialism on the one hand and the historically developed tribal/religious and sexist personality/mentality structures on the other. A Kurdish activist remarked that the transformation of the PKK

> had been condensing from the 1990s onwards [...] This transformation not only meant a transformation [of the ideological goal] from an independent Kurdistan to democratic confederalism but the transformation of mentality structures. It was not simply a political transformation. (Kurdish Activist, interview, 14 July 2019)

The transformation, which would be sealed as democratic confederalism in the 2000s, was developing through the interaction of the organizational needs and ideological interventions throughout the 1990s.

Combined with the lessons learned in the guerrilla war with the Turkish army (Karayılan 2014), the pressure for change resulted in important transformations in the party's organizational structure. For instance, the creation of a separate organization of women fighters and the first ceasefires in pursuit of a negotiated settlement were remarkable developments that would shed light on the processes to come.

> One of the distinguishing properties of the PKK was the independent organization of the women from the men [...] This was not only a theorization but also the [practical] materialization of the women's army and women's organization through the will of the women. (Veteran Kurdish politician, interview, 17 May 2019)

The transformation of the PKK's organizational structure and ideology was happening through the feminization of the Kurdish politics around a well-known motto: 'becoming liberated by fighting, becoming beautiful by liberating oneself, and being loved by becoming beautiful' (Stêrk 2018). Yet, due probably to the intensity of the conflict, the scope of transformation did not reach to the degree of the current framework.[10]

As detailed so far, the transformation was already happening in practice but its acceptance by the organization as a coherent political and ideological project would wait until after Öcalan was delivered to Turkey in 1999. Combined with the organizational turmoil after his imprisonment, the post-Soviet development of radical political thought further pushed Öcalan to end the hesitation between the hegemonic ideology of national liberation and a strong need for a change to ensure the continuity of the PKK (Öcalan 2003: 30).[11] Accordingly, he sought an ideologically acceptable and politically realistic solution for historically deep-rooted problems emerging from the regional experience of capitalist modernity.

This attempt at transforming the organization, in combination with the growing splinter groups after Öcalan's imprisonment, triggered a life-or-death moment for the PKK. The period between 1999 and 2004 was 'the most difficult period [...], a period of painful transformation, and this period [was] happening in the absence of the leader who formed the party, gave it perspective and in practice led it' (Veteran Kurdish politician, interview, 17 May 2019). But eventually from 2004 onwards, Öcalan's leadership was reinstated at the expense of losing around one fifth of the party's members. The unburdened PKK started to experiment with a new organizational structure beyond the Leninist party model in the light of prefigurative and proactive radical-revolutionary politics (Akkaya and Jongerden 2010). Although the problems associated with the Leninist party model persisted to some extent, the PKK-led Kurdish movement transformed into a web of social, political, military/self-defence, and economic organizations, a number of which had already been formed and were active in Rojava well before the civil war in Syria.

The transformations of the global anti-systemic movements, national liberation movements in particular, and the particular ways in which they interacted with locally based party structures and resistance dynamics were constitutive of the revolutionary agency in Rojava. When the geopolitics allowed a power shift, the PYD as a political organization and the YPG-YPJ, the military/self-defence units, were the most prepared and best structured organizations to assume power not only because of the historical development of the Kurdish movement in Syria (as explained above) but also through having an ideological vision of what came next. Everything associated with the Rojava revolution – for instance, the extra-systemic reconstruction of social relations, peaceful co-existence between different ethnic, sectarian and religious groups, gender-libertarian social relations, structurally connected co-operatives, communes, assemblies that organize self-rule – is the outcome of the ways in which the PKK-led Kurdish movement addressed globally present ideological and structural challenges within its ranks.

The geopolitics of the revolution in Rojava

Unsuccessful nation-formation practices, societies forcibly controlled by authoritarian regimes or dictatorships, continuing imperialist interventions, and the continuous deprivation of minority groups were forming the roots of permanent conflicts, and hence social fatigue in the broader region (Bozarslan 2013). Combined with the immediate shock of the neoliberal dismantling of state-led developmentalism, this social fatigue took the form of what was called the Arab Spring. This upheaval unleashed a number of developments which made the Rojava revolution possible. The complex international engagement, however, was also forming the immediate geopolitical *threats to*, as well as *opportunities for*, the survival of the revolution. The geopolitical threats were coming from the politico-social hierarchies in the region while opportunities were arising from the contradictions between different power constellations. In combination with the historical-sociological and ideological lineages explained above, revolutionary agency was constituted by a locally based processual engagement with these geopolitical threats and opportunities. Accordingly, a geopolitical strategy formulated as the Kurdish third way made the revolution possible and continued to form its essence.

The violent intervention of the Assad regime in initially peaceful protests and the involvement of regional and international forces both for and against the regime set the initial configuration of the Syrian war. From the very first days, Russia supported the Syrian regime. The US first supported the moderate opposition, then turned to help Kurdish-led forces after the supplanting of the opposition by jihadi forces. Regionally, Turkey was – increasingly – supportive of the jihadi forces against the Kurds and the Syrian regime, while Iran backed the regime in pursuit of creating a regional alliance stretching from Iran, via Iraqi Shi'as to the Syrian Alawite regime. This background after the start of Syrian war resulted in two interrelated constraints geopolitically surrounding the Rojava revolution. The first (internal) one was formed through the confrontation between the mainstream opposition and the regime. The second (external) one developed alongside the confrontations between the US and Russia in Syria.

First, internally, the regime wanted to instrumentalize the Kurds against Turkey and the jihadists, while the opposition had no views on the Kurdish question. The regime had had a very violent history with the Kurds throughout the past decade and did not recognize their fundamental rights, despite many promises after the Qamishlo revolt (Gauthier 2005). However, given the country-wide uprising, the regime withdrew from Rojava for three reasons largely informed by the experience of previous Syrian regimes in dealing with popular unrest: (a) focusing on the fight in other regions, Aleppo and Damascus in particular, to contain the uprising first and then return to Kurdistan once the fight with the Syrian Arab opposition had been won; (b) leaving the Turkish AKP government to face the 'PKK-linked Kurds', thereby punishing the AKP for its support of the – increasingly jihadi – opposition; and finally (c) making two of its enemies, the Kurds and the jihadists, fight and weaken each other (Gunes and Lowe 2015; ICG 2014; Spyer 2013). The PYD-led Kurds assumed power after the withdrawal of the regime troops. Developments afterwards unfolded in the way the regime imagined that they would. However, particularly their remarkable resistance to ISIS during the battle of Kobanê in 2014, and globally mobilized solidarity actions on their behalf with a massive media coverage, pushed the Obama administration to support the Kurds. The US backing of the Kurdish-led forces became a geopolitical game-changer.

The mainstream Sunni-Arab opposition in Syria, on the other hand, did not have and did not propose any solution to the Kurdish question in Syria for a time after the regime had been ousted (Spyer 2013). Riad Assad, the nominal head of the Free Syrian Army (FSA), rejected the possibility of federalism in an interview in August 2012, saying 'in Syria, there are no Kurdish or Sunni regions. It is all Syrian land' (Khoshnaw 2012). Riad al-Shaqfa, the leader of the Syrian Muslim Brothers, one of the strongest groups, was blunter, stating in September 2012: 'We clearly oppose the ambitions of establishing a Kurdish entity in Syria' (quoted in Caves 2012: 3). It was clear that the mainstream Syrian opposition had no plan for the Kurds, instead asking the Kurds to come under the commandership of FSA without any preconditions which was impossible in view of Kurdish aspirations (Barfi 2013). The Rojava administration did not have a capacity comparable to that of the regime and the state/substate actors supportive of the regime (such as Iran, or the Iraqi Shia). Nor did it have support comparable to that of Syrian opposition from regional (e.g. Turkish) or international forces (such as the US during the early years of uprising). On the contrary, this geopolitical setting was further driving the Rojava revolution into a corner, for it was leaving the Kurds with no friends.

The second geopolitical constraint had to do with the attempts of international forces, the US and Russia in particular, to reorder the region through the global geopolitical contradictions centred on Syria (Unver 2016). Even though the core states are central to these hegemonic relations, they are dependent on converging interests with regional actors, which are conducted by means of continuous negotiations. While all actors try to self-position according to this hierarchical framework, Turkey and the Kurds in particular have benefited from the room to manoeuvre left between Russia and the US. Both of the former have some kind of relationship with both of the latter, unlike, for instance, the Assad regime which has long been cut off from the US. However, the Kurds did not have any leverage against Western states apart from their ability to fight. The implications of Jihadi-Wahhabi Islam and the Kurdish resistance to their attempts at genocide drew the attention of international mass media, which then pushed Western support for the Kurds in their fight against ISIS. Although this support *prima facie* instrumentalized the Kurdish movement, it ultimately also added to its international legitimacy.

The revolutionaries of Rojava engaged with these geopolitical constraints by formulating a third-way policy. Asya Abdullah, co-leader of the PYD, stated in the early days of the Rojava Revolution in 2013, that 'despite the opposition of the regional and international forces, we continued our struggle by opting for a third way and we took big steps towards the construction of democratic autonomy' (Yeni Özgür Politika 2013). Accordingly, the Kurdish third way was conceptualized as an autonomous political strategy of the PKK-led Kurdish movement, beyond the historically confrontational hegemonic power structures of secularist nationalism (i.e. the Assad regime) and Islamist nationalism (i.e. the mainstream opposition) with their varying degrees of international backing. It is asserted to be a political strategy on the path to democratic confederalism, but not the ultimate goal in and of itself.

The geopolitical causality of the Rojava revolution lies in the processual interaction between the contradictions of different political constellations and the Kurdish engagement in this geopolitical setting with a third way policy. Given these two geopolitical constraints, the revolution has been a case of proving its social, economic and most importantly military capacity to sustain and push the regional and international forces to accept the revolution, if not officially recognize it. The unfolding of geopolitics, particularly after the Turkish invasion of Afrin in 2016, further confined the revolution. However, given the focus of this chapter on the constitutive elements of the revolution, an elaboration on these developments is beyond its scope.

Conclusion

I have argued that *the international* was integral to the Rojava revolution all the way down. Building on a historical sociological conception of the international based on the structures of hegemony and dynamics of resistance, I have reflected on how the three particular processes involved in the interaction between *the global* and *the local* shaped revolutionary agency in Rojava: the historical sociology of regional state-formation; the ideological reconstitution in reaction to the upheaval of anti-systemic movements; and the geopolitics of the Syrian war. Accordingly, the historical sociology of state formation after the collapse of the Ottoman Empire, which locked state and non-state polities in a lasting impasse, is the causal precedent of Kurdish deprivation. The various experiences of the Kurds in endeavouring to escape from this impasse against the homogenizing states' repression form the historicity of the revolutionary agency in Rojava.

Conceiving itself as part of anti-systemic movements, the PKK has interactively engaged with the debate within these movements. This engagement has changed along with the transformation in world politics. The strongest impact was brought about by the collapse of the Soviet Union, after which the

PKK-led movement reconsidered the ideological and organizational premises of the hegemonic path to national liberation. This process is central to the ideological reconstitution of revolutionary agency in Rojava.

Finally, obvious constraining conditions pertain to global geopolitics centred on the Syrian war. The constitution of world politics required renewed intervention by the hegemony-seeking powers in the region when regional hierarchies were renegotiated in the post-Arab Spring era. Given the historico-social dynamics, this has reshaped the relations between the states, different identity groups and non-state entities. The involvement of the revolutionaries of Rojava in this constellation with their semantic/ideological and spatiotemporal arsenal is constitutive of the geopolitical constitution of the revolutionary agency.

Notes

1 I thank George Lawson for his detailed comments on the very first draft of this chapter.
2 I do not name my interviewees for obvious security concerns. I have used 7 of the interviews that I conducted as part of my doctoral research.
3 Sources including newspapers and interviews, on which this work is based, are only available in Kurdish, Turkish and French. Thus, all following translations of these sources are provided by the author.
4 I use the term 'PKK-led Kurdish movement' for the network of autonomous movements, parties, civil society organizations, armed groups and so on in four countries (Turkey, Iran, Iraq and Syria) and elsewhere. It refers to the Kurdish political bodies that are inspired by the ideological line of the PKK leader Abdullah Öcalan, but have different organizational structures and, more importantly, carry on autonomous politics according to the (geo)political context of the country they operate in. This, however, should not be interpreted as if political decisions were exclusively made by the PKK leadership and imposed in a top-down fashion. The term covers this organizational complexity and takes the separation between the shared ideology and the autonomous decision-making processes fully into account.
5 On the PKK's relations with local Kurds: 'The family backgrounds of members of other organizations are in the petty bourgeoisie or state bureaucracy. They did not want to shake hands with the people for

whom they were struggling, hesitated to sit in the same place with the ordinary Kurds [...] The PKK, on the other hand, was forcing them to shake hands with the ordinary Kurds and in this way the PKK members won the ordinary people's hearts' (journalist/former activist, interviews, 18 May 2019).

6   On the PKK's use of violence: A number of interviewees mentioned that the PKK's strategically oriented use of violence mainly aimed at opening a space for mobilization in the Kurdish cities and towns, against other contemporary organizations and tribes which were already well-established.

7   A founding member of the PKK defines the importance of the first guerrilla attack on Turkish military bases as 'it was an important step to successfully implementing guerrilla warfare theory in accordance with the character of the period and met the needs of the time' (Karayılan 2014: 62).

8   According to world system scholars, these questions were asked in the West, from the late 60s on, which eventually led to the new social movements against the hegemonic reductionist politics based on identity or class (Wallerstein 2014: 164f.). A similar debate was to take place in Turkey, but only after the second half of 1980s as a result of attempts to understand the ideological roots of the leftist turmoil in the country. For instance, a feminist activist of Turkish background stated that 'we managed to organize a women's march for the first time in 1986. For me this was the end of turmoil caused by the defeat in 1980. This march was decisive.' (Activist, interview, 15 May 2019)

9   In this context, by 'authority' he means senior ranks in the military chain of command.

10 Particularly two books based on talks given by Öcalan (n.d., 1995) published in the early 1990s show the ways in which the interventions in party structure were carried out.

11 Öcalan's analysis of nation-statism 'pushed him [towards transformation]. [...] He reaches radical democracy as a result of analysing power structures and institutions. [Thus,] his main analyses are those of mentality and power. He builds his analysis through the observation of the kind of structures that result from this mentality' (Kurdish activist, interview, 14 May 2019; author's translation).

Resisting World Politics on 'Migration and Development'?
Tracing the Trajectory of Counter Discourses and Movements in Latin America

Mustafa Aksakal

Introduction

This chapter traces the trajectory of Latin American counterdiscourses on the relation between migration and development since the 1950s by juxtaposing them with dominant globalized discourses. It not only provides a different perspective on the discussions on the subject in a particular world region, but also demonstrates how the dominant discourses have been observed, described and countered in this region.

Public discussions on migration and development are nothing new; they emerged in many countries of the global South and North as early as the 1950s. Various migration scholars have outlined these global discussions and identified three major waves of discourse (cf. Nyberg-Sørensen 2012; de Haas 2012; Faist and Fauser 2011; Nyberg-Sørensen et al. 2002). The first, spanning the 1950s and 1960s, took place in a time of labour shortages in many Western countries, and embraced international movements of labour as beneficial for the development of countries of origin by way of their returning migrants. In the 1970s and 1980s a second wave developed that emphasized (under)development in countries of origin as a root cause of migration. The third wave of discourse has been frequently identified as emerging after the 1990s. It was particularly concerned with migrant remittances and the activities of migrant organizations as collective agents that could potentially promote (local) development in their countries of origin.

While this kind of broad overview is useful for illustrating some general trends over time in global policy discourses and public debates, it has its drawbacks too. It tends to assume a kind of global homogeneity where there is none. As the introduction to the present volume underscores, an important feature of globalization is that it proceeds through increasing economic, political and social ties between economic, political and social actors located in diverse world regions. Furthermore, globalization is also characterized by other dynamics, such as practices related to the different ways in which people observe, describe and interpret the world. With respect to migration and development debates, these practices might be differentiated between dominant globalized understandings and discourses (Castles and Delgado 2008) on the one hand, and counterperspectives that provide alternative, and sometimes fundamentally opposed, positions at the local, national and regional levels on the other. The former are the particular viewpoints of powerful political actors that have been circulated globally. The latter are what the present chapter seeks to address in a particular world region: the history of discussions of migration and development in Latin America in terms of producing counterdiscourses to the dominant globalized ones.

Drawing on a range of policy, civil society and academic documents, then, this chapter addresses the discussions related to migration and development that have emerged in Latin America from the 1950s onward. In doing so, the objective is to highlight the contents and structures of alternative discussions and their role in resisting dominant globalized discourses, raising the question of how discussions in Latin America have positioned themselves in relation to those discourses.

Critical and alternative perspectives on migration and development have been articulated by different actors situated in a variety of world regions. Latin America, however, is particularly salient because it is a region with a long historical tradition in the intellectual production of critical viewpoints on development and migration. Since the 1950s, at least four cycles of debates can be identified that have repeatedly served the purpose of providing counterdiscourses to the dominant global ones. Understanding these perspectives can not only help to obtain a more differentiated picture of migration and development discourse in general, but may also facilitate a better understanding of the composition of current global policies and the power structures embedded within them.

The chapter is organized as follows: the next section engages in a brief literature review of the waves of migration and development discussions and introduces the theoretical viewpoint of this chapter. The third addresses four central public debates that were, implicitly and explicitly, involved in discussing migration and development in Latin America. The fourth compares the four discursive cycles and highlights their counterdiscursive features, exemplifying the ways in which they previously resisted or still resist dominant discourses. The conclusion returns to the initial guiding question and argues that these viewpoints might be significant for better understanding the composition of current global policies that often comprise political paradoxes.

Dominant globalized discourses on migration and development

Public interest in, and discourses on, the link between migration and development have now continued for seven decades. Various social scientists have provided a historical overview of the changing nature of these discourses and have identified three major waves (Nyberg-Sørensen 2012; de Haas 2012; Faist and Fauser 2011; Nyberg-Sørensen et al. 2002). To some extent, this chapter also provides an overview of migration and development discussions. Here, however, particular attention is paid to Latin American discussions and the ways in which they have opposed dominant discourses. To this end, this section first focuses on the content, structure and the theoretical foundation of *two* waves of mainstream discourses that emerged during the 1950s and 1960s and then reappeared in updated versions after the 1990s. These insights are later employed as a background for the subsequent analysis of Latin America discussions.

International labour migration and return during the 1950s and 1960s

Throughout the 1950s and 1960s, international economic inequalities, and especially access to employment (Kindleberger 1967), were considered the main causes of South–North migration. This view of labour market scarcities in countries of the global South was also reflected in considerations of migration outcomes. It was expected that labour migration could help industrialized countries solve the 'excess of labour demand' problem and marginalized countries overcome the 'excess of supply' issue (OECD 1978: 19). For the industrialized countries, it meant increasing the elasticity of their labour supply, countering supply bottlenecks particularly in agriculture, mining and domestic service (UNECE 1963). For the marginalized it implied exporting unemployed people, thus limiting the costs resulting from unemployment (Kindleberger 1967: 199f.). Unemployed people would have the possibility of being employed and potentially earning higher incomes by moving to industrialized countries. In the long run, they would gain human capital, namely new skills, during their stays in destination countries (UNECE 1963). This meant that migrants would accumulate financial *and* human capital that would be imported to their countries of origin through financial remittances and, especially, through the investments and professional expertise they could offer on their return, which would, supposedly, lead to economic development (Faist and Fauser 2011).

This first discursive phase was significantly shaped by two different, yet in some ways complementary, theoretical approaches, namely neoclassical theory and modernization theory. Common to both approaches is that they 'evaluate the movement of people from labour-abundant to labour-scarce regions and countries – along with a presumed transfer of capital in the opposite direction' (de Haas 2012: 13), increasing efficiency and productivity in all regions and consequently providing benefits for all. From a neoclassical perspective, it has been argued that economic differences between regions represent the main drivers for cost-benefit calculations (e.g. expected wages) and subsequent outmigration. Human capital, therefore, represents a particularly important resource because mobile people aim to accumulate and make use of their existing skills as profitably as possible during their stays abroad (Massey et al. 1998). From a modernization theory viewpoint, it has been contended that migrants are important forces of innovation and change. On the one hand, they bring money back to their home countries. On the other, returnees are also identified as transmitters of novel ideas, know-how and professional attitudes. Both aspects were associated with the quick diffusion of wealth and modernization in poor and traditional societies (de Haas 2010).

As King and Collyer (2016) observe, the dominant migration and development discourses of the 1950 and 1960s continued until the 1990s to assume that migration can generate economic and human capital benefits for countries of origin. However, some 'demystification' of the assumptions underlying these discourses occurred through a range of empirical studies made during the 1970 and 1980s. What became increasingly clear was that the benefits of labour migration for the countries of destination outweighed those for the countries of origin, in effect creating a kind of development aid from countries of the global South to wealthy countries of the global North (see Castles and Kosack 1973).

Temporary migration and remittances from the 1990s to the present

Migration and development scholars have identified the latest period of broader discourses as emerging after the 1990s. This ongoing wave of discussion has, on the one hand, adapted to the *Age of Migration* (Castles et al. 2014), highlighting the diversification of source and origin countries and patterns of migration. On the other hand, as Castles (2008) noted, the new phase of discussions has also partly revisited older theoretical and political ideas of the first wave. This becomes evident in the World Development Report 2008 in which international migration is discussed as a realistic pathway for poverty reduction in marginalized regions (World Bank 2007). Formulated differently, international migration was still considered an engine of progress that might trickle down to the poorer segments of society. Despite some similarities, the latest wave of discussions, however, covers additional topics related to the circulation of migrants, money and ideas that were received earlier with little or no attention, as well as dealing with the increasing relevance of countries of origin as partners (Faist and Fauser 2011; King and Collyer 2016). So, while in the initial period returning migrants' investments were emphasized, now financial remittances have moved to the foreground. Temporary and circular migration are therefore considered the most efficient ways to ensure the flow of remittances as it is expected that temporary or circular movers not only have the strongest ties to families back home, but also the highest commitment to supporting them and thereby contributing to economic development (EC 2005). In addition, social remittances – understood as the transfer of ideas, knowledge and attitudes – are emphasized as important for propelling development in countries of the global South (OECD 2006). This is considered to have been achieved through temporary returns, brain gain and brain circulation. Migrant organizations are celebrated as important players involved in philanthropic activities and collective entrepreneurship, which is regarded as stimulating both economic and social development (UN 2006). Finally, world political arenas have developed (e.g. the High-Level UN Dialogues on Migration or the Global Forum on Migration and Development), where dialogues between political actors from countries of both origin and destination for migrants have been institutionalized, indicating the acceptance of countries of origin as partners (Ban 2007).

Some core ideas from the previously noted neoclassical and modernization approaches still receive some attention, such as the emphasis on economic development or modernization through the transmission of ideas, attitudes and knowledge from advanced to peripheral societies. However, political discourses have also become more diversified through the emergence of different political logics (Nyberg-Sørensen et al. 2002). In the 1950s and 1960s migration was meeting the complementary needs of countries of the global North and South (i.e. the excess of labour demand and supply), but after the 1990s migration discussions were concerned with different issues. For instance, as Guarnizo (2017: 457) observed, past South–North labour migration has significantly shaped public conversations, institutions and societies in many destination countries. This has been expressed, for instance, in tendencies to xenophobic reactions to migrants; the proliferation of right-wing ideologies and political parties has also influenced the latest discourses on migration and development. As Castles and Ozkul (2014) alleged, temporary migration is discursively promoted in some discourses because temporary permits convey the message to the local population that the settlement of immigrants and their access to social entitlement are restricted.

Differing political logics are often mirrored in discursive contradictions: while in certain discussions some migrants (e.g. irregular migrants) are addressed as a threat to the security, identity or cohesion of immigration states (Nyberg-Sørensen 2012), in others they are celebrated as development heroes (Delgado 2018). This fact has been acknowledged through the denomination of this link as a 'nexus' (Nyberg-Sørensen et al. 2002), conveying the notion that 'a set of complex interdependencies and two-way causality that may have contradictory effects' co-exist (Carling cited in Bastia and Skeldon 2020: 4).

More importantly for the purposes of this chapter, the previously noted discourse highlights that political actors have indeed observed, described and interpreted migration and development dynamics in immigration *and* emigration countries. However, this has been done from a very particular viewpoint, meaning that, rather than representing entirely global discourses, they often express *globalized* viewpoints because they focus on processes from a particular perspective, that of *the global North*. In addition, the latest globalized discussions have been criticized by some scholars because prevailing power asymmetries between immigration and emigration regions are reproduced in discourses. It has been alleged that representatives of powerful countries discursively promote an unequal division of roles, so that countries and institutions of the global North are suspected of setting the political principles and priorities, and actors of the global South of merely enforcing these agendas (Castles and Delgado 2008). This indicates that discourses are more than verbal communications. From a Foucauldian perspective, not only is knowledge production in discourses related to power, so are the ways in which discourses are linked to diverse practices (e.g. the practices of international organizations) (Foucault 1991). Against this backdrop, migration and development discourses are not only globalized, but also often represent dominating viewpoints, in which inequalities are reproduced.

Discussions in Latin American have historically been opposed to these dominant globalized discourses in many ways that will be addressed in detail in the remainder of this chapter. In many academic contexts these opposing discussions have been frequently reduced to certain neo-Marxist and dependency perspectives. A closer look at these discourses reveals, however, that debates on migration and development have had a long-standing trajectory in the region and have even, in some cases, been linked to social movements, which I address as counterdiscourses. The terminology draws on Karl Polanyi's (1973 [1944]) seminal study *The Great Transformation*. He observed that the political and economic transformations in 19th-century England involved a double movement, referring to dialectical dynamics between liberal public policies and opposing responses from society. Inspired by Polanyi's ideas, this chapter follows the perspective of this book: on the one hand, it traces the ways dominant globalized discourses on migration and development are historically observed, described and opposed in a variety of Latin America debates and, on the other hand, it shows that discourses in this region represent a significant component of global discourse in light of broader globalization processes.

Counterdiscourses on migration and development in Latin America

Discourses on the migration and development relationship had already begun in Latin America in the 1950s. This section is concerned with answering questions related to the content and structure of the discussions as well as the ways in which migration and development were associated. In particular, it aims to uncover the ways in which these discourses instilled difference and opposition to dominant globalized viewpoints. In general terms, it can be argued that, from the very beginning of these discussions, the unequal development of world regions within the global economy was a major concern. As the following review of the most important cycles of discourse in the region shows, the specific link between migration and development has been addressed more implicitly in some periods, and more explicitly in others.[1]

Regional asymmetries, industrial development and migration concerns (1950-1960)

The first wave of Latin American discussions was initiated in the 1950s by various intellectuals directly and indirectly linked to the Economic Commission for Latin America and the Caribbean (ECLAC), with the institution's director, Raul Prebisch, playing a major role in developing what came to be known as the 'Latin American structuralist approach' (in short: 'LA Structuralism'). LA Structuralism represents a theoretical framework which explains, through considering 'structural differences' between countries, a range of macro-economic dynamics, such as the problems associated with the long-term deterioration of the terms of trade in peripheral countries (Jenkins, 2013). Prebisch and his colleagues observed that core countries are historically more industrialized and hegemonic, which is manifested in the production and export of manufactured goods. By contrast, peripheral Latin American economies have an agro-mineral character that is expressed through the export of natural and agricultural resources to core countries. In other words: '[W]hile the centres kept the whole benefit of the technical development of their industries, the peripheral countries transferred to them a share of the fruits of their own technical progress.' (Prebisch 1950: 10). From this point of view, the result is an asymmetric economic relationship between the centre and the periphery to which Latin American countries with structural and institutional differences, unequal exchange and a deterioration of terms of trade were exposed (cf. Kay 2018). As the head of ECLAC, Prebisch was also interested in developing a strategy for the promotion of economic development in Latin America. From a political standpoint, he conceived of economic progress as a way to increase the standard of living for the population by systematically increasing productivity in the region. This was not possible if Latin American countries remained in their traditional roles as producers of primary goods because it made them increasingly dependent, vulnerable and subordinate players in the global economy. From his viewpoint, promoting development involved industrialization which, in turn, required a strong state dedicated to actively promoting progress in the country. The role of the state, then, was to implement political measures related to protectionism, subsidies and investments in the infrastructure of the domestic industry to support the development process, also known as, the 'import substitution industrialization' (ISI) (Kay 1989). Essentially, the underlying idea was to create developmentalist states that protected and promoted domestic industry in Latin American countries, and to improve the life chances of the members of these societies. This means that the fruits of these endeavours were envisaged as trickling down from the companies to the industrial labourers through increasing wages and, consequently, decreasing causes of labour migration. Regarding human mobility, Prebisch was also aware that a constantly growing rural population entailed not only rural–urban migration, but also industrial development as underlined in the following quotation:

> agriculture absorbs a decreasing proportion of the increase in the population of working age, with the result that industry and other activities have been able to increase their employment more [...]. There have, however, been instances in which the rapid growth of industry during recent years has brought about an actual transference of workers, with unfavourable consequences for agriculture. (Prebisch 1950: 43)

While this reflects the outcomes of industrialization on agriculture, it is worth noting that discourses within ECLAC in subsequent years were also directed toward the demographic and social effects that rural–urban migration had on peripheral countries and on urban societies (Ducoff et al. 1965). Moreover, discussions on the role of the developmentalist state sought to find strategies to attract highly skilled migrants. It has been emphasized that to attract skilled foreign workers, more than sporadic economic progress is required. To achieve long-term socio-economic development in Latin American countries, Bertola (2016: 246) noted, the implementation of effective developmentalist policies was needed. This in turn required the building of 'economic, social and political structures'. From this point of view, development was perceived as a useful means to attract more qualified immigrants. Furthermore, it was argued that an additional role of the state is to create and implement coherent recruitment strategies, namely, attractive migration policies for 'encouraging immigration of specialized labour' (Perez 2016: 69).

This approach was developed at around the same time that the first migration and development discourses emerged in the Global North. It is striking that both discussions were similar in that the emphasis was on economic development through industrialization but focused on this idea from different angles, namely, from origin and destination region perspectives. As previously noted, an asymmetric relationship between core and periphery countries that led to unequal outcomes was the main focus. From this vantage point, (internal) migration was not addressed as a natural consequence of emerging regional disparities and rational choices, but rather as an issue situated in the broader economic development processes of the global economy. Industrial development was thought to have side effects related to urbanization and the depopulation of rural areas that might have required state intervention (ECLAC 1957). At the same time, highly qualified immigration was perceived as relevant for accelerating industrial development.

The almost simultaneous emergence of this Latin American discussion and the first wave of dominant globalized migration and development discourses indicates that counterdiscourses do not always represent a concrete response to dominant discourses. In fact, discourses may result from different types of observations and interpretations of development, which may afterwards be instrumentalized as tools to counter dominant viewpoints.

Debates on dependency, underdevelopment and migration (1970-1980)

In the mid-1960s, dependency theories gradually gained traction in public discourses in Latin America and evolved from regional discourses to internationally known and accepted critical migration and development debates during the 1970s and 1980s. While the core ideas of the centre–periphery paradigm of LA Structuralism were kept alive in nascent dependency theories, the approach roughly developed in two theoretical directions: the structuralist and the Marxist strands. Indeed, both strands provided analytical tools for explaining the relevance of dependency in the development processes of countries of the global South, but they focused on the underlying mechanisms differently. For instance, from a structuralist viewpoint, Furtado (1973) observed that both the technologies and the determination of consumption patterns in peripheral countries were controlled by core countries. He considered these 'dependent patterns of consumption' as keys for explaining the preservation of underdevelopment and dependence in peripheral countries. From a more Marxist position, Marini (1973) observed that dependency in peripheral countries was accompanied by the 'super-exploitation' of the domestic labourer. According to this viewpoint, the core–periphery division in the global economy and the resulting unequal exchange would lead to decreasing profit rates among domestic capitalists. To compensate for this economic loss linked to unequal exchange, the capitalists would overexploit the local labour force. In turn, this overuse of labourers would hinder the switch from absolute to relative surplus values as the dominant productive relationship in society, which would reinforce the dependency of these economies. Independent from the particular strand of dependency theory in play, these approaches often considered that earlier noted capitalist macro-dynamics had fundamentally transformed the ways in which society was organized, such as the forms of (re)production and relationships. Resulting structural imbalances thus produced an industrial reserve army inclined to migrate either internally or internationally (Portes 1978).

A further crucial issue related to the migration and development link that dependency scholars emphasized was the phenomenon of brain drain. From this point of view, conditions of underdevelopment were not solely connected to the overexploitation of domestic labourers, but also represented a powerful factor pushing especially well-educated and qualified society members to the more developed and industrialized regions (Frank 1967). In the case of Argentina, Oteíza (1971) revealed that the outflow of qualified persons could be linked to differences in wages, infrastructure, social prestige, and political instabilities and repression between countries of origin and destination. These circumstances have been associated with barriers to development as reflected in a policy document by ECLAC (1975: 10):

> The emigration of scientists, professionals and skilled labour in general is a common feature of all the countries of the region which has been accentuated over the last few decades and is favoured by the emigration policies of the developed countries. [... I]t is known that this emigration represents a substantial economic loss in terms of training costs and of the productive resources thus taken from the national economy.

The quote illustrates the ways ECLAC addressed intellectual and economic losses related to training, human capital and taxes. In subsequent years, the previous discussions were continued by updating the contents to fit the current circumstances but also became more diversified through the inclusion of alternative viewpoints.

The debate on development from within and unequal exchange (1990-2000)

Discussions on neoliberal globalization have emphasized the politically promoted trend toward an increasing circulation of capital and goods and a decentralization of production (Harvey 2007). This global development has also shaped discussions on migration and development in Latin America. As a consequence, classical structuralist and dependency theories lost their analytical power to explain development processes. Moreover, after the 1980s, migration processes moved toward the more globalized, accelerated and diversified dynamics identified by Castles and colleagues (2014) as the 'Age of Migration'. These conditions involved the need to adjust the analytical lens to changing economic, political and social circumstances. These challenges were met by the further development of perspectives toward neo-structuralist and neo-dependency approaches, as noted earlier.

Neo-structuralist approaches emerged in Latin America as a response to the proposed macroeconomic policies under the Washington Consensus and its adjustment programmes. Like previously discussed LA Structuralism, the neo-structuralist perspective in the 1980s also focused on 'endogenous structural factors' (Sunkel 1993: 7).[2] A systematic, theoretical and practical revision was carried out in 1990 in the context of ECLAC and its policy document *Changing Production Patterns with Social Equity*:

> [T]he 1980s represented, in historical terms, a turning point between the previous pattern of development of Latin America and the Caribbean and a phase which is not yet fully defined but will undoubtedly be different and which will mark the future development of the region [...]. The challenge is none other than to find the path that leads to development. (ECLAC 1990: 2)

Briefly summarized, the approach foresees a development process that is 'from within', or a change in the productive structure of the economy from the export of raw materials to the export of industrial goods. As in the previous structural approach, several functions appertain to the state. Its role changed from that of a developmentalist actor to one entrusted with the tasks of seeking new opportunities in the global economy, observing and governing the market, promoting private–public partnerships and open regionalism as well as implementing social policies to increase equity in society (Kay 2018). As in LA Structuralism, migration was implicitly considered to be part of the theoretical framework of the neo-structuralist perspective. This signifies that the macroeconomic conditions were perceived as an important factor that decreased the life chances of society members and could simultaneously cause internal or international migration. By contrast, adapting to the contemporary economic rules of the game meant, by definition, reducing migration pressures and avoiding a brain drain. In short, the focus was solely on the causes of outmigration, namely, development conditions, thus creating a rather indirect link to migration. While neo-structural intellectuals have been hesitant to directly address the link between migration and development, this does not hold true for representatives of the neo-dependency school.

In globalized discourses, free trade is often associated with increasing economic development in countries of the global South. In relation to migration, this means there is an expectation that, after high levels of short-term outmigration, there will be reduced migration in the long run due to the general improvement of the socio-economic situation of the origin-country population (Martin 2016). Moreover, and as discussed above, financial remittances are seen in this perspective as also promoting development (World Bank 2018).

These kinds of viewpoints are sharply challenged by several neo-dependency scholars. They observe that transnational corporations represent increasingly important global players forcing developing countries into a new kind of dependency. As Delgado and Marquez (2007) suggest, this situation becomes clear when one considers the maquiladora sector in Mexico, which expanded in times of free trade under the North American Free Trade Agreement (NAFTA). Maquiladoras are productive units that are largely disconnected from the Mexican economy and represent industrial extensions of large transnational corporations originating mostly from the USA that carry out labour-intensive assembly work. Because these companies enjoy an attractive production environment via tax breaks and low wages, they indirectly export labour. In addition to this 'indirect export' of labour, there is also a direct exportation of labour expressed in migration flows toward the US, composed of a kind of 'reserve army of the unemployed' (cf. Delgado and Marquez 2007). The underlying labour-export-led model clarifies why (against neoclassical considerations) relatively high levels of inequality (underdevelopment) persist in Mexico and why the country has, in recent history, risen to be the largest migrant-exporting country in Latin America. From this viewpoint, the role of financial transfers can be seen as placing the onus of development performance on the shoulders of migrants, thereby, creating additional economic dependencies.

The Buen Vivir discussion (2000-present)

Good Living or *Buen Vivir*[3] represents another important wave in which migration and development have been intensively discussed. As an indigenous philosophical perspective, *Buen Vivir* has a long trajectory in the Andean region. However, the viewpoint has resurged as a migration and development discourse in recent years and became increasingly popular around the 2000s in Latin America. This social philosophy represents a holistic perspective on human wellbeing which has important implications in the understanding of the migration and development link. In general terms, *Buen Vivir* expresses an indigenous worldview on the ways society is organized around the environment, the community and a certain way of living that is based on socially determined needs (Chuji et al. 2019). This perspective was taken up in academic, political and civil society discourses in the Andean region and led to some social movements during the 1990s as well as later political changes in Bolivia and Ecuador after the 2000s.

The philosophical starting point of *Buen Vivir* is similar to the previously noted discourses, and is related to a fundamental critique of past and present Western development thinking and globalized debates:

> [The perspective represents] a substantial questioning of contemporary ideas of development, and especially their attachment to economic growth and their inability to solve the problems of poverty, without forgetting that their practices lead to severe social and environmental impacts. (Gudynas 2011: 2; author's translation)

While many of the previously discussed counterperspectives identify development issues in relation to asymmetric dynamics, dependency and underdevelopment, *Buen Vivir* critically addresses the ways in which prosperity is discussed and expressed in Western discourses, politics and economic practices. But what exactly are the main characteristics of this perspective and how is development perceived by it? Before addressing this question, it might be worth noting that *Buen Vivir* represents a framework in which multiple academic approaches, civil society and policy discourses and practices co-exist (Vanhulst and Beling 2014). This becomes especially evident in political debates that have evolved in Bolivia and Ecuador where *Buen Vivir* has been, although with slight differences, recognized as a set of guiding principles for state action. Gudynas (2011) identifies these characteristics as follows: firstly, the approach considers development as a non-linear process, recognizing the plurality of development ideas and paths in human history. Secondly, the emphasis is on a new relationship between nature and human beings. Nature has an intrinsic value and the excessive exploitation of it through certain means of production and consumption is, therefore, condemned. Thirdly, the perspective rejects the reducing of social relations to marketable goods or services and emphasizes rather the relevance of social relations and interactions in communities that are based on reciprocity and solidarity. Finally, because this perspective rejects the primacy of economic development and its measurement by property or income levels, it stresses non-material wellbeing, such as happiness and good spiritual living. In short, inspired by non-capitalist indigenous visions of wellbeing, *Buen Vivir* underscores the importance of ecologically, socially and socioeconomically sustainable community developments. Two concepts in *Buen Vivir*, namely (in)equalities and inclusion seem to be particularly interesting with regard to discussions on migration and development.

As Villalba (2013: 1430) notes, '*Sumak Kawsay* [Buen Vivir] corresponds to the Andean indigenous ontology', leading to very different understandings of advancement in society. This perspective foresees a decisive transformation in the way human beings define, produce and consume their basic needs away from ideas and practices related to development and thinking that are linked to European modernity. This includes a shift in how relationships to others and to the environment are formed and maintained through economic, political and social practices (Chuji et al. 2019), and embracing wellbeing (i.e. happiness and a good spiritual life) (Villalba 2013). A rigorous implementation of the above-mentioned principles may resolve many of the currently existing inequality-related dynamics because it includes a systematic shift in the perception of outcomes as well as the means to achieve such outcomes. Against this backdrop, it would also be unlikely that particular development conditions, such as regional economic differences, would reproduce certain drivers of migration. An example in favour of *Buen Vivir* is the idea of food sovereignty reflected in the following statement by a Bolivian intellectual:

> How do you achieve a good life? By satisfying the basic nutritional needs, and this by controlling production. The *Ayllu* [author's comment: *a type of extended family, working collectively in a commonly held terrain*] community strictly regulates the system of agricultural production and other resources, the decisions made by the authorities after consultation with the people are carried out with speed, opposition is punished. With the achievement of good production at the same time, one of the fundamental objectives, *suma manq'aña*, namely the principle of eating well, is achieved. (Choque cited in Gudynas 2011: 6; author's translation)

The quote shows how agriculture is approached as an integral part of community development. Rural production is not only considered a means for satisfying basic needs, but is also linked to social relationships and decision-making processes in the community. The academic and civil society discussions on food sovereignty impacted political discourse and were finally implemented in the Bolivian Constitution in 2009. Article 255 proclaimed food sovereignty for all Bolivian citizens, including the prohibition of privatization of rural areas as well as a ban on biotechnologies and toxic substances suspected of harming human health and the environment in agricultural production. This gives farmers more power to decide what, how and where to produce, and it protects them politically, potentially eliminating a range of inequalities in rural areas (e.g. exclusion or exploitation) and, therefore, some important drivers of rural outmigration. It also invites us to embrace the role of social actors in rural development differently: it does not suggest outmigration as a pathway out of rural underdevelopment, as proposed by some international organizations, but rather aims to empower rural dwellers economically and politically.

In addition, the link between migration and development was approached in a different manner. Migrants were looked at from an equity and rights perspective, rather than as the threats to, or heroes of, development that they are frequently identified as in globalized debates:

> [*Buen Vivir*] promotes the creation of Latin American and Caribbean citizenship, the implementation of policies that guarantee the human rights of border populations and refugees, and the protection of human rights of Latin Americans and the Caribbean in countries of transit and destination. (Acosta 2009: 25; author's translation)

The citation shows that the migration and development link is considered an integral process in which the inclusion of all human beings is a major priority. From this viewpoint, citizenship is embraced as universal membership. This includes solidarity with migrants, meaning a respectful and tolerant interaction with foreigners. Some of these ideas were also considered in the Ecuadorian National Plans of Development. The significance of inclusion was underscored as a 'harmonious integration' (cf. SENPLADES 2010: 110) through promoting the formal relations in the region. Moreover, the constitution claims to integrate returning migrants to 'protect migrant workers' (ibid.: 80). From this vantage point, migrants have not been solely viewed in terms of consequences for countries of origin and destination, but rather as subjects that may conceivably need support and safeguarding.

Buen Vivir has been critically addressed, and it has been pointed out that the political implementation of this perspective by the governments of Ecuador and Bolivia was certainly not free of ambiguity and various problems (see, for example, the issues of food security addressed by McKay et al. 2014). Nonetheless, *Buen Vivir* evolved into one of the most important alternative perspectives in Latin America and, in many ways, challenged dominant globalized discourses on migration and development. Although there have been political turnarounds recently towards more reactionary governments in Bolivia and Ecuador, the *Buen Vivir* discourses in academia, policy-making and civil society have opposed and still oppose the deep-seated mainstream understanding that prioritizes (economic) development and material wellbeing. The consideration of relational and emotional aspects in development processes opened up a different vantage point on the causes of migration. In embracing migrants and their needs in an inclusive and solidarity-based perspective, this vantage point clearly counters (neo)liberal understandings that perceive migrants as national security threats in destination regions or as cash cows for remittance-based developments in origin countries.

Discussion: Countering dominant globalized discourses

The previously presented four periods of discussion not only show that public discourse on migration and development has had a long historical trajectory in Latin America, but also that a multitude of actors have approached the nexus from different angles.

With regard to the former aspect, the first three approaches focus mainly on economic (under)development as an important factor in migration. In the early structuralist approach, migration was addressed as a consequence of industrial development and then later in relation to the brain drain. It was also acknowledged that the human capital represented by skilled migrants was needed for industrial development. Therefore, the emphasis was placed on promoting development both to avoid outmigration and to attract skilled foreign labourers. LA Structuralism served as the central theoretical groundwork for discourses related to dependency theories. In the second wave of discussions, several social scientists explicitly considered internal and international migration as a consequence of dependency and underdevelopment. The third wave of LA discourses largely represented theoretical revisions of the earlier discussions. While neo-structuralist approaches concentrated on development as an endogenous process in which migration was addressed in a way similar to earlier discussions, the neo-dependency perspective concentrated on the relevance of global capital and on the activities of transnational companies, particularly, in the framework of free trade. In contrast to these largely macroeconomic perspectives, the discourse on *Buen Vivir* represents another vantage point on migration and development which can, therefore, be identified as the fourth and exceptional wave of the debates. As a holistic and humanistic as well as non-material perspective, it underscores the role of overarching goals such as universal (human) rights, solidarity and inclusion as central to society, and represents principles that are associated in many ways with the migration and development nexus.

As for agents, multiple actors have been involved. In the earlier structuralist approach, the discussion was mainly concentrated around ECLAC members and state representatives who observed and, in some cases, followed the recommendations of the UN institution. In the following decades, ECLAC remained an important player in public discussions. In the dependency discourses, academic actors became increasingly involved in public discourses (Kay and Gwynne, 2000). In the 1990s especially, civil society took a central role in counterdiscourses, which was related to at least two dynamics: in the post-Washington Consensus, non-governmental organizations were awarded central roles as agencies in development practices, and were thus financially and rhetorically promoted (Veltmeyer and Petras 2000); the 1990s likewise witnessed the emergence of diverse 'new social movements' (Delgado and Veltmeyer 2017) in Latin America that were initially organized by farmers, rural workers and indigenous groups. Afterwards some of these movements expanded globally because activists all over the world showed their solidarity with them (Petras and Veltmeyer 2011). A case in point is the Zapatista Army of National Liberation, which started its activities in Mexico, symbolically in the same year that the North Amercian Free Trade Agreement (NAFTA) was implemented, as a local indigenous social movement resisting global neoliberal discourses and policies. Finally, it is worth noting that after 2005 some leftist governments evolved as new players reproducing counterdiscourses in the context of the socialism of the 21st century (Delgado and Veltmeyer 2017). Ecuador and Bolivia implemented central ideas of *Buen Vivir* in their political constitutions around 2008 and 2009.

In sum, all these actors have observed the global economy, dominant globalized discourses and related manifestations in the form of economic and political practices, and have reacted, in one way or another, with counterdiscourses and sometimes with political and social movements. Needless to say, there have been variations in observing, describing and interpreting globalized discourses and economic and political dynamics in Latin America. The previous analysis provided an overview of the most important cases in which the global economy and migration processes as well as migration and development discourses have been interpreted from alternative and often opposing points of view. It underscores that dominant globalized discourses were challenged in most of the critical discussions on migration and development in Latin America. From a Foucauldian viewpoint, it might even be argued that most Latin American discourses have identified globalized discourses as symbols of imposition, reproducing power asymmetries. Consequently, the previously addressed Latin American discussions mostly developed opposite viewpoints, which this chapter terms counterdiscourses.

The Latin American structuralist and *Buen Vivir* approaches represent particular discussions. While the former viewpoint was initially developed to explain dynamics in the global economy and afterwards adapted to migration and development discussions, the latter viewpoint represents an ancient indigenous philosophy, which has gained public acceptance over the past three decades. Nonetheless, when considering the entire trajectory of discussions, it can be argued that these discussions in Latin America represent an impressive history of resistance to dominant globalized discourses, policies and practices. The results also indicate that Latin American discussions represent an important component of global discourses on migration and development.

Conclusion

This chapter has been devoted to public discourses on the link between migration and development in Latin America, investigating the ways that public discourses were positioned in relation to dominant globalized discourses over the past decades. Considering the historical trajectory of Latin American debates, it has become clear that very diverse and rich reflections on development and migration have evolved. It is striking that, with the exception of the *Buen Vivir* approach, the vast majority of the selected perspectives concentrated on the link between asymmetries, dependency and economic underdevelopment and migration. This means that many discourses have reflected on North–South relationships and perceived this link to be unequal, as well as a process that most likely provokes outmigration. Put differently, they produced materialistic perspectives on development and migration. Nonetheless, the previous discussion shows that the debates on migration and development symbolized discursive waves of political counter practices, including discourses and, partly, political and social movements that were theoretically and politically opposed to dominant discussions on migration and development. In this way, they represent an important component of global discussions in the past and in the present, and are therefore more than just 'pessimistic' views of the link, as assumed by some social scientists (e.g. de Haas 2010). This is because of the long discursive tradition in which different viewpoints have developed.

There are several benefits from understanding these dominant discourses and their counterdiscourses. On the one hand, they can provide insights into different modes of observation, description and interpretation, especially the ways in which these practices are shaped by political interactions and mutual references. On the other, they can facilitate a better understanding of current dynamics in global migration policies. In addition, the juxtaposition of the two viewpoints can, for instance, provide new insights for analysing the paradoxes in recent global discourses, such as the Global Compact for Safe, Orderly and Regular Migration launched in 2017.

Notes

1   The aim of this analysis is not to provide a comprehensive overview of alternative migration and development discourses in the region, but rather to selectively focus on the most significant discussions. The underlying selection criteria of these four periods of public discussions are related to the variety of political actors involved, the political resonance on the institutional, civil society and academic levels in the region, and the concrete references to previously noted dominant globalized discourses. Moreover, it is worth noting that the distinction between the four discursive waves follows analytical purposes. In fact, many of the presented waves are related, meaning that rather than representing clearly separated discursive phases, they have built on or even overlapped with each other.
2   The Washington Consensus represents a range of economic policy recommendations related to the Structural Adjustment Programme, aiming to promote liberalization, deregulation, privatization and free trade, thereby resolving development issues in Latin American countries.
3   'Sumak Kawsay' in Kichwa or 'Suma Qamaña' in the Aymara language.

'Sovereignty' and 'Intervention'
Metaphors of Russia's Loneliness in a Global World

Sergei Akopov

Introduction

This chapter engages in debates about mapping the global from the perspective of contemporary Russian politics. It particularly focuses on the question of how the nexus between 'sovereignty' and 'intervention' has been articulated by Russian state and bureaucratic elites in their discourse on contemporary domestic and foreign affairs. Its main research question is: What do political metaphors of Russia's 'sovereignty' and 'intervention' tell us about the mechanisms of the 'organized politics of loneliness', as a specific way of relating to (and imagining) the world, in contemporary Russia?

In relation to the subject of this volume I would, firstly, like to contribute to research on how (as indicated in the introduction) transnational connectivity is limited and even actively resisted by actors that foster the isolation of nation-states by appealing to border protection, anti-globalization resentment, and concepts of global enemies. Today this often occurs as part of the general claim for national sovereignty or what Seyla Benhabib (2016: 109) has criticized as 'the new sovereigntism'. I argue that the Russian case adds to this general debate.

Secondly, I would also like to open up a discussion with several other contributors to this volume. For example, in his chapter Aziz Elmuradov asserts that Moscow's recent conception of the global has largely been defined by an idea that the Western-led liberal world order is in decline and that, instead, Russia should call for a multipolar, pluralistic world with a 'multiplicity of politico-cultural forms and multiple centers of international influence' (Chebamkova 2017: 1). In this chapter I explore what the price paid by Russia for advancing such an ethical and ideological position in the international arena might be. For example, does Moscow's rejection of universalism inevitably push Russian elites to ontologize the global 'loneliness' of Russia and other 'great civilizations' in the world arena? Should Russia practise self-help in order to protect its 'lonely sovereignty' in a hostile world? In the latter case, can Russia's declared 'geopolitical loneliness' (Surkov 2018) serve as a justification for interventionism and revisionist world politics, while civilizational dialogue de facto turns into a 'dialogue on our terms'?

My argument will proceed as follows. In the next section, I will explain the theoretical framework of my research, which is based on the idea of sovereignty as a symbolic structure (Jens Bartelson), and the link between 'sovereignty' and 'intervention' (Cynthia Weber). I will then explain the methodology of discourse analysis of political metaphors and how it can illuminate the 'politics of loneliness'. In the empirical part I will proceed to investigate the principal 2014 'Crimean speech' that sheds light on the discursive articulation of 'sovereignty' and 'intervention' within Russian politics.

Of course, before the 2014 Ukrainian crisis there was the 1990s crisis in Yugoslavia, the 2008 war in Georgia, the 2008–2009 campaign for the independence of Kosovo, and so on. However, before 2014 Russia usually managed to find 'global alliances' with several Western states. This was most evidently the case in Russia's joint opposition with France and Germany to the US-led invasion of Iraq in 2003. It was only after the conflict over Crimea that the West was unified in its decision to impose sanctions on Russia, prompting Russia to reply with countersanctions. The case of Crimea opened the floodgates to mutual accusations of interventionism. The disputes over the suspension of several Russian athletes from the Winter Olympic Games in PyeongChang, Russia's alleged intervention in the US elections, and the 2018 chemical weapons scandal in Salisbury constitute just a small number of cases out of many in this respect. Those countries who either abstained or stayed neutral with regard to Russia soon became key partners of Russian foreign policy within the BRICS alliance between Brazil, Russia, India, China and South Africa, as well as the Shanghai Cooperation Organisation (SCO) and the RIC Forum linking Russia, India and China. The empirical analysis in this chapter will take the 'Crimean speech' as its starting point.

'Sovereignty' and 'intervention' as performative and discursive practices of the local and the global

In the literature it is quite common to problematize 'Westphalian' accounts of the nature of sovereignty as a myth of International Relations (IR) (Albert 2016: 118) and sovereignty itself as an 'essentially contested and essentially uncontested' (see Bartelson 1995) concept. Jens Bartelson (2014: 39) sees sovereignty as a symbolic form by which Westerners have perceived and organized their political world during the modern period. According to him, this 'fetishism of sovereignty' implies that today everything that can be constructed as a threat to domestic political order 'can be twisted into an argument for further interference and intervention in the name of the overarching objectives of international peace and order' (ibid.: 99). Consequently, the governmentalization of sovereignty has amounted to 'a stealthy rewriting of the *nomos* of Earth that has turned the modern international system into an empire in its own right' (ibid.). In other words, sovereignty reveals itself 'through the effects that it generates' (Epstein et al. 2018: 804), for which reason we need to theorize further on the performative nature of sovereignty.

As noted by Tanja Aalberts (2016), like any other concept the concept of 'sovereignty' is meant to structure the reality around us. However, behind this lies the more complex question of how 'sovereignty' actually corresponds to that empirical reality. Referring to the analytical philosophy of Wittgenstein, Aalberts points towards a performative nature of sovereignty. In her view, 'sovereignty' not only describes, but also *constitutes* a certain reality (ibid.: 184). Moreover, although sovereignty tends to be seen as the founding principle of the modern state, there is no comprehensive account of sovereignty that is universally applicable to all cases of statehood. In this chapter, I agree that the use of the concept of 'sovereignty' can act as a powerful figurative expression (ibid.: 195), performed within a practice of exercising political power, and also that 'sovereignty' can be interpreted and studied as a discursive practice (ibid.: 192).

The performative nature of sovereignty resides in the fact that it does not so much describe a reality, but rather is itself (political) action towards the construction of a reality. Performativity can also be manifested in an attempt to represent something that is conditional and conventional (like, for instance, modern Russian collective identity) as unconditional, natural, universal, or even as the only 'normal' political order. Cynthia Weber described this as the phenomenon of 'simulating sovereignty' and of 'performative states', where ideas of sovereignty and legitimized interventions are mutually constituent. As Weber emphasized in relation to US invasions in the Caribbean, 'in the sovereignty/intervention pairing, it is sovereignty which serves as the foundational concept and intervention which is meaningful only in relation to sovereignty. The construction of sovereignty as both a guarantee of the meaning of intervention and as a term that is meaningful in and of itself is done by theorists' (Weber 1992: 201f.).

Drawing on works by Jean Baudrillard, Weber points out that the latter's notion of 'simulation' can also be applied to discourses of sovereignty and intervention, because 'just as in simulation no ultimate foundation exists to ground indicators, so too with discourses of sovereignty, no "domestic community" can be distinguished and made to serve as the foundation of sovereign authority within a state' (ibid.: 215). According to Weber, the only way for sovereignty not to be seen as referring only to itself is the existence of another category – the category of 'intervention'. Weber calls intervention 'an alibi' of sovereignty, because intervention always implies a violation of some sovereignty (ibid.: 215). She outlines two alternatives for states to speak on behalf of the source of sovereign authority. Both of them reflect attempts by states to exert effective control over political representations. The first alternative is a 'political' representation that involves a presumed exchange between the state and its citizenry. In this case, a citizenry 'authorizes the state to serve as its agent so long as the state honours its obligation to stand for and further the interests of that citizenry both domestically and internationally' (ibid.: 216). However, according to Weber, what makes this relationship between the state and its citizenry possible is a second type of representation, 'symbolic representation' understood as 'the act of portraying officialized myth [...]. In this case, what is portrayed is the mystical source of sovereign authority, "the people". Symbolic representation is a strategy whereby the sovereign authority of the state is "written" or invented in a specific form which serves as the grounding principle of the state' (ibid.).

At the time (the early 1990s), Weber's ideas on the *simulation of sovereignty* were new in IR, but not in the social sciences more generally. From Judith Butler had already come the ideas that the power of language can performatively constitute identities in fantasy, and that, for example, 'genders can be neither true nor false, but are only produced as the truth effects of a discourse of primary and stable identity' (Butler 1990: 136). When we look at sovereignty as a set of discursive practices and symbolic representations, I suggest that political metaphors can become useful tools to unveil particular frames that a speaker is enacting in order to gain the support of the social groups that he or she is addressing.

Metaphors of security as tools for framing the 'politics of loneliness'

In political philosophy the concept of 'loneliness' is often defined through its juxtaposition with 'solitude'. The former is considered to be a negative state, because it has to do with painful rejection of the individual. By contrast, the latter – solitude – is not driven by estrangement, but rather a positive notion, as through solitude we can attain more self-awareness or greater creativity (see also Akopov 2020). Hannah Arendt has explicitly drawn attention to this difference: 'the lonely man finds himself surrounded by others with whom he cannot establish contact or to whose hostility he is exposed. The solitary man, on the contrary, is alone and therefore 'can be together with himself' (Arendt 1994: 476). Some scholars replace the dichotomy between solitude and loneliness with a similar opposition between 'loneliness' and 'aloneness', agreeing that a person who is alone does not feel abandoned but rather is full of enthusiasm (Singh 1991: 111). In psychology, similarly, Clark Moustakas distinguished between productive 'true loneliness' and 'negative loneliness'. While the former is equivalent to our earlier definition of solitude, the latter is characterized as 'loneliness anxiety' and is accompanied by a system of defence mechanisms that distract people from dealing with their crucial life questions. Instead, loneliness anxiety motivates people to constantly seek activity with others (Moustakas and Moustakas 2004). Counterintuitively, public gatherings in large crowds may not be the most effective ways of coping with loneliness. Crowds can become lonely as well, and 'lonely crowd' societies are usually characterized by a high level of conformity and 'other-directed people' (Riesman et al. 2001).

The ultimate idea of this theoretical endeavour is 'to insert [loneliness] into the reading of international relations, a conception which has so far remained outside the analytical focus of IR theorists' in a very similar way to the one in which Felix Berenskoetter (2007: 647) described his aim to insert the concept of 'friendship' into IR theory. That appears logical not only because 'loneliness' is an emotion that ontologically grounds the need for friendship (both individually and collectively), but also because loneliness satisfies both criteria offered by Berenskoetter for concepts of international political theory: presence within academic circles and public discourse, on the one hand, and the ability to grasp key features of social relations tied to their 'experiential content', on the other (ibid.). An example of the latter is the article 'The loneliness of the half-breed' published in 2018 by Vladislav Surkov, a former First Deputy Chief of the Russian Presidential Administration, in which he affirms the slogan of Russian Tsar Alexander III: 'Russia has only two allies: its army and navy', something he considers 'the best-worded description of the geopolitical loneliness which should have long been accepted as our fate' (Surkov 2018).

However, a detailed introduction to the concept of loneliness and what it means for IR discourse is beyond the scope of this chapter. Here, I want to focus on a more recent case of the 'politics of loneliness', and specifically on how sovereignty and intervention have been vocalized by Russian state elites in their discourse on Russia's identity since the so-called 'Crimean spring' (2014). Put briefly, the 'politics of loneliness' can be linked to the idea, explained in the previous section, of the performative nature of sovereignty. In my understanding, the political discourse on sovereignty can play a performative function by absorbing the collective loneliness of the local community and redirecting it towards an 'external enemy' (or threat) in the global community. Most often it is done to strengthen vertical state control and to centralize power 'in the name of the nation' (Laruelle 2009) or 'state-civilization' (Tsygankov 2016). This securitization occurs through the means of language – specifically by means of metaphors that allow us to bridge claims for the defence of national sovereignty and justifications of interventionism in world politics.

These so-called 'metaphors of security' became an effective unit of analysis to study Russia's 'puzzling' collective political subconscious (see Chilton 1996: 47). Here I am interested not in random metaphors, but rather those that can be observed within well-established frames of political communication and channels of political mobilization. For example, those that unpack widespread anxieties, traumas or nostalgia for Russia's lost greatness (see Samokhvalov 2017). By exploring metaphors, we literally let the language of Russian official discourse speak for itself, allowing tropes to take us beneath the surface of rational ad hoc argumentation, towards the unknown mechanisms of the emotional construction of social solidarity (Bleiker and Hutchison 2014), the organization of hate (Ahmed 2004), or the hidden depths of affective political communities (Hutchison 2016), which help to reveal how the Russian political community envisages the link between national and global politics.

Certainly, the language of official discourse cannot speak on behalf of all Russians. It cannot reflect perspectives and positions regarding the 'world making' of the entire Russian community. However, it can at least mirror certain trends in public opinion and help to reproduce key frames and perspectives. This is not a new idea, particularly if we relate such an investigation of political metaphors to classical frame analysis, which explains conceptual frames as ways of organizing experience and structuring an individual's perception of society and identity. According to Erving Goffman, the manner in which the role is performed 'will allow for some "'expression" of personal identity' (Goffman 1986: 573). Therefore, for Goffman, there is a relation between persons and roles that 'answers to the interactive system – to the frame – in which the role is performed and the self of the performer is glimpsed' (ibid.).

Originally the idea of frames came to Gregory Bateson, who was observing fighting games between monkeys in the San Francisco Zoo. He believed that the monkeys exchanged metacommunicative signals, letting other members of the group know whether a particular fight was a 'fight for real' or rather a 'game-fight' for fun. We can, probably, find similarities between how monkeys exchange their metacommunicative signals and how politicians frame their rhetoric towards potential voters by using metaphors as signals to indicate how much their fight for national sovereignty is a 'fight for real'. In other words, a widely accepted political metaphor can become a 'metacommunicative frame' outside of which a speaker's messages may be simply ignored (Bateson 1987: 193).

Like Goffman and Bateson, George Lakoff (see Lakoff and Johnson 1980) also explored framing as a strategy in political communication promoting specific interpretations of political reality. According to Lakoff, frames determine our opinions and values as mental structures that influence our thinking, often unconsciously. That is because communication itself comes with a frame. There is an important connection between frames and metaphors. Authors suggest that metaphors are very important cognitively because they are widely used to convey personal meaning and worldmaking. For example, what Lakoff and Johnson described as a 'conduit metaphor': a speaker can put ideas or objects into words or containers and then send them along a channel, or 'conduit', to a listener who takes that idea or object out of the container and makes her own meaning of it (see ibid.).

Why do some 'conduit metaphors' connected with security generate real emotional resonance among their recipients while others entirely misfire? Based on Lakoff and Johnson, we could suggest that this happens when powerful metaphors become assets that allow a variety of ways to make meaning for a significant portion of the politically mobilized population. The sense of loneliness, anxiety, trauma and nostalgia for the great past becomes a perfect reservoir that can be drawn on to construct metaphors of securitization, while the latter can cumulatively shore up new social alignments that create new political realities. In this chapter I suggest that political metaphors should be considered as metacommunicative signals targeted towards the (direct/indirect) reactivation of different frames of 'loneliness anxiety' in the social imaginary of Russian citizens. Or, as Russian scholar Olga Malinova (2012: 4) puts it, political leaders expect that their arguments will fit particular frames to provoke a desirable reaction from the audience, which is limited by the established semantic repertoires. For Lakoff (2006) the elements of the communication frame include the following: a message, an audience, a messenger, a medium, images and a context. In our case, such a 'message' will be a Russian official discourse of sovereignty; the audience – government servants and those members of the Russian population who consume this discourse; the medium – the Russian president, who articulates images and metaphors that will become the subject of our discourse analysis in the next section.

Discourse analysis of metaphors of 'sovereignty' and 'intervention' in the 'Crimean speech'

As discussed in the section above, we are looking at political metaphors of security that frame sovereignty in a way that helps to absorb, deploy and redirect the collective emotion of 'loneliness anxiety', which can also be used for the justification of interventionism. If, following Weber, we consider justified intervention as 'an alibi' of sovereignty, then, in the case of modern Russia, it is logical to pick as a starting point for discourse analysis the 2014 'Crimean speech'. The first step is to look at the speech and distinguish metaphors of sovereignty and intervention that reveal how Russian elites envisaged both *the global* and *the national* (local). To synthesize these metaphors, I will use a technique of initial active coding derived from the methods of grounded theory. In grounded theory it is recommended to test whether the developed codes are representative. Thus, in a second step (next section) I test this speech against other speeches, undertaking a systematic analysis among the pool of all the Official Addresses of the Russian president to the Federal Assembly (1994–2020).[1] I will suggest that the identified metaphors offer an indication of the particular ways in which Russian elites construct 'symbolic representations' of sovereignty in order to make an authoritative claim to represent the Russian people in local and global affairs. A final graph will help to discuss the results in a comparative perspective in the conclusion.

The 'Crimean speech' was made on March 18, 2014 in the Kremlin, where the Russian President addressed the Russian parliament. I have used that speech to create twenty 'open' codes of 'sovereignty':

a) Integration, gathering together (*sobiranie*); Reunification of Russia regardless of the opposition of the West; Primordial unity of Slavic countries (panslavism); Ancient Rus as a common heritage; Inseparability of Crimea from Russia.
b) Glorification of Russian military (for example, historical victories in Crimea).
c) Soviet 'sovereignty parade' as a negative phenomenon.
d) Victimization of Russian nation as being forcefully divided and historically split apart. Metaphor of '*the sack of potatoes*' as symbol of lack of recognition of Russian-speaking diaspora.
e) Speculating on Russia's trauma of the 1990s.
f) (Relative) deprivation of Russia's population.
g) Opposition between the suffering ordinary people and irresponsible elites and highly paid 'global nomads'.
h) Unmasking and unveiling of nationalism (case of conflict in Ukraine); References to fascism and WWII.
i) President as a protector of ordinary people, who 'does not abandon his men' (paternalism).
j) '*The elastic spring*' metaphor – Russian resilience and need to be assertive; Sovereignty and self-determination; Sovereignty as immunity from the West.
k) Importance of maintaining political stability and seeking world order within the system of the UN.
l) Soft power and foreign intervention via 'colour revolutions'.
m) Sarcasm and hypocrisy of the West; Condemning exceptionalism of the USA.
n) Gratefulness to the countries of the East / BRICS for support for Crimea becoming Russian.
o) '*Keeping our house in order*' metaphor (political and legal order in Russia).

p) Collectivism and collective will; Solidarity and 'spiritual bracing' (*duhovnie skrepi*').
q) Russia facing a threat from the 'fifth column' (*'this disparate bunch of "national traitors"'*).
r) Legal aspects of sovereignty (Case of Kosovo, Ukraine's illegal revolt, Crimean Referendum etc.).
s) Ungratefulness of the West.
t) People as the ultimate source of every authority and sovereignty.

Following the logic of building grounded theory I synthesized and reorganized these twenty initial codes into six groups (constellations): the three first groups (1–3) represent metaphors of 'sovereignty', while the second three (4–6) represent 'justified interventions'. I illustrate them below:

The first group I brought together under the metaphor *the defender of ordinary people*. This trope accentuates the 'loneliness anxiety' of citizens seeking the paternalistic protection of a strong leader: 'We *could not abandon* Crimea and its residents in distress. This would have been a *betrayal* on our part' (Putin 2014). After that accumulated collective emotion can be redirected to construct perceptions about the outside world: 'However, what do we hear from our colleagues in Western Europe and North America? They say we are violating norms of international law. Firstly, it's a good thing that they at least remember that there exists such a thing as international law – better late than never' (ibid.). Defending the common people and, in their name, defending political stability against the hypocrisy of political elites (i) can be expressed in the Russian catch phrase 'we do not abandon our men' ('*mi svoih ne brosaem*').

The second group of symbolic representations falls under the metaphor of *spiritual ties* for national unification (p). Here the primordial unity of Slavic countries and panslavism (a) in general play a key role in promoting the historical civilizational unity of three Slavic countries 'where Prince Vladimir was baptized. His spiritual feat of adopting Orthodoxy predetermined the overall basis of the culture, civilization and human values that unite the peoples of Russia, Ukraine and Belarus' (ibid.). Russia is being threatened by a 'fifth column' (q) that may put its *unity under threat* – a valuable language tool to justify the need for sacral sacrifice in the best traditions of the scapegoating mechanism when violence can be diverted onto another (external) object, 'something it can sink its teeth into' (Girard 1979: 4). The (re)unification of Russia, along with the recovery of its national sovereignty (a) (regardless of how this might complicate its international relations) and the glorification of its military, plays a key role here (b). It appropriates nostalgia for lost self-esteem and national pride: 'This is also Sevastopol – a legendary city with an outstanding history [...] Crimea is Balaklava and Kerch, Malakhov Kurgan and Sapun Ridge. Each one of these places is dear to our hearts, symbolizing Russian *military glory* and outstanding valor' (Putin 2014).

Thirdly, the *house in order* metaphor unites under a single frame codes like the importance of domestic *stability* (o) and how the world's stability is being challenged by the decline of the UN (k). Stability should be achieved, according to Putin, via the collective will of the people as the ultimate source of legitimacy (s): '*We see* that the overwhelming majority of people in Crimea and the absolute majority of the Russian Federation's people support the *reunification* of the Republic of Crimea and the city of Sevastopol with Russia ... because the people are the ultimate source of all authority (ibid.). The expression 'we see' plays a performative role here, symbolically uniting into a single political body the president and 'his men', so that neither of them feel themselves to be 'lonely' anymore.

The fourth group redirects claims to sovereignty towards justified interventionism, employing an allegory of *the elastic spring*. That includes codes for Russian resilience, the need to be assertive against the West/NATO, or immunity from the West (j) coupled with sarcasm over Western exceptionalism (m). An image that threatens Western partners with a Russian 'spring' that will strike back at them is emblematic in that sense: 'They are constantly trying *to sweep us into a corner* because we have an independent position [...]. But there is a limit to everything. And with Ukraine, our western partners have crossed the line, *playing the bear* and acting irresponsibly and unprofessionally' (ibid.). The metaphor of 'playing the bear' gives away another psychological mechanism – comparative victimization: 'After all, they were fully aware that there are millions of Russians living in Ukraine and in Crimea [...] Russia found itself in a *position it could not retreat from*. If you compress *the spring* all the way to its limit, it will *snap back hard*' (ibid.).

The fifth group I marked under Putin's metaphor of *the sack of potatoes* (d), which speaks directly to Russia's 'geopolitical loneliness' described earlier. Regretting the marginalization and division of the Russian nation, the president noted: 'Millions of people went to bed in one country and awoke in different ones, becoming ethnic minorities overnight [...] while the Russian nation became one of the biggest, if not the biggest, ethnic group in the world to be *divided* by borders' (ibid.). Criticizing Russia for its lack of assertiveness in world politics, he added: 'I heard residents of Crimea say that back in 1991 they were handed over *like a sack of potatoes*. This is hard to disagree with. And what about the Russian state? […] It humbly accepted the situation' (ibid.). In this group I also placed codes like speculating on Russia's trauma of the 1990s (e) and the further victimization of the Russian nation as being forcefully split apart (d). They seem to be based on an idea of Russia's relative deprivation (f).

Finally, the sixth group – the idea of *'moral debt (duty)'* – is based on the ungratefulness of the West to Russia (t). It addresses Russia's sense of alienation and isolationism from the negative 'Other', but perhaps also what Aziz Elmuradov in his chapter to this book describes as a deep, historically rooted sense of insecurity, which results in Moscow's permanent demand for a great leader (*'vozhd'*) and 'great power politics'. According to Putin, the actions of the West were aimed against Ukrainian, Russian and Eurasian integration, despite Russia's attempts to engage in dialogue with the West. Instead of reciprocal steps 'they have lied to us many times, made decisions behind our backs […]. This happened with NATO's expansion to the East, as well as the deployment of military infrastructure at our borders. They kept telling us the same thing: "Well, this does not concern you". That's easy to say …' (ibid.). Below we can compare how the 'ungratefulness of the West to Russia' contrasts with Russia's 'gratefulness to the East' (n): 'We are grateful to the people of China, whose leaders have always considered the situation in Ukraine and Crimea by taking into account the full historical and political context, and greatly appreciate India's reserve and objectivity' (ibid.).

The six key metaphors of Russian sovereignty and justified intervention identified above remain instrumental for our further investigation. As we can see, the first three groups are meant to accumulate and absorb domestic 'loneliness anxiety', and the last three aim to redirect it towards envisioning *the global* (West and East). A further round of saturations is needed to see whether the initial coding of these six metaphors and, most importantly, the mechanisms of the 'politics of loneliness' that they contain, has any relevance to a wider cache of speeches to the parliament.

Metaphors of 'sovereignty' and 'justified intervention' in the annual addresses of Russian presidents (1994-2020)

Since 1994 the Russian president has delivered an address to the Russian parliament almost every year, outlining major plans for the county's development in the upcoming year. His listeners usually number around 1300 people:

members of the Federation Council and Russian government, deputies of the State Duma, heads of the constitutional and supreme courts, the governors of Russian regions, heads of the Russian Orthodox Church and major media outlets, and so on. The 1994–2020 collection of speeches to the Russian parliament looks like a valid pool against which we can test the symbolic representations of Russian sovereignty that we identified earlier in order to build more grounded conclusions about the 'politics of loneliness'.

In Table 8.1 I have systemized every mention of 'sovereignty' or 'sovereign' in the annual addresses of three Russian presidents. After each year I have provided in brackets abbreviations of the names of the Russian presidents; for example, '1994 (BY)' for speeches of Boris Yeltsin, '2000 (VP)' for Vladimir Putin and '2008 (DM)' for Dmitry Medvedev.

Table 8.1 Employment of 'sovereignty' in 1994–2018 addresses of Russian presidents

Year	Nº	Representation of sovereignty inside and outside Russia
1994 (BY)	6	*Inside:* Sovereignty of the multinational people of Russia granted by its constitution that should protect their equality (1) and guaranteed by Russian armed forces that protect territorial integrity (2) *Outside:* Problem of building united monetary system with Belarus (3); if necessary defending Russia's legitimate interests 'firmly and harshly' (4); Russia is not required to request permission from the world community for its UN peacekeeping operations within the CIS (5); in relation to European security – against the expansion of NATO without Russia (6)
1995 (BY)	15	*Inside:* Ensure sovereignty, independence and unity of Russia (1); sovereignty and need to overcome crisis improving the quality of life (2); sovereignty and building proper federalism and municipal management (3–4), sovereignty against separatism (5); sovereignty vs. 'banditism' in Chechnya as loss of territorial integrity and power fragmentation (6–13); defending sovereignty (14) and the stability of state borders (15)
1996 (BY)	6	*Inside:* Sovereignty of nationalist movements led to the fall of the USSR (1) while 'paralysed' Russia could not become a 'foothold' against nationalism of former USSR republics (2); President Boris Yeltsin protects Russian people as source of real sovereignty in 1993 conflict with the Supreme Council (3); satisfaction that finally in 1991–1993 the Soviet 'parade of sovereignties' was channelled into the Federal Treaty of Russia (4) *Outside:* Alma-Ata agreements on the creation of CIS from sovereign states (5); tendency for integration prevails now over the former 'run-away' of some CIS S. states (6)

1997–1998 (BY)	0	
1999 (BY)	2	*Inside*: Russian sovereignty declaration underpins new Russian parliamentary tradition (1) *Outside*: Protecting sovereignty vs solving problems by force, with methods 'from the Stone Age' (2)
2000 (VP)	2	*Inside*: 'Challenge for Russian state sovereignty' vs global terrorism getting inside the country, but also aspiring geopolitical recomposition of the world (in case of Chechnya) (1) *Outside*: Attempts to infringe upon the sovereign rights of post-Soviet states under the guise of 'humanitarian interventions' (2)
2001–2005 (VP)	0	
2005 (VP)	4	*Inside*: Our values determine our sovereignty and we will stay strong (1); Russia chose democracy itself and decides how/when to build it itself (2); gratitude to soldiers defending sovereignty during WWII (3) *Outside*: those who 'buried' sovereignty of Russia ahead of time made a mistake (4)
2006 (VP)	0	
2007 (VP)	3	*Inside*: National spiritual unity as grounds for sovereignty (1); 'State sovereignty is also determined by cultural criteria', wrote D. Likhachev (2) *Outside*: We will only be able to preserve our statehood and sovereignty if our citizens see, feel, and are confident that all the state's efforts of are aimed at protecting their vital interests – improving their lives, improving their welfare and safety (3)
2008 (DM)	1	*Inside*: Any 'reformatory itching' is inappropriate, Sovereignty of people and constitution should remain intact for a long time
2009 (DM)	0	
2010 (DM)	1	*Outside*: the size of sovereign debt is minimal. The level of Russia's international reserves today is significantly higher than it was at the end of 2008
2011 (DM)	0	

2012 (VP)	5	*Inside*: Not disruption of sovereignty but continuity in Russia's political development, promotion of direct democracy, including people's initiatives via the Internet online (1) *Outside*: Russia should remain sovereign and influential in C21st world, keeping its national and spiritual identity (2); Sovereignty as strong diplomacy and military might (3); To be sovereign we should multiply and be younger, more creative and morally better (4); Unity, integrity and S. of Russia vs separatism, nationalism, Russian sovereignty vs outside intervention including through foreign agents (5)
2013 (VP)	1	*Outside*: Russia will aim for leadership in defending international law, seeking respect for national sovereignty, independence and the unique identity (*samobitnost'*) of its peoples
2014 (VP)	7	*Inside*: This year we overcame hardships together proving that we are a mature nation, a really sovereign and strong state, that can defend its compatriots (1) and respect the sovereignty of Ukraine (2-3) *Outside*: Russian sovereignty vs. sovereignty loss by states in Europe (4-5); Sovereignty vs dissolving, getting lost in the world (6) *Outside*: Eurasian Union as integration, based on keeping national identity of its states (7)
2015 (VP)	0	
2016 (VP)	1	*Outside*: Sovereignty as unity based on patriotic values vs. sanctions against Russia
2018 (VP)	1	*Outside*: Technological delay as loss of sovereignty that is equivalent to the loss of economic energy
2019 (VP)	3	*Outside*: Russia has been and always will be a sovereign and independent state (1). It will either be that, or will simply cease to exist. Unlike some countries, without sovereignty Russia cannot be a state (2). For the first time our reserves fully cover not only the sovereign debt (3), but also private borrowings.
2020 (VP)	5	*Inside*: The opinion of our citizens, as the main source and bearers of sovereignty (5) must be decisive. *Outside*: Russia can be and can remain Russia only as a sovereign state (1). Our nation's sovereignty must be unconditional (2); National citizenship to be an obligatory requirement for those who hold positions of critical significance for national security and sovereignty (3); The 2020 amendments to the Russian constitution will help to create a solid system that will be absolutely stable in terms of its external contours and will securely guarantee Russia's independence and sovereignty (4).

I then attributed each mention of sovereignty to one of six above-mentioned metaphors and calculated their total number. Cases that I could not ascribe to any of these groups I assigned the label '*other frames*'. Following the logic of R.B.J. Walker, I have split these metaphors into '*internal*' and '*external*' ones, applying Walker's (1993: 159) famous 'inside/outside' dualism of 'order' vs 'anarchy'. As we remember from Weber (1992: 201), discourses of sovereignty imply discourses of (legitimate/justified) interventions. Looking at the three 'internal' metaphors in the left column, we can see that they can be coupled with justifications of 'external' interventions in the right column (Table 8.2).

Table 8.2 Numbers of symbolic representations of Russian sovereignty 1994–2020 projected onto 'internal' and 'external' political communities

Sovereignty projected onto the national sphere (Inside)	Sovereignty projected onto the global (Outside)
'The defender of (the will and voices of) the common people' being victimized – 7	Russian diaspora treated as a 'sack of potatoes' – 5
'The spiritual ties' of Russia – 5	'The elastic spring' of Russian resistance – 16
The need to 'keep our house in order' – 21	'Moral debt' of the 'ungrateful West' – 2
Other – 3	Other – 4

This coupling seems logical: the metaphor of *the defender of common people* can be redirected towards the need to protect the mistreated *Russian diaspora abroad*. Once unified by its *spiritual ties*, Russia can be mobilized (like an *elastic spring*) into resistance to the Western liberal world order. Finally, the commitment to *keep our own house in order* is mutually supportive of the obligation not to trust the hypocrisy of the *ungrateful West*. The results of Table 8.2 are again graphically displayed in Figure 8.1.

Generally, the six metaphors mentioned above relate to the utilization of sovereignty in the texts of the 1994–2020 addresses of Russian presidents, though to different degrees. Figure 8.1 shows that 21 mentions of the term 'sovereignty' fall within the symbolic frame '*keep our house in order*'. This is a rather wide symbolic pool in which we can emphasize the representation of sovereignty as building strong centralized federalism and opposition to separatism, 'banditism' and the loss of territorial integrity (alluding to the two Russian wars in Chechnya). Another noteworthy aspect is the close link between claims for sovereignty and the idea of a strong Russian state (*derzhava*),

Figure 8.1 Metaphors of 'sovereignty' in addresses of Russian presidents 1994–2020

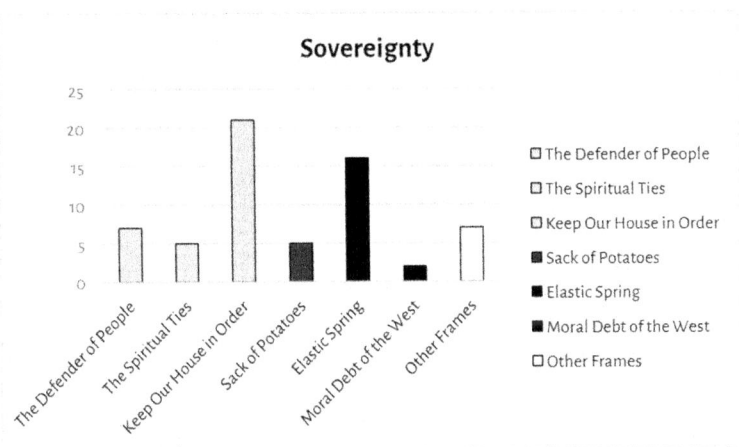

as well as its financial independence from foreign creditors (see, for instance, Medvedev's declaration in 2010 that Russia's 'sovereign debt is minimal').

The second most numerous group is *the elastic spring* of Russian resistance, with 16 examples. While the previous group largely related to justifications of 'internal' interventions (like wars in Chechnya), *the elastic spring* expresses how Russia envisages 'justified interventions' in its 'external' relations, in particular, concerns about 'humanitarian interventions' and accusations that NATO controls European countries for whom 'possessing sovereignty is too much of a luxury' (see Table 8.2).

According to Figure 8.1, the metaphors *'defender of common people'* (seven mentions) and *'spiritual ties'* (five mentions) were almost equally influential. The latter relates to the sovereignty of the Russian state and its leadership of the spiritual unity of the Russian nation, based on the preservation of its unique civilizational identity. The former is more concerned with the representation of the president as a main defender of the interests of 'common folk'. For example, in 1993 Boris Yeltsin (1993) 'protected the interests of the Russian people' in his conflict with The Supreme Council, which 'acted against the will of the people'. In a comparable way, in 2014 Vladimir Putin (also in patriotic unity with the people) defended Russian interests in conflict with NATO and against the sanctions imposed by the West.

Metaphors representing the Russian diaspora abroad, treated as a '*sack of potatoes*' (five examples), usually refer to them as compatriots (*sootechestvenniki*), whether they live in Latvia, Estonia or Ukraine. References to the '*moral debt of the ungrateful West*' (two mentions) emphasize the notion of the West's long-expected attempt to break down Russian statehood and sovereignty. Both narratives started to evolve in Russian discourse during the first term of Putin's presidency. For instance, back in 2005 he said, in relation to the task of 'keeping state sovereignty': 'It seemed to many that our young democracy was not a continuation of Russian statehood, but its final collapse. That it was just a prolonged agony of the Soviet system. Those who thought this way made a mistake' (Poslanie Prezidenta 2005).

In 2007, in Munich, Putin developed this idea, claiming that the Organization for Security and Co-operation in Europe (OSCE) had degenerated into 'a vulgar instrument designed to promote the foreign policy interests' of Western states alone (Putin 2007). According to the Russian president, 'it is obvious that such interference does not promote the development of democratic states at all [...]. We expect that the OSCE be guided by its primary tasks and build relations with sovereign states based on respect, trust and transparency' (ibid.). In 2014 Putin was already pursuing a similar line of argumentation by condemning the 2008–2009 interventions in Kosovo and US exceptionalism, which 'prefers not to be guided by international law' but rather 'by the rule of the gun' (Putin 2014). 'Here and there, they use force against sovereign states [...]. To make this aggression look legitimate, they force the necessary resolutions from international organizations, and if for some reason this does not work, they simply ignore the UN Security Council and the UN overall' – a narrative later used by Putin to deflect US criticism of Russia's intervention in Crimea.

Eventually this logic grew into the full-scale opposition of Russia to the 'global West': despite many efforts of 'those who in the past 15 years have tried to accelerate an arms race and seek unilateral advantage against Russia' they still have not 'managed to restrain Russia' (Poslanie Prezidenta 2018). The passage above demonstrates that symbolic representations of the *moral debt of the ungrateful West* and *the elastic spring* are interconnected. Pointing to this interconnectedness is valuable for explaining the 'politics of loneliness'.

Russia's 'lonely' sovereignty: conclusion and discussion

The word 'sovereignty' or 'sovereign' was used 63 times in the addresses of Russian presidents to the Russian parliament between 1994 and 2020. In his Official Address to the Federal Assembly on 15 January 2020, the Russian president used the word sovereignty six times (more than in any of the speeches in the previous years). 'Sovereignty' in that speech was related to different subjects: the sovereignty of the 'Russian state', the 'unconditional' sovereignty of the Russian nation, sovereignty as a 'guarantee of national security and independence', sovereignty and social opinion as a 'source of power' (Presidential Address to the Federal Assembly 2020). Given the manifold ways in which sovereignty has established itself in the world of Russian political discourse we can pose the question: What is the reason for the constant return to sovereignty by different Russian presidents?

One of the approaches to answer this question is to treat 'sovereignty' as a 'floating signifier', 'an object presupposed by hegemonic articulatory logics' (Laclau 2000: 75); but what makes one 'floating signifier' more powerful than another? A second approach looks at 'sovereignty' as a symbolic form (Bartelson 2014), but a symbolic form of what? Or, perhaps, sovereignty can be approached as a tool for mediation between an authoritarian political regime and the perceptions of a given populace, where 'going outside the regime is not an option' (Gill 2015: 28, 50). But what makes the populace trust the narrative of the regime? Without disregarding the three approaches mentioned above, in this research I was testing Weber's (1998: 92) idea that political speeches 'may be analysed as performative enactments of a state's sovereignty'. My discourse analysis aimed not just to show how metaphors of security become political representations of Russia's sovereignty, but also how they reflect the perceptions of Russian elites on the nexus between *the national (local)* and *the global* – the subject of investigation in this volume.

The findings of this research seem to indicate multiple interconnections between a group of metaphors that play the role of containers for the accumulation of political support inside the local community and a (second) group that redirects and diverts the 'fear and anxieties' of the national populace towards construction of the image of a hostile global environment (in particular, towards the anti-Russian conspiracy of the hostile West). There is something very existential that plays the role of a 'floating signifier' of Russian sovereignty and stands behind its symbolic form, functioning as a mediation tool between Russia's authoritarian politics and its populace. It is hard to say for sure what that is, but, as I have tried to explore in the discussion above, it seems credible to suppose that Surkov's narrative of 'Russia's geopolitical loneliness' is not as innocent and accidental as it may sound.

Once we insert loneliness into Russia's puzzling equation between claims for its national sovereignty and justification of its outside interventionism, it looks as if our circle can be squared. Surkov compares Russia's cultural and geopolitical identity with that of someone born into a mixed-race family: 'Russia is a Western–Eastern half-breed nation. With its double-headed statehood, hybrid mentality, intercontinental territory and bipolar history, it is charismatic, talented, beautiful and lonely. Just as a half-breed should be' (Surkov 2018). The image of 'lonely Russia' created by Surkov mirrors all six metaphors of Russian sovereignty identified in this research. Russia is independent and assertive (*the elastic spring* metaphor), Russian-speaking people are divided and victimized (*the sack of potatoes*). That explains the demand for Russia's unity through shared *spiritual ties* as well as the idea of stability and *order in our house*. Last but not least is the symbolic representation of the Russian president who *defends and does not abandon his men* against the hypocrisy of the *ungrateful West*. The latter perfectly fits into the conclusion reached by the former main ideologist of the Kremlin: 'What will the forthcoming loneliness look like? Will it be the loneliness of a middle-aged bachelor at the edge of the dance floor? Or the happy loneliness of the front-runner, an alpha nation that has made rapid headway to leave all other peoples and states far behind?' (Surkov 2018).

How can 'lonely sovereignty' justify intervention? In my view, it makes sense even on the level of our daily life. When we feel anxiety about being lonely, we can justify to ourselves things that others would find hard to accept. Notably, the same can happen with collective 'loneliness anxiety': loneliness can be fantasized as a sacral sacrifice for staying true to our home community and national identity, even if it is the price to be paid for alienation from the global world.

Notes

1   All the texts of the Official Addresses of the Russian president to the Federal Assembly (1994–2020) were retrieved from the Russian Legal database 'Consultant Plus' (http://www.consultant.ru).

Russia and the EU in a Multipolar World: Invoking the Global in Russian Terms

Aziz Elmuradov

Introduction

Over the past decade, Russia's relations with the European Union have evolved from competition to conflict. With the Ukraine crisis as a culmination point, many scholars explain the conflictual stand-off as a result of a long-term crisis rooted in the internal structure of EU–Russia interaction (Casier 2016; Chaban et al. 2017; Haukkala 2015). While such a perspective contributes to a better understanding of the conflict, there is more to the confrontational dynamics between the two sides. World politics can be traced back not only to the pursuit of national interests, but also to differing ways of envisioning the world. To a considerable extent, the current conflict with Russia is a conflict of worldviews. In line with the theme of this volume, the following chapter takes this epistemic dimension of world politics seriously. The world and the global are not fixed realms but are constituted in the practices of concrete actors who create their discursive horizons of the world and the global through symbolic representations, narratives and models. This chapter, therefore, focuses on practices of worldmaking inherent in Russian foreign policy discourse. Retracing popular modes of mapping the world from the Russian perspective, I will show how a multipolar worldview informs the relationship between Russia and the Western world.

Russian foreign policy discourse is greatly affected by major trends and trajectories under way in world politics. Russia finds itself in an increasingly dynamic global environment. The world is more volatile and uncertain today than at any time since the fall of the Berlin Wall. In a broad sense, 'disorder', 'breakdown', 'the rise of the rest', 'post-West', 'post-liberal' and even 'post-truth' (D'Ancona 2017) have become widespread mantras of the day rampantly used by global elites to define the magnitude and potential trajectories of the shifting global context. In addition, Russia's immediate international environment is also dynamic – sometimes more so than Russia itself – politically, economically and demographically. With the EU in flux, China on the rise, and the US-led liberal world shaken, what challenges does such a world subject to fluid change present to Russia? How does Moscow's perception of global change shape its approach to interaction with the EU? To deal with these questions, this chapter argues that it is crucial to explore Moscow's long-standing normative thinking: a doctrine of a 'multipolar world', centred on the principle of balance of power. This multiplex edifice of views underpins Russia's contemporary understandings of the global political space and is thus relevant to its perceptions of the EU.

Moscow's conservative turn

Moscow's current mode of envisioning of the world and the global must be put into the context of a broader policy shift. This new policy course is marked by the so-called 'conservative turn', also called a 'Eurasianist' or 'civilizationalist' turn, an important dimension of which is re-envisioning the world order. On the one hand, there is a sense of uncertainty accompanied by a mixture of concern and excitement about what Russian politicians describe as a global shift of power. The rhetoric in Moscow remains mired in the spirit of the 'decline of the West'. Some Russian leaders run to overgeneralizations that 'the rise of the rest' and the 'shift of global power to the East' is an inevitable course of history. Looking forward to these global transformations, Russia's Foreign Minister Sergey Lavrov says that 'after five or so centuries of domination of the collective West, as it were, it is not very easy to adjust to new realities that there are other powerhouses. It is not Russia that is shaping this world order, it is history. It is the [global] development itself' (Lavrov 2018b). According to policy experts Sergey Karaganov and Dmitry Suslov (2018), there is 'no way Russia can avoid or sit out this process', or else whatever new world is created, 'it will be created without Russia, or even against it'. Russian president Vladimir Putin claims that 'it is now being decided how the world will look in the future, in the coming decades. Will this be a world of monologue and the rule of force, or a world of dialogue and mutual respect?' (Kremlin 2018).

In this narrative, the EU 'has failed to create a politically unified space capable of acting in concert on the international stage and is unlikely to achieve this in the future' (Bordachev 2019). It is 'certainly fighting to make sure that it is not lost in this new world order' (Lavrov 2018b), but 'the ability of Brussels to influence this world is waning' (Kortunov 2019a). In Russian political circles, there is a proverbial saying: 'Europe is an economic giant, but a political dwarf.' This attitude lingers in the air. If previously the EU was portrayed as a difficult but still indispensable partner for a host of reasons including Russia's own 'modernization', over the past decade the paradigm has shifted from inferiority to superiority, to estrangement and even to a certain sense of indifference. Russia and the European Union are 'certainly not in confrontation—unlike Russia and the United States. They are, however, experiencing estrangement and, in some cases, alienation' (Trenin 2019).

In matters of world politics, the EU is perceived as impotent due to its technocratic inertia and resultant inability to respond effectively to the challenges of the dynamic world and, worse still, to its increasing dependence on 'Atlanticist moods' in matters of strategic importance, to its own disadvantage. In effect, what is questioned is not the role that the EU could play globally as 'one of the independent poles', but its very ability to recompose itself in a timely manner in order to play that role. Adding to these, there is a sense that the European project is in deep crisis – a perception buttressed by the rise of anti-Brussels sentiment in a number of European countries. The EU was 'struggling internally even as international relations ... entered a period of unusually high turbulence. The sharp turn in U.S. policy has made the breakdown of the international order ... an irreversible process. That order was most suited to European interests and its collapse poses a serious challenge not only to the philosophy of European foreign policy, but also to Europe's worldview' (Trenin 2019). But there is 'not much that Russians can realistically expect from Europeans. Despite their valiant efforts, they [European leaders] will not turn the EU into a geopolitical and strategic counterweight to the United States. They will probably not produce leaders of the stature of not only de Gaulle, Brandt, and Churchill, but even of Chirac, Kohl, and Thatcher' (ibid.).

By contrast, Moscow is and must be ready for 'creative participation' in the global transformation. Imbued with a powerful sense of righteousness, Russia 'will remain a country that is able to ensure its survival' either with support from allies or, if necessary, all on its own (Bordachev 2019) or even as a 'lonely power' (Shevtsova 2010; see also the chapter by Sergei Akopov in this volume). The major challenge Russia faces today is to reinvent itself as an indispensable global player. This is obviously a long-term vision that surpasses the time frame of the current presidential term. However, in Moscow's eyes the process has already started. The Western liberal order is waning as it is losing its monopoly over 'universal' norms and values, and the centre of gravity in world affairs is shifting to the non-West. According to a widespread view, the emerging world order should 'fully reflect the changing balance of powers and the existing West-centred institutions should either undergo a profound transformation or be replaced by more universal, more inclusive and more representative organizations' (Ivanov 2019). The world should 'fully reject the concept of Western (i.e. liberal) universalism in favor of developmental pluralism', and the emerging concept of modernity should 'imply opportunities for preserving national traditions, culture, specific economic, social and cultural models distinctly different from the Western examples' (ibid.). At times Hobbesian and at other times Lockean, Moscow's worldview is crucial, and it is to its ideological roots that I now turn.

Multipolar world

From the Russian perspective, two paradigms can be distinguished that oppose each other in contemporary world politics. One is believed to advocate cultural, economic and political globalization conducted under the guidance of the Western world, including the EU. The other, which Russia itself advocates, is a more particularistic approach that calls for 'a balance of interests, multiplicity of politico-cultural forms and multiple centers of international influence' (Chebankova 2017: 1). The latter worldview – multipolarity – has been reinforced as Russia's main world political view advanced in the international arena. Its proponents claim that such a conception of world politics can only have 'a dialogical character, in contrast to the unipolar world order that is mostly based on the normative monolog of liberal democratic states' (ibid.). According to this view, the European Union, by proclaiming the ideas of democracy, individual freedoms and human rights as the main principles of its foreign policy, 'imposes these on everyone else, not caring much about how this may affect people of other cultures. European pretensions of "universality" do not allow for a dialogue with "others"'. In these conditions, 'normal diplomacy as an art of compromises is impossible' (Tsygankov 2018).

In what follows, I will explore the *geopolitical*, *historical* and *civilizational* dimensions of this worldview while contextualizing their implications within Russia's self–other-definitional discourse towards the EU. In doing so, I follow the line of argumentation that the underlying justifications of sovereignty and the balance of power retain their centrality to an understanding of Russia's EU discourse – also in its global context. As genealogical repertoires of foreign policy thinking, the concepts of sovereignty and the balance of power largely inform Russia's relationship with the EU. As we will see, these concepts also underlie a set of deep-seated convictions and beliefs about the nature of Russia's role and its relationship to the wider world.

Geopolitical mappings

Multipolarity is a *geopolitical* concept centred in the idea of the balance of power essential to Russia's self-identification as a sovereign power in world politics. In grossly oversimplified terms, this implies that if there is no balance of power, there is no full sovereignty. It is by virtue of history and geography that it is an imperative for a country such as Russia to maintain full sovereignty over its domestic as well as foreign policy. The concept is most often associated with the figure of Yevgeny Primakov (1929–2015), a veteran Russian politician, diplomat, architect and arch-representative of this worldview. According to this concept, Russia should be an independent centre of power and a crucial global player with its own understanding of the world order and should build a foreign policy based on its own strategy, and not just in conformity with or opposition to someone else's worldview (Primakov 1996). From this perspective, major powers see the world through their own lenses and cognitive maps: America's *neoliberalism*, Europe's *normative power* and China's *tianxia*. Russia is no exception. The main factor influencing Russia's world political attitude is a desire to feel less like the periphery of Europe and more like the independent centre of Eurasia. Primakov's legacy was to strengthen the multi-vector nature of Russian foreign policy, essentially abandoning the unilateral orientation to the West that prevailed in the first half of the 1990s. Primakov put forward a plan for the development of a strategic triangle taking in Russia, China and India as a practical mechanism for promoting global multipolarity, a concept that later led to the establishment of BRICS. He argued against the expansion of NATO into Central and Eastern Europe and in favour of creating a new European security architecture for a reunited continent without dividing lines. All these ideas laid the foundation for Russia's foreign policy formulation for the subsequent period.[1] The principles he formulated alongside the notion of multipolarity have since then constituted the basis of Russia's foreign policy concept, including its 2016 version (ERFUKNI 2013; MFARF 2016). These principles entail the pursuit of national interests, pragmatism and a multidirectional policy that suggests a readiness to cooperate with any country around the world where there is a reciprocal willingness based on mutual respect, equality and a balance of interests.

Although framed in these terms, the world according to Moscow is characterized at the same time by great power politics in which it is predominantly these 'major powers' that lay down the rules of the international order, 'acknowledge' and 'respect' each other's 'national interests' as a 'sphere of privileged interests' and, while they may compete with one another, also cooperate to uphold the global order. It is a world where smaller actors need to know their place for their own good and tolerate a tacit restriction on their sovereignty. According to proponents of multipolarity, a vast majority of existing nation-states are simply not able to independently ensure even their own security and economic growth, not to mention any significant contribution to the formation of a new world order. Thus, in both the present and future multipolar world, only a handful of countries – the major powers – have 'real sovereignty'. President Vladimir Putin stated this view of the world in his speech at the St. Petersburg International Economic Forum on 2 June 2017: 'There are not so many countries that have sovereignty. Russia treasures its sovereignty, but not as a toy. We need sovereignty to protect our interests and to ensure our own development. India has sovereignty; China is such a country; but not many' (Kremlin 2017). As for the European Union, Russia would like to see 'a responsible international player capable of pursuing an independent foreign policy in the interests of European nations' (Lavrov 2018a). For Russia, the European Union 'as a political actor has a positive meaning when a united Europe appears as a subject sovereign with respect to the United States, an independent center of power. [...] in the foreseeable future this condition is not feasible in practice' (Trenin 2018).

It seems the Russian officials do not so much lament the EU's acting on geopolitical motives, rather they deplore exactly the opposite – the EU's not being sufficiently geopolitically mindful. The Russian elites do not hide their surprise at how little autonomy and decisive leadership Europe really exercises when it comes to the big decisions in world politics. Lavrov recalled that 'we for some previous years overestimated the independence of the European Union and even big European countries' (Lavrov 2014). Some critics argue that, contained in their 'post-modern ecosystem, Europeans lost their curiosity about how Russia sees the world and its place in it, [...] failing to grasp that what they saw as a benevolent power could be viewed by others as a threat' (Krastev and Leonard 2014: 3). What happened to Europeans? They are 'largely absent on issues of military security in Europe: their silence in response to Trump's decision to withdraw from the INF Treaty was deafening and very telling' (Trenin 2019). 'The West today is more afraid of plastic bottles than Russian missiles' (Kortunov 2019b).

The Russian discourse on the multipolar world order also reveals its view of the broader structure of European security architecture. Like its envisioning of the global order, Moscow's concept of Europe is multipolar and pluralistic. According to Richard Sakwa, there are two opposing paradigms of European political space envisioned by Brussels and Moscow respectively. The first is a *wider Europe*, 'the idea of the continent centred on the EU and European space is represented as Brussels-focused, with concentric rings emanating from the west European heartlands of European integration' (Sakwa 2015). In Moscow's view, the paradigm of a *wider Europe* is not, in reality, truly European. It is Atlanticist, that is, deeply embedded in the Atlantic community. The EU-centred wider Europe is becoming absorbed into the Atlantic system, jeopardizing its own normative foundations and lending its policies a geopolitical dynamic that the EU was established precisely in order to transcend (ibid). More than a cosmetic update, European leaders face the historic task of rethinking the entire 'European project' because it is becoming less and less European (Kortunov 2018a).

The second paradigm, according to Sakwa, is based on the idea of a *greater Europe*. This would be a continent united in its systemic diversity. Instead of an EU-centred Europe, the idea supposes a multipolar continent, with more than one centre and without a single ideological flavour. This is a more pluralistic representation of European space, and draws on a long tradition,[2] including Gorbachev's 'common European home'. The idea of a new European Security Treaty, announced by Dmitry Medvedev in 2008, called for the realization of such a vision – a genuinely inclusive new security order – arguing that new ideas were required to ensure that dividing lines were not once again drawn across the continent. In 2010 in Berlin Putin made a similar plea for a geopolitical unification of all of 'Greater Europe' from Lisbon to Vladivostok, to create a genuine 'strategic partnership' (Putin 2010).

In contrast to the unipolar and exclusive nature of European geopolitical space, the Russian leaders take the multipolar and inclusive nature of Asia as a positive example. 'As for the multipolar or unipolar nature of Asia, it is not unipolar; we see and understand this very well. The leaders of the Asian countries today have enough common sense to enter precisely this mode of working with each other. And we are ready to work in the same mode with everyone' (Kremlin 2016). Unlike relations between Russia and the EU, 'Russian–Chinese relations are a very flexible form of interaction, which the two sides can calibrate and customize depending on the particular area of cooperation. The sides are not constrained by any highly detailed bureaucratic procedures, protracted decision-making mechanisms, limitations of national sovereignty and so on' (Ivanov 2019). The Chinese–Russian partnership is 'not directed against any third countries ... has nothing to do with "dividing Eurasia" [and] does not imply relations between a "senior partner" and a "junior partner"' (ibid.). There may be asymmetries in their relations, but 'these asymmetries do not make the relations hierarchical with the leading power imposing its will on the satellite power' (ibid.).

For Russia, China's rise is an illustrative example justifying its view of the emerging multipolar world. Firstly, Chinese experience shows no linear dependence between the effectiveness of economic modernization and political liberalization. China is 'at the vanguard of a global normative revolution, as Western-led conceptions of universal values give ground to competing models of development' (Salin 2011). Secondly, the Kremlin sees China's rise as instrumental in shifting the global centre of gravity from the Euro-Atlantic to the Asia-Pacific region. According to Fyodor Lukyanov, Research Director of the Valdai Discussion Club, justification for Moscow's 'shift to the East' has nothing to do with Russia's attitude towards Europe but with

> the objective fact that only a country with solid and acknowledged positions on the Pacific may seek to become a great power in the XXI century. Russia needs to hurl all effort to implement a complex strategy of re-orientation towards Asia Pacific [...] as it does not any longer make sense for Russia to keep regarding all its actions through the prism of its relationship with Europe. (Lukyanov 2014a)

Historical imageries

Multipolarity also has a *historical* dimension. This is particularly relevant in the case of Russia, since Russian elites draw on historical imageries in order to justify the need to shape the present-day international order. Historically, Russia has been both a maker and a taker of the rules upon which the international order is based. Adherents of multipolarity in Russia like to refer to the experience of the 'Concert of Europe', but this time not on a European but a global scale; the actors are different, but the basic tenets are conceived as similar. Russian foreign policy expert Bobo Lo summarizes the view aptly:

> The great powers determine the arrangements and rules of international politics, and, crucially, abide by them. No single power may be allowed to threaten the status quo or assume disproportionate power – Napoleonic France in the nineteenth century, the United States today, and China in the future. Smaller states know their place, and frame national policies with due regard for the interests of the major powers. The latter do not interfere in one another's domestic affairs. And security – or at least their security – is collective and indivisible. (Lo 2015)

Indeed, the Russian elites use the past to argue how Russia as a great power has contributed to European stability. For example, in Putin's rendering, unlike [the Treaty of] Versailles, concluded without Russia and ultimately leading to the Second World War, Russia's very active participation in Vienna Congress 'secured a lasting peace' and manifested 'generosity and justice' (cf. Kremlin 2013). The Russian view suggests that useful lessons should be learnt from the Concert of Europe, that is, the defeated should not be treated too harshly, and that Russia should not be excluded from the negotiating table.

Given Russia's own active participation and resultant sense of historical pride, it is little wonder that Russian leaders boast of the Congress of Vienna and the concert of European great powers as the standard example of an effective security system. Russian Foreign Minister Sergey Lavrov refers to it, asserting that 'Russia became a saviour of the international system' at the Congress of Vienna, the formation of which 'led to development of the continent without serious military conflicts for 40 years' (Lavrov 2018c). Sergey Karaganov, one of the leading foreign-policy experts in Russia, has elevated the Vienna system to the status of something worth emulating. '[U]shering in the most glorious era in the history of the European continent', the main reason why the Congress of Vienna worked was that 'the postwar arrangement was relatively fair and did not humiliate France in defeat'. And then he goes to lament that 'there was nothing like the Congress of Vienna following the Cold War, although the solemn language and commitments of the 1990 Paris Charter had the makings of a historic accord for "eternal peace". Now Russia with its globally minded elite, topnotch diplomacy and geographical position can do a lot to help build this world, a new Concert of Nations, for the benefit of itself and its partners' (Karaganov 2015). Another prominent expert, Fyodor Lukyanov, recalls that 'what is needed is precisely a genuine professional diplomacy in the spirit of the 19th century, a diplomacy that is familiar from textbooks but whose actual practice has been virtually forgotten' (Lukyanov 2014b).

Some critics contend that the design of the 'European Concert' cannot be replicated under modern global conditions. According to Andrey Kortunov, Director of the Russian International Affairs Council, although the 'European Concert' was fully multipolar and really helped to preserve peace in Europe for a long time, it is impossible today to repeat the experience. Today the situation is completely different. 'In the 21st century, the differences between the great powers affect the foundations of the world order, the basic concepts of international law, and even more general questions – the ideas of justice, legitimacy, the 'big meanings' of history' (Kortunov 2018b). In the author's opinion, there is a simple reason why the 'European Concert' is a naïve example for how the balance of power might be maintained in the contemporary world. And this reason is the flexibility characteristic to the great powers of the past: Great European powers could afford the luxury of promptly changing the configuration of unions, coalitions, and alliances to maintain the overall balance of the system.

> Could we imagine such flexibility today? Could we suppose that over the course of two or three years, Russia would be capable of swapping its current partnership with China for an alliance with the United States? Or that the European Union, as it faces increasing pressure from the United States, would re-orient itself towards strategic cooperation with Moscow? Such scenarios look improbable at best and absurd at worst. (ibid.)

Kortunov argues that 'the magnificent multipolar façade often disguises the same steel-and-concrete bipolar structure of global politics, reflecting the Soviet mentality that has not been entirely overcome' (ibid.). For instance, Moscow's contemporary view of the 'East–West' dichotomy reflects the rudiments of the Soviet mindset. Such a mindset does not fit into the declared multipolar picture of the world, but it is a very convenient way for Moscow to construct opposing imageries of 'West' and 'non-West'. Nevertheless, some parallels the expert draws do resonate with the mainstream perceptions and beliefs of Russian political elites. The question is posed: 'Why did the 1814–1815 Congress of Vienna result in a stable European order, while the 1919 Treaty of Versailles became meaningless 15 years after it was signed?' (ibid.). In answering this question, Kortunov finds fault with the nature of democratic political leadership. In contrast to the Concert devised by absolute monarchs, Versailles was crafted by the leaders of the Western democracies who depended on national public sentiment, which in turn demanded that they 'punish the Germans'. In this reading, Kortunov laments that today's politicians are even more dependent on public sentiment and that 'the chances of seeing new examples of Alexander's magnanimity and Metternich's insight today are slim' (ibid.).

Civilizationalist vocabulary

Multipolarity under Putin has acquired a new *civilizational* dimension. Russian political elites refer approvingly to Samuel Huntington's theory of the 'clash of civilizations'. Just as there are several centres of global power, so there are various civilizational 'poles'. The 2013 Russian Foreign Policy Concept talks of 'global competition [...] on a civilizational level,' with 'an increased emphasis on civilizational identity' (ERFUKNI 2013). In proposing a 'dialogue between civilizations,' Moscow is declaring to the West that 'our values are just as good as yours'—different, but in no way inferior. The 2016 Foreign Policy Concept also unambiguously commits to this aspect: 'competition has been ... gaining a civilizational dimension' with 'attempts to impose values on others'; 'promoting partnerships across ... civilizations' is regarded as a priority; the 'civilizational diversity of the world and the existence of multiple development models have been clearer than ever' (MFARF 2016).

Emphasizing the civilizational dimension of world politics in this way raises the possibility of further cultivating the notion of civilization as a subject of international politics. Multipolar world ideologists consider civilizations as a new subject of international politics (Chebankova 2017). In this reading, 'civilizational development' is seen, as Putin said in a speech to the World Russians People's Council in 2018, as 'the foundation for the multipolar world' while Russia is as 'an authentic civilization, a unique one, but one which does not aggressively claim its exceptionalism' (Kremlin 2018). Referring to a prominent Russian thinker of the 19th century, Nikolai Danilevsky, Putin stated that 'no civilization can call itself supreme, the most developed one' (ibid.). Some Russian intellectuals (Mezhuev 2012; Tretyakov 2012) claim that Danilevsky's ideas could be invoked in defence of the equality of the world's political cultures, their peaceful co-existence and recognition.

Moreover, Russia's elite considers this civilizational ideology to be a distinct intellectual product that it can offer to the world (Tsygankov 2016). The idea is to reconstruct the discourse on international affairs in such a way that the ideas of particularity, cultural-historic context and the multiplicity of political forms can be incorporated. Whether such a worldview could contribute to global stability remains an open question. Some argue that the theory of the multipolar world could be developed into a stronger and more coherent political ideology, given its substantial metaphysical and political basis (Chebankova 2017).

The Russian political elites continue to speak of the multipolar world both as a desirable goal and as a modern-day reality. It is one thing for Moscow to embark on a quest to shape the world on the basis of preconceived ideas of multipolarity and another thing to effectively handle the real world constituted by instantaneous and unpredictable processes rather than order or linearity. In a way, the changing global context has been a dream come true moment for Russia. But even when dreams come true, one has to live up to them. The tension between *the normative* – a genuine change to a multipolar world – and *the instinctive* – inherent belief in the Hobbesian nature of world politics – continues to influence Russia's world political attitudes. On the one hand, Moscow speaks of a need to adapt to a world in transition, one that is increasingly globalized and interdependent. On the other, the instinctive element in Moscow's reaction to the pressures of a dynamic world is to draw back to what it knows – classical interpretations of great power politics. Assertive in the pursuit of its goals, the course of Moscow's foreign policy has been condemned in the West. While the Russian elites denounce the 'demonization' of Russia, the general feeling is that they take a certain psychological satisfaction from the fact that Russia is back on the world stage, perhaps 'disliked by some but ignored by none' (Lo 2018). The major legitimating reason for retaining the present course and taking it further is the conviction that it has been widely successful. This is not just the view of the Kremlin and the Russian political elite. It is also shared by some Russian liberal critics, the public and even some experts in the West. 'Russia may be on "the right side of history" in opposing moral interventionism – a position in which it is supported by China and India' (Lo 2018). In Russia, recent foreign policy successes in the Middle East and the partnership with China are stressed in contrast to the failures of Western policymaking.

All this being said though, it is important to note that such preconceived ideas about the inherent and normative nature of world politics do not hang in thin air. Immersed in them, Russia's discourse on the multipolar world is simultaneously flavoured by human personality to an uncommon degree. It is common to speak not just of Putin but also of 'Putin's Russia'. Russia's story has become the story of the President himself, a story of which he is a diligent student and that he preaches at every opportunity. This tonality cannot go unmentioned as it intimately pertains to a deeper understanding of the political philosophy within which Putin's worldview is rooted. His perception of Russia's place in the world is certainly not a modest one, neither is his emotional appeal to it: 'As a citizen of Russia and the head of the Russian state I must ask myself: Why would we want a world without Russia?' (Solovyov 2018). He took Yeltsin entirely seriously, in his own way, when the latter, on leaving office because of ill health, told him to 'take care of Russia'. It is no lie that the 'Putin consensus' has gained wide support, implicitly or explicitly, across the broader Russian political spectrum and, perhaps more importantly, that that support is based on the 'gut instinct' of many in Russia, who have come to believe that if there is anyone who should represent modern Russia, it can be no one else but Putin. 'Divorced to marry Russia', that is the kind of admiration he enjoys among many of his compatriots, with some even calling him *vozhd*, meaning a leader of exceptional power and authority. The philosophy behind his foreign policymaking reflects the characteristics of Putin, not only the views and ideas that he cherishes but also the methods he favours of putting them into action. Like Yevgeny Primakov, his political godfather, his political philosophy is not only to defend national interests as such, but also to manage to do so under the most unfavourable conditions, even when the country's capabilities are at a low ebb. As Putin himself observed, speaking at Primakov's funeral, it is important 'to keep listening to Yevgeny Primakov's voice' and 'to remember his lessons' (Kremlin 2019a). Furthermore, Putin's world politics is one which seeks to remain vigilant and alert to developments in larger forces and moods, global and local. Wisdom then consists in finding the balance between the need to 'swim with the currents' or 'appear to be swimming with them', and 'to steer' them in a needed direction, if necessary, to intervene in order to make the difference. 'Blackbelt' in his martial art,[3] practitioners of politics close to Putin do not deny his claim to an equal ranking in matters of foreign policy. It is these qualities, too, namely a conservative and survivalist persona aligned with Russian strategic culture and historical experiences that reaffirm traditional principles of world politics.

Conclusion

Summing up, Moscow's conception of the global context over the past decade has largely been defined by the idea that the Western-led liberal world order is in decline. This decline is constructed as a result of a historical process that, in Moscow's eyes, has already started. The liberal order is losing its monopoly over 'universal' norms and values, and the centre of gravity in world affairs is shifting to the 'non-West'. Instead, a particularistic approach is proposed that claims to call for a balance of power, multiplicity of politico-cultural forms and multiple centres of international influence. This worldview – of a multipolar world – has been reinforced as Russia's world political doctrine and advanced in the international arena: 'The world should fully reject the concept of Western (i.e. liberal) universalism in favour of developmental pluralism' (Ivanov 2018). Proponents of this view claim that such a conception of world politics can only have a dialogical character. Framed in these terms, the world according to Moscow in significant ways remains rooted in great power politics.

Notes

1. All Foreign Policy Concepts since 2000 derive from global security and geopolitical considerations developed by Yevgeny Primakov. The terminology of multipolarity has shifted lately toward an emphasis on 'polycentrism'. The 2013 Foreign Policy Concept speaks of the transition to a 'polycentric system of international relations.' Practically speaking, there is no substantial difference between the two concepts.
2. Giuseppe Mazzini's idea of a 'United States of Europe'; Gaullist ideas of a broader common European space from the Atlantic to the Pacific; Gorbachev's idea of a 'common European home'; Nicolas Sarkozy's return to the idea of pan-Europa; the Valdai Club's idea of a 'Union of Europe'.
3. In Putin's own analogy, 'Judo teaches self-control, the ability to feel the moment, to see the opponent's strengths and weaknesses, to strive for the best results. I am sure you will agree that these are essential abilities and skills for any politician' (Kremlin 2019b).

Back from the USSR
Envisioning the Global Through Journey Narratives

Lucy Gasser

Making worlds and their horizons

This chapter traces the worldmaking practices of four journey narratives by travellers from the global South in the Soviet Union. Animated by postcolonial theory and decolonial aims, it contributes to envisioning the global by understanding literature as practising a 'species of world making' (Bell 2013: 257) and seeks to identify the narratives of the global that latently structure the normative horizons of these writings. It articulates the worldmaking practices of British imperialism's 'civilizing mission', and looks at writers from Britain's former colonial dominions who displace and contest them. Rabindranath Tagore and Bisham Sahni from the Indian subcontinent and Pauline Podbrey and Alex La Guma from South Africa each had the opportunity to travel in Soviet Russia and its socialist satellites and penned nonfictional accounts of their experiences. The chapter argues that these formerly marginalized texts furnish resources for productively contesting colonially determined narratives of the global and hone a capacity for pluralizing aspirational horizons. This serves the decolonial aim of dismantling the legacies of imperial ways of producing (knowledge of) the world.[1]

British imperialism's so-called civilizing mission entailed a narrative that did a great deal of work for the colonial project. It told a story in which the Western European colonial metropolis was located as the centre of both the imperium and the world: this was the node whence all that was laudable in European civilization and needed to be exported to the colonies originated. It served as the moral pretext that sought to disguise and legitimate the exploitation that was in fact constitutive of the empire: it was the ethical imperative that bade the more 'advanced' European civilization to come to the aid of its junior siblings in the colonies, to be caretaker of their resources.

Dismantling this faulty structure and its various articulations has been the work of much postcolonial scholarship, not least Edward Said's enormously influential *Orientalism* (1978). Yet I want to propose the value of considering the ramifications of the civilizing mission anew by turning a critical eye on the spatio-temporal mappings underwriting its discursive production of the world. Moving from a clearer delineation of these, I trace how the writings of a number of travellers to the Soviet Union from the global South not only multiply thwarted the colonial arch-narrative's violently ascribed cartographies and temporalities, but furnished the resources and honed the capacity to envision a plurality of alternative aspirational worlds.

My intervention here takes the form of a number of juxtaposed and interrelated readings of accounts of journeys in the Soviet Union and its satellites. These journeys were broadly situated within the geopolitical time of the Cold War, though one account – Rabindranath Tagore's *Letters from Russia* (1930) – significantly predated it. Tagore's epistles are read alongside Bhisham Sahni's *Today's Pasts* (2004) in order to demonstrate how their worldmaking practices constructively repudiate the civilizing mission. Pauline Podbrey's *White Girl in Search of the Party* (1993), in turn, complicates their 'corrective'. Finally, reading Alex La Guma's *A Soviet Journey* (1978) against the grain, I argue for the value of insisting on plurality when envisioning narratives of world. The writer-travellers should not be taken as representative or as giving exhaustive accounts, but as instantiations of viewpoints that produce alternative spatio-temporal mappings of both *colonial* narratives and much-studied *postcolonial* trajectories of 'writing back' to the imperial centre (Ashcroft et al. 1989).

The civilizing mission's projection of the global constitutively informed and shaped its discourses and narratives. Its particular practices of worldmaking entailed positioning the European capital as the centre whence the kind of civilization deemed desirable was to radiate outward to the colonial peripheries. Spatial marginality was thus ascribed to the colonial 'outposts'. A neat expression of this is offered by the cartographic forays that culminated in the Mercator projection that in many (Western) contexts became the most frequently occurring world map, and thus most commonly held envisioning of the world. This projection places Western Europe top and centre, dramatically understates the size of the African continent, and glibly divides the Pacific. The interplay between what is construed as literal and metaphorical centrality is evident, as is the marginalization – again, both literal and figurative – that comes with being located on the periphery.

Germane to the approach of drawing out these alternative mappings is Pheng Cheah's proposal, in *What is a World? Postcolonial Literature as World Literature*, that world literature be thought of as 'literature that is an active power in the *making of worlds*, that is, both a site ... and an agent that participates and intervenes in these processes' (Cheah 2016: 2; emphasis added). The making of worlds and the discourses that sustain them are determined by the power structures that produce them. As Duncan Bell (2013: 261) observed, worlds can 'be taken by force, made and remade in the image and at the behest of others. Imperialism, according to this account, is a technology for the taking and (re)making of worlds'. Each of the texts discussed here entails practices of worldmaking, and my readings work to configure the horizons that determine these worlds, as well as their normative content: specifically, the contours of their normative horizons. Imperial legacies leave not merely cartographic traces, but also temporal ones, as succinctly communicated by the Greenwich Meridian's positioning in London. Cheah points to how centrality works not only in the ways space is charted, but in the ways time is measured: The subordination of all regions of the globe to Greenwich Mean Time as the point zero for the synchronization of clocks is a synecdoche for European colonial domination of the rest of the world because it enables a mapping that places Europe at the world's centre (Cheah 2016: 1).

This maps time as literally emanating outwards from a temporal centre – a node that determines global punctuality – in the capital city of the British empire. Grafting this on to the civilizing mission elucidates how the mapping of time works in that narrative. In colonial stories, London was to be understood as the determining co-ordinate of temporality: belatedness and backwardness – those oft-reiterated accusations levelled at the colonies – were to be determined in relation to this centre. This fitted the narrative of the civilizing mission, since it was necessary to establish the colonizers' putative superiority over the colonized in order to justify their ruling over the latter. This superiority was, and indeed often still is in a variety of different contexts today, articulated in temporal terms, as an expression of the advanced nature of European civilization and culture.

Both these temporal and spatial dimensions work to determine derivativeness. The peripherality of the colonies is derived from the assigned centrality of the imperial capital; the belatedness of the colonies is derived from the more admirable advancedness of European civilization; the colonized are taught to consider themselves always in a species of alterity derived from Europe. In addition, the colonized are cast in these arrangements as passive: as the *object* of the civilizing mission, that which needs to be civilized.

The designation of being *before*, *ahead of*, or *more advanced than* is implicitly premised in the civilizing mission on an understanding of progress, and it is on this that my first readings will pivot. It is important to interrogate these ascriptions of progress and progressiveness, as they are reborn in subsequent narratives. The colonial narrative would have it that the imperial centre is the home and origin of progress, and that colonialism brings progress to the colonies to help them along. This co-optation of 'progress' insinuates itself into other narratives as well, particularly those of Europe's global positioning. The European centre was able to model itself as 'owning' progress. This formed an integral component of the 'structure of legitimation around colonialism: Indigenous societies could not have survived without the advent of white education, infrastructure, etc' (Lentin 2019). The seeds sown here germinate in later notions that there is something inherently progressive about Europe, 'underpinned by a wider conception of Europe and the West as the general birthplace of the so-called "rights of man"' (Lentin 2004: 14).

In *Provincializing Europe: Postcolonial Thought and Historical Difference*, Dipesh Chakrabarty (2000: 20) enunciates the need to 'release into the space occupied by particular European histories… other normative and theoretical thought enshrined in other existing life practices and their archives. For it is only in this way that we can *create plural normative horizons*' (emphasis added). The articulation of 'plural normative horizons' is useful to the task in hand. The 'normative' grasps the directionality, the implied forward thrust of progress at stake. The image of the horizon is apposite for the spatio-cartographic metaphorics at work in my argument, which understands the idea of the horizon in the spirit suggested by Vijay Prashad's (2007: xvii) view of what the Bandung conference of 1955 did for its Afro-Asian participants: 'The horizon produced by the Third World enthused them'. The conference's imaginative power was that it created an alternative framework of the possible, enabled a different configuration of what might be striven towards – and this was full of animating energy.

The horizon then delimits the world that can be imagined, the fringes of the imaginable, and thus marks also the figuration of the aspirational. One might hope to *progress* towards one's aspirations. The horizon of a world, moreover, may be determined by its centre. As such, efforts to destabilize and disarticulate Eurocentric narratives like the colonial civilizing mission can be well-served by locating not only alternative centres, but by also calibrating the alternative horizons they might bring into existence.

Chakrabarty's injunction to create a plurality of such normative horizons is implicitly a denial of the will to exclusivity embodied in the civilizing mission's agenda: *only* the European colonial power could represent the 'right' way to progress; and there was only one kind of desirable progress. Temporality, construed in the linear terms of these narratives, allows only one route to the future: the one charted by the European frontrunner. Chakrabarty's call is for a multiplicity of horizons to be opened out in the space long occupied exclusively by European historiographies and epistemologies.

Tracing the articulations of imagined worlds as configured by the traveller accounts I come to below, facilitates a mapping of alternative horizons and, concomitantly, alternative understandings of progress and progressiveness than those derived from (Western) Europe. Narratives of progress entail that there is something to be progressed towards. The civilizing mission had a clear sense of what that should be – at least a clear agenda on what it wanted to market it as being: if the colonies tried very hard, they might one day arrive where the colonial centre was *already*. But progress was also actively envisioned by agents in the global South, in ways that neither took their home countries as intrinsically peripheral, nor unquestioningly accepted the horizons ordained by coloniality. Specifically, global South travellers in the Soviet Union offer a rich resource for alternative imaginings of the horizons of desirable progress. Significantly, they orientate these in relation to co-ordinates that do not deem the imperial capital to be central at all, rather bypassing it altogether and triangulating their positions according to alternative compass points. It is these alternative mappings that I seek to excavate in the following readings.

Rabindranath Tagore, Bhisham Sahni, Alex La Guma and Pauline Podbrey all had the opportunity to garner first-hand experience of the Soviet Union. Each provides traces of these experiences in their written accounts: for Tagore, this took the form of the letters he sent home during his travels; for La Guma, it was a travelogue written for and published by the Soviet publishing house aptly dubbed Progress Publishers; Sahni and Podbrey articulated their impressions in autobiographies. Their sojourns in the USSR and surrounding countries span a large temporal framework, and they embarked on their journeys with different agendas and priorities, which inflect their narratives of this space accordingly. I sketch their delineation of alternative normative horizons through readings that juxtapose first Tagore and Sahni to illustrate how they thwart received colonial narratives and open up an alternative aspirational space in the Soviet Union. I then turn to Podbrey in a reading that highlights a possibly necessary critique of some of the more wilfully utopian impressions generated by the first two. Finally, I integrate some observations of what can be gleaned from the contestation of a will to exclusivity through a reading of La Guma's account.[2]

Against colonial worldmaking: Rabindranath Tagore and Bhisham Sahni

Rabindranath Tagore (1861–1941) was, at the time of writing his correspondence from Russia in 1930, already an established and internationally respected man of letters. He has been dubbed, by Indian literary historian Sisir Kumar Das, 'the most towering Indian of the century next only to Gandhi' (2015: 8). Tagore was born into a relatively privileged household in Calcutta in 1861 and, as a result of inheriting significant property, he did not have to work for a living. To many, he is best known as the winner of the 1913 Nobel Prize for Literature for the English translation (some might say adaptation) of *Gitanjali*. Tagore was deeply critical of the British Raj in India, in 1919 renouncing his knighthood in response to the massacre at Jallianwala Bagh, where the British Indian Army opened fire at peaceful protestors. He was a strong advocate for Indian independence from British colonial rule, though, unlike many who supported this, he was not a proponent of nationalism as its antidote.

Both a passionate poet and teacher, in *Letters from Russia* Tagore positions education as the most central of his concerns. He had been invited a number of times since 1925, and 'in spite of ill health he was fairly determined to make the visit when the VOKS (All Union Society for Cultural Relations with Foreign Countries) again invited him in 1930' (Bhattacharya 2017: 249). Despite plans to travel further afield, his journey lasted only about two weeks, and was limited to Moscow and its surroundings due to his poor health. His experiences were determined by the fact that he was on an official tour, and all his communications were mediated by interpreters. His letters were published more or less as they arrived, in *Prabasi*, a well-regarded centrist Bengali literary journal, and shortly afterwards in 1931 in a collection as *Russiar Chithi*, in the original Bengali. The letters were sent home to an India-in-the-making; the correspondence is personal but intended for a wider audience, as Tagore expresses a wish for his native land to learn from his observations. Excerpts appeared in English translation, but a full-text English version only became available in 1960 – partially due to the efforts of the British colonial government (see Bhattacharya 2017: 238). I work from the English translation made by Sasadhar Sinha.

Bhisham Sahni was born in 1915 in Rawalpindi, in today's Pakistan, and moved to India after Partition in 1947. Most of his written work, which includes short stories, novels and several plays, is in Hindi, though his mother tongue was Punjabi and he was taught in Urdu. He was a well-respected writer and political activist, as well as being younger brother to Indian film and stage actor Balraj Sahni. Bhisham Sahni was politically engaged for most of his writing career, participating in the Quit India Movement in 1942, serving time in jail, campaigning against communal violence, and working variously with the Indian National Congress Party, the Indian Peoples' Theatre Association (1946–50), the Progressive Writers' Association (1976–86), and serving as head of the partly Soviet-sponsored Afro-Asian Writers' Association. He spent seven years in Moscow, working as a translator at the Foreign Languages Publishing House from 1956 to 1963. Though sympathetic to socialism, Sahni never joined the Communist Party of India, partially due to his perceiving in the party a lack of a coherent agenda against communalism.

Sahni's autobiography *Today's Pasts: A Memoir*, originally written in Hindi and published in 2004, was published in English in 2015 in a translation by Snehal Shingavi. This is the translation from which I work. Though not ardently pro-Soviet, in his text, he presents himself as evidently and lingeringly sympathetic to communism. He writes with the benefit of hindsight and delineates a tale of at least some disillusionment, while nonetheless locating in the Soviet Union of his memory lingering potential.

Some 74 years separate the original publication dates of these two texts. Such a lengthy interval serves to make the overlap of some particularly resilient narratives all the more remarkable, though, of course, they neither experienced the same USSR, nor presented a homogenous imagining of it in their writings. Both set out with positive expectations, which surely influenced what they chose to register. Key amongst their agreements are a shared attitude to the question of education and an indictment of Western European greed, both of which run directly counter to the narrative of the colonial civilizing mission.

Both Tagore and Sahni find cause to laud the Soviet Union for its accomplishments in the field of education. Though the civilizing mission depended on a purported ethical imperative to *bring* education (and religion) to the colonies for its legitimating structure, both of these Indian travellers represent the USSR, rather than the colonizers, as being at the forefront of educational 'progress'. Tagore, especially, wished to learn from the achievements made in the sphere of education, and expressed his intention to take the practices he witnessed on his journey back to his school at Santiniketan in Bengal (Tagore 1960: 49, 52). The Soviet world he produced could serve as a model to emulate for Indians due, in his construction, to the two regions' many similarities: 'Only a decade ago they [the Russians] were as illiterate, helpless and hungry as our own masses: equally blindly superstitious, equally stupidly religious' (ibid.: 27). Sahni, too, was profoundly impressed by the USSR's accomplishments in literacy and education; indeed, both his children went on to attend university there.

The understanding of progress presented by the texts also has a cultural dimension; as indeed did the civilizing mission. Rather than locating the most advanced, desirable, and aspirational version of culture, or stage of 'civilization', in the colonial metropolitan 'centre', Tagore and Sahni find evidence not only of the equal standing of the Soviets, but of their being ahead on this spectrum. Certainly, one could take issue with their implicit or explicit definitions of 'culture' and 'civilization', but it is worth noting that, however their texts choose to define the markers, the Soviets are more advanced in the implied developmental trajectory.

Tagore observes that those who participate in cultural events are 'wage-earners, such as masons, blacksmiths, grocers and tailors. And there also come Soviet soldiers, army officers, students and peasants' (ibid.: 56). The Soviet Union, for him, is to be lauded not only for making this possible for its citizens, but for possessing and producing citizens who are able to find such high culture desirable – which again speaks to the question of education. He notes: 'One cannot imagine Anglo-Saxon peasants and workers enjoying it so calmly and peacefully until the small hours of the morning, let alone our people' (ibid. 51). The Soviet Union emerges, in this sense, as culturally superior to the 'Anglo-Saxons'.

The attribution of cultural advancedness is a subset of the attribution of civilizational development, which speaks to the envisioning of the kind of civilization that more closely approximates the one that the authors deem worthwhile. A second major accord, then, between Tagore and Sahni's accounts is in their locating in the Soviet Union an important rebuttal of the greed and decadence of the colonizers. The colonial centre is indicted for a 'glut', born of its Western European civilization and violently exported to the colonies.

Tagore sees the global problems of capitalism and colonialism – and they are not to be divorced from each other. He notes: 'Not much statistical intricacy is involved to see that during the last hundred and sixty years the all round poverty of India and England's all round prosperity lie parallel to each other' (ibid.: 103) – and finds a 'radical solution' (ibid.: 3) being sought in Russia. Europe and its 'Western civilization', by contrast, are rendered contemptible for belying their barbarism: 'behind the scenes everything is topsy-turvy, filthy and unhealthy, dense with the darkness of sorrow, misery and evil deeds. But to us outsiders, looking through the window of the shelter we obtain, everything appears proper, elegant and everybody well-fed' (ibid.: 7). This Europe wilfully forgets its own history where 'they burnt innocent women as witches, killed scientists as sinners and remorselessly crushed freedom of religious belief and denied political rights to religious communities other than their own' (ibid.: 62), and hypocritically points the finger elsewhere:

> It is proclaimed to the people of the world that Hindus and Mussulmans cut one another's throats ... but once upon a time even Europe's different communities were engaged in murderous strifes which have now turned to desolating wars between different European countries... displaying the primitive mind of suicidal stupidity, before which our petty barbarism must bow its head in awe. (ibid.: 16)

In the contrast, this Europe emerges as the home of greed and decadence, which it exports to its colonies: 'The pride arising from the difference in wealth has come to our country from the West' (ibid.: 8). As a welcome antidote to this, the Soviet Union has created an environment for 'the complete disappearance of the vulgar conceit of wealth' (ibid.: 9), where there 'is no barrier of greed' (ibid.: 108). Sahni, too, indicts Europe and the West for the 'glut of consumer goods in the capitalist world' (Sahni 2015). Together, Tagore and Sahni participate in producing a narrative of the decadent wicked West, as well as a faith in the lack of greed and corruption associated with communism. The dissatisfaction of some Soviet citizens with the scarcity of goods available to them is, indeed, for Sahni observing the Union in the 1960s, rather to be blamed on the increasing openness to the outside world under Khrushchev which allowed them access to capitalist frames of comparison.

Implicitly, this indictment on the part of Tagore and Sahni entails an understanding of civilizational progress as moving towards a more equitable distribution of resources. This too runs overtly counter to colonial narratives of the colonial centre as a beacon guiding less developed peoples to the desired destination, or as a role model for the colonized to emulate. The civilizing mission was premised on its artificial manufacturing of a moral high ground for the colonizers. Tagore and Sahni's accounts completely dispel this myth, locating their guiding lights rather in the Soviet Union, which in their iteration serves in many ways as the antithesis of the colonial power.

The European colonizer's greed is furthermore accompanied by negligence and cowardice, as articulated by Sahni through his development of a historical narrative in which the West comes off poorly. Despite his experience of some disillusionment with its original promise, Sahni (2015) still concludes that the world 'will have much to learn from the Soviet Union'. This conclusion is at least partially accounted for by his narrative of the geopolitical terrain of the Cold War – which, in turn, is knitted to a particularly inflected narrative of the Second World War:

> The British government had turned its entire attention to the war, and was becoming increasingly cruel and cold towards India. So much so that when Bengal was overwhelmed by the famine and more than three million people died, suffering, the British government remained unmoved even as the world watched. (ibid.)

The Bengal famine in 1943 reveals, for Sahni, Britain's indifference to its colony. Let down by the British who are understood as having at least some responsibility to what is at this point still part of the empire, in Sahni's envisioning Indians begin to find a favourable alternative in the Soviet Union:

> During the course of the war, the popularity and the influence of the Soviet Union had grown worldwide. It was the Soviet Union that suffered the worst effects of the Second World War. England and America delayed opening up a second front while Hitler's forces invaded deep inside the Soviet Union. Then the war took a turn, and the Red Army routed Hitler's forces all the way back to Berlin. Such a total reversal had never been seen before. It changed everything. Young people were drawn to left-wing thinking in large numbers. (ibid.)

The British, already condemned for their failure to intervene during the famine in Bengal, are implicitly cast as cowardly for their reluctance to open a second front, while the Soviet Union 'suffers the worst effects' only to heroically save the day by beating Hitler all the way back to Berlin.

If this is not sufficient reason for the colonial oppressor to cede the moral high ground, the final blow is dealt in the portrayal of the Soviet Union as representing a more advanced position in relation to questions of social justice: specifically, in combatting sexism and racism. The Soviet Union emerges in Tagore's letters as a space that has improved the lot of both women, and racialized peoples: a reputation it held in many parts of the world and for a notably long time (see, for instance, Sandwith 2013).

In Tagore's letters, Soviet Russia has solved, so it is suggested, the problems of multiple co-habiting nations and of racism. He notes, 'that in their State there is no difference whatsoever of race and colour' (Tagore 1960: 39); the Soviet project is one that creates and fosters 'community which includes also the swarthy skinned peoples of Central Asia. There is no fear, no concern that they too should become strong' (ibid.: 48). This is a sentiment that will be echoed by first prime minister of India Jawaharlal Nehru some 16 years later in *The Discovery of India* (1946): 'Russians are almost totally devoid of racialism' (Nehru 1994: 549). In these articulations, it is in the Soviet Union that the 'progressive' politics of anti-racism and anti-sexism are understood as taking place.

The Soviet Union thus emerges as a space that has achieved solutions to problems which Tagore's and Sahni's homeland is still grappling with, and consequently as a site of aspiration and even envy. It is to the Soviet Union that Sahni and Tagore would have their countrywomen and men look for guiding principles and concrete strategies on the road to an aspirational future. Tagore's discursive construction proffers the advancedness of the Union, in terms of education, culture and social justice, linking it and what it represents to the future. The Soviets, for him, are 'determined to raise a new world' (ibid.: 10); 'Russia is engaged in the task of making the road to a new age; of tearing up the roots of ancient beliefs and customs from its ancient soil' (ibid.: 115). Sahni, too, is moved by its bearing a torch to the future: 'Whenever attention was cursorily paid to the Soviet Union's problems, the mind was also drawn to their accomplishments. When Sputnik – the first satellite – was launched by the Soviet Union and mankind was brought closer to the heavens, the entire world rejoiced' (Sahni 2015). Technological progress crystallizes the Soviet Union's general 'aheadness'. Sahni associates the USSR's advances into space with its position at the vanguard of progress and its connection to the future. It is its affiliation with the future that offers the final, and perhaps most obvious, instantiation of the Soviet Union's representing a vision of desirable 'progress' for these two travellers. It opens up an alternative normative horizon in the worlds cumulatively produced by these two travellers' accounts and the readings offered here. They not only resist and contest the civilizing mission's demarcations of global centrality and civilizational aheadness, but situate an alternative horizon for their aspirational future.

After displacement of the civilizing mission: Pauline Podbrey

Pauline Podbrey was born into a Jewish family in Lithuania in 1922, and emigrated with her family to Durban in South Africa in 1933. Her father was a committed communist and from a young age she moved into leftist political activism, joining the South African Communist Party and doing a great deal of work with various trade unions. The latter caused her to meet H.A. Naidoo, a well-known South African-Indian trade unionist whom she later married. Due to apartheid legislation that made it technically illegal for Naidoo to move from Durban to Cape Town, where the family settled in 1943, as well as difficulties relating to their interracial marriage, Podbrey and her family escaped to London in 1951, and on to Hungary in 1952, where she and Naidoo worked for Radio Budapest until their return to England in 1955. Consequently, she experienced the Soviet republic in the context of the discontent that led to the uprising of 1956, but left prior to the actual revolt and occupation.

In her memoir *White Girl in Search of the Party*, written in English and published in 1993, Podbrey recounts her experiences of the Soviet Union as viewed with the benefit of hindsight, after the dissolution of the USSR. Her imaginative production of Soviet space is profoundly influenced by her relationship to communism. As a young activist in South Africa, her image of the Soviet Union is an idealized one: she imagines this space as the fulfilment of a grand aspirational dream, at the forefront of progress: 'I was convinced that the Soviet Union was leading the world in all spheres, art, science, industry, the emancipation of nationalities, women, agriculture' (Podbrey 1993: 27). In terms of progress in the various spheres of culture, technology and, importantly, social justice, the Soviet Union is leading the way: it is here that she locates her normative horizon.

When offered the opportunity of working at Radio Budapest, Podbrey expresses her enthusiasm for the opportunity to participate directly in the actualization of such a noble ideal:

The thought of living and working in a socialist country excited and thrilled us! In our dreams we'd never hoped for such a privilege. To experience at first hand the struggles and achievements of building socialism, to share in the life of a people engaged in this historic task, to be part of their movement to create a workers' paradise; it all seemed to us too good to be true. (ibid.: 157)

From a vantage point shaped by her white South African upbringing, then, the Soviet Union looks like a dream of a better future. This is where the communism that inspired and drove Podbrey and her fellow activists in South Africa is actually being put into practice. Later she opines, '[t]he Soviet Union was a dream of Utopia common to the right-thinking persons all round the world, the Fatherland to which we all owed allegiance for moral, ethical and ideological reasons' (ibid.: 186). Her language – 'paradise', 'Utopia' – articulates this space as an idealization and aspiration.

South Africa, by contrast, is not quite so far ahead in Podbrey's portrayal. Indeed, it is also 'behind' its former colonizer Britain. When Podbrey struggles to find a hospital that will deliver her mixed-race baby, she is pleased to find a British matron at a nursing house willing to take her on: 'Here, we told ourselves, is a woman of principle. It just goes to show, we said, how much more civilized the British are, how much more advanced than we South Africans' (ibid.: 129). It transpires that the matron is primarily financially motivated, and backtracks when the other patients express displeasure. But Podbrey's imagined South Africans, due to their racism, are less 'civilized' and, implicitly, more backward, than the British – though of course the 'civilizedness' of the British matron is directly undercut by her prioritizing money. Podbrey's attributed backwardness is understood in relation to an imagined progressive, socially just society. This envisioning of South Africa as behind both the Soviet Union and the West represented by Britain, undergoes a sharp change as Podbrey comes to experience first-hand the 'paradise-in-the-making' constituted by socialist Hungary.

Her disillusionment becomes inevitable as she describes the dismantling of the precious image of the 'glorious future' that the Soviet Union had represented for her. The utopian vision she had looked to for inspiration in South Africa is shattered by the lived reality of Budapest. At the radio station, she experiences, and indeed participates in, the construction of a false image of the USSR. She witnesses the fabrication of desirable news: 'In the absence of any real news two Yugoslav comrades were set to work next door to us manufacturing items of "news"' (ibid.: 168); and the dogmatic strictures imposed when it comes to party propaganda: 'a report of a speech by Comrade Stalin, no matter how indigestible the English translation ... had to be broadcast verbatim' (ibid.: 168).

With regard to the Soviet Union's advancedness in terms of social justice, Podbrey is forced to question her until then strong belief in the USSR's overcoming of the problem of anti-Semitism. In this regard, her voice serves as a necessary corrective to the utopian envisioning of Tagore and Sahni's attribution of progressiveness in this sense. At first reacting indignantly to claims of anti-Jewish feeling in response to the Slansky trial in Czechoslovakia, she is subject to censoring by her supervisors in a manner that suggests a less than clean slate. Her colleague Istvan, who is also Jewish, disappears mysteriously from the station and though no clear reason ever emerges, it is speculated that 'he had failed to confess to a bourgeois Jewish merchant father' (ibid.: 182).

The vision of the Soviet Union as a space that has overcome the problems of racial discrimination is also belied by her experience. She relates an incident that happens to her husband, H.A., when he encounters some Romani people on the street:

> 'Oh sir,' he [the spokesman of a group of Romani] begged, 'take me back with you to your land. I want to be with my own people, with black people, like you and me'. 'But in South Africa,' H.A. tried to explain, 'the black people have a bad life, they don't have equal rights with the whites, they suffer from discrimination and prejudice'. 'Same as here, same as here...' Our only previous contact with gypsies had been in restaurants, listening to their seductive, soulful melodies or foot-tapping to their wild, abandoned, exciting strings. Were they really an oppressed minority? (ibid.: 189)

While the 'wild, abandoned, exciting strings' strike a rather exoticizing note, Podbrey's appreciation of their position is an important step in her disillusionment with Soviet communism as she recognizes discriminatory treatment and signals the racialization and racism present within Europe and the Soviet Union, revealing that this is in fact not the dream of a race-free society it was purported to be. This serves as a significant contestation of what – in Tagore's and Sahni's cumulatively produced worlds – might have been represented as the Soviet Union's paving of a smooth road to an aspirational future of social justice. Racism, counter to that narrative, is alive and well in the Soviet space of Podbrey's account.

The narrative of the USSR's having overcome sexism is also shown up as false. It is, arguably, Podbrey's experience of communist control over women's reproductive rights that pushes her disillusionment to its culmination. Unintentionally falling pregnant during her time in Budapest, she expresses her expectations as a woman and a communist: 'I'd have thought that in a Socialist country women had the right to decide what to do with their own bodies' (ibid.: 171). This, she learns, is lamentably not the case. Indeed, it is her experiences in insisting on her right to an abortion and her final but difficult success in this endeavour, that signals for her the disintegration of everything she had believed communism to mean: 'I felt ashamed to be benefiting from such a hypocritical system, one in which abortions, like other prizes, were at the disposal of the privileged, like me. The class differences of other countries seemed trivial by comparison' (ibid.: 172). Podbrey is disillusioned not merely by the system's failing her as woman, but by its betrayal of the principles of equal treatment. This is chillingly revealed by the juxtaposition of the story of the typist Lydia, who is forced to seek out an illegal abortion and ends in prison. Interestingly, this becomes a turning point in the text's evaluation of South Africa. Podbrey says, 'I'd had two abortions [in South Africa] but nothing prepared me for the indignity to which I was now subjected by this doctor and his nurse' (ibid.: 171). In apartheid South Africa, it seems, she was able to access abortions, and was treated with less indignity.

She also signals the exceptionalism of the South African Communist Party amongst the communist parties of the world, noting 'just how special they [the communist party leaders] were in the international Communist arena we were not to discover until later' (ibid.: 142). The South African communists were warm and welcoming of all fellow travellers; British communists, for instance, were less congenial. Finally, after the colossal disappointment and disillusionment Podbrey experiences as a result of her time in the Soviet bloc, she concludes very much in favour of the South African brand of communism she had initially fallen in love with: 'That was a part of my life I could be proud of – the South African Communist Party was the only organization which stood for total equality... But life under a Communist regime had opened my eyes to the evils inherent in such a system' (Podbrey 1993: 201). Consequently, in the world of Podbrey's text, socialist Europe emerges as the home of a failed dream: a false vision of desirable progress. This causes her to shift her normative horizon away from that once-utopian image back to South Africa, which – however diseased on a governmental level – emerges as having more closely approximated that horizon and thus as the locus of a true, or ideal, vision of communism yet to be achieved.

In conclusion: Beyond a will to exclusivity with Alex La Guma

Tagore and Sahni's repudiation and displacement of the civilizing mission, and Podbrey's contestation of its Cold War inverse are valuable in dismantling the legacies of colonial worldmaking. It does not, however, enact structural change when different placeholders merely rehearse the same trajectories: as when the Soviet road to socialism replaces the colonial road to capitalism. And while Podbrey's locating an aspirational ideal in South Africa is productively resistant to dominant norms, the structure underlying this serves to replace one horizon with another. In conclusion, then, I offer a reading against the grain of what is at face value a profoundly clear-cut ideological text: Alex La Guma's vehemently pro-Soviet *A Soviet Journey* (1978). In its particularly stringent reproduction of binary politics and prescriptive socialist trajectories, this travelogue is explicitly mapping a single alternative normative horizon. Nonetheless, contrary to the travelogue's more obvious agenda, I want to end by arguing that this text signals the possibilities inherent in resisting a will to exclusivity, and thus latently reveals a capacity for configuring horizons in the plural.

Alex La Guma (1925–1985), born in District Six in Cape Town, was a South African writer and anti-apartheid activist. He was a defendant in the notorious Treason Trials, and was forced into exile in London in 1966. A life-long communist, he was also an active member of the Soviet-sponsored Afro-Asian Writers' Association, publishing in their quarterly journal *Lotus*, and winning the Lotus Prize in 1969. La Guma was chief representative of the African National Congress in the Caribbean when he died in Havana in 1985. He went to the Soviet Union in 1975 as a guest of the Union of Soviet Writers, and this journey, along with experiences gathered on trips in 1970 and 1973, furnished the material that would result in his travelogue (see Field 2010: 210), a text whose aim is overtly to present a positive image of the communist project being pursued there. Originally published by Progress Publishers in Moscow, the book belongs to the 'Impressions of the USSR' series and forms a part of the image of itself the Soviet Union was interested in presenting abroad.

La Guma positions himself as a staunch communist, enamoured of the Soviet project and convinced that his home country has much to learn from it.

Not only does he wish to disseminate knowledge about the USSR in a positive light, but he explicitly presents it as practising a viable alternative to the global capitalism of the West, which is yoked to the ongoing colonial oppression he sees his and other countries suffering under. In a typically pro-Soviet sketching of 'progress', the USSR facilitates the 'catching up' of its 'non-European' (La Guma 1978: 34f.) brethren, allowing them to bypass capitalism and enjoy, by association with the rest of the Union and as also suggested by Tagore and Sahni, closer proximity to the future.

While overtly promoting this trajectory, the text nonetheless dissolves the exclusivity on which it is theoretically premised. Throughout his journeys in the Soviet Union, La Guma makes and fosters connections with Soviet citizens, enlivened by the mutual sympathies that he presents in the text as existing in simple interactions and conversations and in the interest and empathy displayed by those he encounters. This produces an imagined something shared that binds them, cultivating connections, affinities, sympathies and grounds for alliances. These are fed by a capacity to allow different stories to co-exist without cancelling each other out, allowing them, rather, to supplement each other. Significant in this world's imagining of pasts and origin stories, then, is its lack of a will to exclusivity. While Europe's imperial civilizing mission required the quashing of other stories than those of Western European reason and religion, and Soviet propaganda foresaw only the Soviet route to a desirable future to the exclusion of other ways, La Guma's meetings with the peoples of Soviet Eurasia suggested varied stories that were happy to live alongside one another. In Kazakhstan, his guide Amangeldeh relates how the local mountains came to be: 'There is a legend which says that when the world was born, God looked down on Kazakhstan and saw the flat empty steppes. He felt sorry for those living in such desolate emptiness, so he took a handful of rocks and tossed it down as a sort of compensation and so we got the Blue Mountains.' (ibid.: 114f.).

In response, La Guma offers a different narrative of the origin of mountains:

> There is an African folk-tale, from Tanzania, I think, which gives another explanation for how mountains came to be. It says that long ago the earth was smooth and flat and even all over, but one day she arose to talk to the sky. When the two of them had finished their chat the earth took leave of the sky and started to return. But she did not reach home all over. Some parts of her became tired on the way and stopped where they were. (ibid.: 115)

La Guma's 'another explanation' claims no exclusive universality and no supremacy for itself. On another occasion, he relates the story of how stars came to be:

> 'Stars were first made in South Africa, you know'. I told him that South African tale of the young African girl who sat warming herself by a wood fire one night and played with the ashes, taking them in her hands and flinging them up to see how pretty they were when they floated in the air. As they floated away she put more wood on the fire and stirred it with a stick and the bright sparks flew everywhere and wafted high into the night. They hung in the air and made a bright road across the sky, a road of silver and diamonds.
> 'It's still there,' I said. 'They call it the Stars Road or the Milky Way.' (ibid.: 131f.)

La Guma ends his anecdote: 'if we invented the stars, it must have been your people who invented the sun' (ibid.: 132). The account of his journey imagines and produces a world that is shared and inclusive, in which different (hi)stories can accommodate each other and need not strive to win out over each other. By allowing these different stories to co-exist, La Guma's travelogue works to contest a will to exclusivity and so unleash the potential of a plurality of normative horizons. This is, finally, structurally different in a way that mere displacement cannot be.

In conclusion, the juxtaposition of these readings serves to unfold how these travel accounts can serve as resources not only for contesting violently ascribed colonial narratives, but as sites of productively imagined alternatives. The centres of their worldmaking practices are not located in the former colonial centre, which itself is moved to the periphery of their envisioning of the global. As such, the aspirational horizons animated by the worldmaking activities of these travel writings lie, for Tagore and Sahni, not in Britain's imperial capital, but in the potentialities opened up by the Soviet Union. The alternative horizons opened up by them are complicated and undercut by Podbrey's account. Her contestation of too utopian a representation of the Union's achievements in social justice is valuable to guard against one exclusive route to prescriptive progress merely being replaced by another. La Guma, finally, signals the capacity of his worldmaking not only to forego the will to exclusivity on which colonial narratives such as the civilizing mission are premised, but to display its utter expendability in the world he chooses to imagine. Implicit in this is also the value of plurality indicated by Chakrabarty's call to create *plural* normative horizons in place of Eurocentric prescriptions whose structuring principle is exclusivity. An insistence on plurality and structural change in thinking about exclusive narratives of the global works in the service of dismantling the legacies of colonial epistemologies.

Notes

1 I am grateful to the members of the RTG 'World Politics' for their insights and comments on earlier drafts of this chapter.
2 I build here on previous work, parts of which have appeared elsewhere, though in pursuit of different arguments to the one I make here (see Gasser 2019a, 2019b).

Beyond a Global Horizon
Vers la pensée planétaire (1964) and the Discourse of Planetarity 1930-2020

Michael Auer

Introduction

> Today the planetary is on everyone's lips, and yet they don't know what they are talking about. They think the planetary is the global: what concerns Chicago and Singapore at the same time, or whatnot and whatnot. ... By planetary I mean errant thinking, an errant world'. (Axelos in Gauvin 2009: min. 43, author's translation)

With these words taken from a 2009 *France Culture* interview, Kostas Axelos cautions against confounding what he calls the planetary with globalization. Now, it is certainly questionable whether planetarity is indeed the talk of the town. However, in her 2005 book *Death of a Discipline*, Gayatri Spivak also urged the errant thinking this paradigm stands for (the word planet comes from the Greek 'planâsthai': 'to err, to wander') and thus revived a discourse that goes back to Weimar Germany and the likes of Ernst Jünger, Carl Schmitt and Martin Heidegger (cf. Apter 2006: 60). Likewise Achille Mbembe announced he would offer 'Reflections on Planetary Living' in his opening speech at the 2020 Ruhrtriennale that was cancelled due to COVID-19. The critique of a 'technological escalation' and 'unshackled markets' he wanted to articulate there (Mbembe 2020a) brings to mind the early developments of planetary thinking provoked by Ernst Jünger's (1930) essay on 'The Total Mobilization' of all resources, economic and technological as well.[1]

In this chapter, I would like to sketch the alternative way in which planetarity addresses the developments that are today commonly referred to as globalization. It gives voice to a fundamental critique of the presuppositions implicitly guiding discourses of globalization and to the global horizon that allows for such presuppositions, without falling into a merely negative critique of globalization. Instead, planetarity needs to be understood as a distinct practice of worldmaking, one that grants a novel kind of perspective and agency. This is why its analysis proves an important contribution to this volume, a contribution I am tempted to characterize as a supplement to the phenomenological and epistemological paradigms that are key to the project. As a particularly economic approach to the complex discursive field of planetary thought and action, I will focus on the book *Vers la pensée planétaire* (*Toward Planetary Thinking*) that Kostas Axelos published in 1964.[2]

Axelos, a Greek communist revolutionary and exile who lived in Paris since 1945, provides somewhat of a 'missing link' between the conservative revolutionaries of Weimar and today's postcolonialism. He was influenced by Heidegger's phenomenology and the so-called 'Kehre' (turn) away from it and he was implicated in the shift to post-structuralism that French thought underwent since the 1960s. Axelos contributed to this shift by questioning the Freudo-Marxist presuppositions upon which many French (and also quite a few German) left-wing intellectuals had relied since the end of the Second World War. That *Vers la pensée planétaire* is supposed to play an active role in this intellectual and political shift is already clear from its title vector 'toward planetary thinking'. Indeed, by means of a rereading of Freud and Marx, the book seeks to inspire the 'step and leap' (Axelos 1964: 27) from a 'Western and European modernity' to what it envisions as a new 'planetary era' (Axelos 1964: 307), one that moves beyond the global horizon which gave rise to this modernity. That is to say that Axelos's project engages in a specific practice of worldmaking, a practice that leaves behind not only the grand narratives of modernity, but also the *horizon* of the *globe* in and from which they gain their 'sense' and 'self-evidence'. Thus, one might characterize the contribution the discourse of planetary provides to this volume as a distinctly post-phenomenological and post-structuralist attempt at world-making.

In what follows, I will show that planetarity moves beyond the global horizon thanks to a non-dialectical notion of becoming ('devenir') aporetically oriented toward a decentralized universe. In order to think such a becoming, Axelos playfully engages central political, philosophical and psychoanalytical arguments which allow him to swerve away from the globe's (phallo-)heliocentrism. In a second step, I will unfold the political implications of *Vers la pensée planétaire* and the understanding the book has of its own agency in the passage to a 'planetary era'. My closing remarks will turn to what I suggest calling the prefigurative style of Axelos's thinking and writing, a style whose figurative dimension does not point back (or forward) to a literal dimension. As the future – or better: 'what is to come' ('l'à-venir') – remains structurally open, the book uses prefigurations in a manner that anticipates the way Gayatri Spivak will later speak of literature's planetary promise: it 'cannot predict, but it may prefigure' (Spivak 2005: 49).

In order to outline what is at stake in the 'planetary ... leap' (Axelos 1964: 27) let me begin by outlining the globe as a different horizon of world-making.

The global horizon and total mobilization

Axelos rejects the global because it implies a model of circularity and circulation bound to the emergence of heliocentrism. Although already implicit in the metaphysical heliocentrism that goes back at least as far as Plato's parable of the sun and the cave, an actually global horizon can only emerge thanks to the 'Copernican and Galilean revolution' (Axelos 1964: 311). Throughout the Middle Ages the distinction between the sublunary realm of physics and the superlunary world of astronomy (or metaphysics) developed in Greek thought continued to prevail. It was only with modern astrophysics and its empirical heliocentrism that the movements of heavenly and earthly bodies were conceived of as following the same laws. One of the major points of Hans Blumenberg's monumental study *The Genesis of the Copernican World* is that the heliocentric model of the universe should not be misconstrued as a decentralization and humiliation of the human being. On the contrary, the shift away from a geocentric worldview allowed the human subject to imagine itself in the solar centre of the world with the earth (and all other stars) revolving around it (see Blumenberg 1987: 540ff.).

This imaginative dimension is complemented by the geographical and technological inventions of the modern age. The discovery of the Americas, the circumnavigation of earth and the innovations in cartography established a global political economy that could be mapped onto the globe; in the words of Carl Schmitt: 'For the first time in history, man was holding the terrestrial globe in his hand, the real one, as if it were a ball' (Schmitt 1997: 33). The universal model of bodies revolving around a solar centre and the political economy of circulation and accumulation began to reinforce one another, letting a global horizon emerge in which Europe could stage itself as a quasi-solar centre that accumulated the surplus gained from the global circulation of wares, persons, peoples and ideas. In other words, the figure of the globe is bound to a nascent Eurocentrism. The human being that Schmitt sees venturing out to grasp the globe as a whole is clearly marked as a European male. In *The Nomos of the Earth in the International Law of the Jus Publicum Europaeum* (originally published in 1949), Schmitt argues that free trade in a liberal world market is complicit with the emergence of Europe as a political geography of nation-states set apart from the rest of the earth (Schmitt 2003: 140ff.), which is why the modern world is both global and Eurocentric (see Schmitt 2003: 86f.). Schmitt here articulates an influential geopolitical argument that ties the emergence of global capitalism to the political, legal, scientific and technological developments in Modern Europe in a way that is already intimated in *Capital* where Marx once speaks of a 'terrestrial globe' which has been 'monopolized' by the 'revenue' system and its cycles (Marx 2000: 531). In the 1990s, Jacques Derrida referred to precisely this geopolitical paradigm when he addressed the European 'cape' as an articulation of 'capital' in the monetary and in the political sense (as 'capital' and 'capitale') (Derrida 1992: 35f.). In the global horizon of a 'European and Western Modernity', scientific objectification and economic reification from an outside – and in this sense transcendent – point of view go hand in hand. The common logic of heavenly and earthly cycles finds a philosophical justification in the (transcendental) *ego cogito* that imaginatively positions itself at the centre of the universe in an attempt to mobilize, and dispose of, everything (including all empirical egos) around this phantasmatic Archimedean point.

The consequences of such a complicity of Copernican astrophysics, modern subject philosophy and the Eurocentric political economy of colonialism and imperialism come to the fore once modernity has run its course and has, in a certain sense, already moved beyond itself. What 20th-century history shows for Axelos is that neither the universe, nor global capital, nor the so-called subject has a fixed centre. As a result, these points of reference are decentralized and dispersed in multilateral networks. From now on 'everything influences everything else, opening the field for all possible combinations and interferences' (Axelos 1964: 303). The expansion of such networks follows a 'double movement' that 'continues to accelerate,' as it simultaneously fosters 'abstraction' and 'automation' as well as 'dislocation' and 'non-adhesion' (ibid.) in such a way as to strip off any reference to an empirical centre (such as Europe or the sun). However, it does so without breaking with the cyclical model that initially arose from such a centre. The cycles continue to reinforce one other because the interactions and interdependences, the connections, correlations and the mutual concessions, the coordinations, the integrations, the operating, operative, and operational operations, the intercommunications and telecommunications, the reciprocal implications, the causes and causalities all act one upon the other and upon the whole of their ensemble. (ibid.: 303)

This network of networks (of networks…) sprawling across the entire global sphere is an experience Axelos shares with the Weimar intellectuals as well as with Derrida (1992: 42) who sees the European 'cape' paradoxically coming to a head in the decentralized networks of an 'extreme capillarity'. Consequently, Axelos characterizes this double movement of automation and dislocation using a famous phrase coined, and popularized, by Ernst Jünger in 1930: 'total mobilization' (Axelos 1964: 303). This is probably the most acclaimed formulation by this right-wing German writer. Not only did Carl Schmitt and Martin Heidegger readily embrace the phrase because it addressed the most urgent developments of the 20th century (see Schmitt 1999: 10 and Heidegger 2004: 10ff.), it also made, as Beatrice Hanssen (2006: 86) has pointed out, 'an indelible impression' on Walter Benjamin. In a book review that deals with the collection of essays in which Jünger's essay on 'The Total Mobilization' appeared – and that is extremely hostile to that volume in every possible respect – Benjamin stated that all 'precise formulations, genuine accents or solid reasoning' speak to a 'reality' which is 'that of Ernst Jünger's "total mobilization"' (Benjamin 1979: 126; for Benjamin's marginal role in the discourse of planetarity see Wohlfahrt 2002: 70 and Auer 2013: 45ff.). That even Benjamin acknowledged that Jünger's phrase has a significant bearing on reality signals why the term was later able to cross into the left-wing political camp, attracting, for example, Paul Virilio (1995: 135) or Michael Hardt and Antonio Negri (2000: 26, 421).

What Jünger means by total mobilization implies nothing less than the end of the global worldmaking practices outlined above. Unbridled technological progress levels all political hierarchies and dissolves all geopolitical boundaries, thus spelling the ruin of Eurocentrism and the sovereign nation-state alike. Schmitt draws the consequences this has for international law and politics. Western modernity distinguished between economy and politics along the legal lines of a liberal society (and its *bourgeois*) on the one hand and the sovereign state (and its *citoyen*) on the other. These classifications were all, in turn, mapped onto the geopolitical lines Europe drew to separate itself from the rest of the world (cf. Schmitt 2003: 140ff.). As soon as these lines differentiating a European centre from its global periphery became obsolete, the fundamental distinctions organizing the global horizon – such as public vs. private sphere, domestic vs. foreign policy – were superseded as well. For Schmitt, this moment was reached at the Washington Meridian Conference of 1884. The Greenwich Meridian agreed upon there drew a geopolitical line that no longer defined legal spaces, but rather technologically unified the earth in terms of time and space. That Schmitt so prominently referred to the Meridian Conference is the reason that the discussion of planetarity in 1950s Germany revolved around global and planetary lines (cf. Auer 2013).

Planetarity speaks to a situation in which technological and economic innovations override all conventional political categories. Jünger and Schmitt see the end of the nation-state leading to a planetary 'civil war' in which transnational nongovernment agents fight each other on the legally unregulated battlefields that modern technologies carry onto the entire planet: 'For the first time, earth as a ball, as a planet, has become a battleground, and human history presses on towards a planetary order' (Jünger 1948: 43). What Schmitt and Jünger thus diagnosed in the 1930s to 1960s appears today in the guise of failing states, Net Wars, (cyber)terrorism or GPS-based drone warfare. It is in addressing challenges such as these that a discourse of planetarity develops which is not only interested in diagnostics, but also articulates a new kind of politics in a time threatened by worldwide warfare. Needless to say, the suggestions Schmitt, Jünger, and Heidegger, Virilio, Derrida and Spivak make for a possible planetary 'order' or 'disorder' vary significantly (and not even the German authors agree on this). In what follows I will focus on two poles of this discourse: a politics of enmity associated primarily with Carl Schmitt and a politics of friendship first introduced as such in *Vers la pensée planétaire* (but already implicit in Jünger or Heidegger, although with different consequences (cf. Auer 2013).

Axelos, who was introduced to the discourse of planetarity in the 1950s at the very latest, is also convinced that Eurocentrism and the sovereign nation-state belong to the past. 'Planetary Politics' (thus the title of the final chapter of *Vers la pensée planétaire*) begins once the distinction between domestic and foreign policy no longer holds (see Axelos 1964: 298). Since a globalized world admits of 'no outside anymore' (ibid.: 298), 'sovereignty' has become a power that 'no person or institution could wield any longer' (ibid.: 302). When interpreted within a global horizon, such a situation would inevitably call for an 'administration' – or management, governance – 'of the globe' and its cycles of 'production, distribution, and consumption' (ibid.: 309). It is remarkable that the Cold War did not make a difference in this respect; despite the fact that *Vers la pensée planétaire* was published in 1964 during the Vietnam War and only a few years after the Cuban Missile Crisis. Beyond the ideological differences however, Axelos sees both the United States and the USSR as headed towards this kind of globalized management of circulation and accumulation.

That alone serves to show that planetarity was not a Cold War discourse and explains why it revived after the fall of the Iron Curtain. That was the case with Derrida, whose *L'autre cap* (translated into English as *The Other Heading*, not literally as 'the other cape') was prompted by the end of the so-called Second World. In it he mentions the articulation of the European cape and head (*caput*) as political and economic capital because he sees himself witnessing 'a planetarization of the European model' (Derrida 1992: 36) which might be opening itself 'not only to the *other cape* and especially to the *cape of the other*, but also perhaps to the *other of the cape*' (Derrida 1992: 15, translation modified by the author). The techno-political dispersal in networks of decentralized capillaries fosters, and exacts, an orientation toward transnational and post-Eurocentric encounters. And such is the case of Gayatri Spivak, whose plan for a planetary study of literature, in a double twist, employs Area Studies to wrest Comparative Literature from its Eurocentric bias and employs Comparative Literature to wrest Area Studies from its Cold War investments in a US *raison d'État* (see Spivak 2005: 1ff.). These are anti-state and anti-Eurocentric strategies that seek to institutionalize the discourse that Axelos introduced to France in the 1960s and that tries to conceive of 'a universe that has surpassed the solar system' (Axelos 1964: 307), instead 'breaching the cape that still conceals the abstract landscape of the planetary era' (ibid.: 311).

Since this attempt to break with the political economy of the globe – and the contemporary notion of globalization it gives rise to – raises the question of how a planetary 'avant-garde' can gain and give orientation in such an abstract landscape, it entails a new understanding not only of politics, but first and foremost of thinking and its relation to action.

The errant trajectories of 'planet-thought'

Axelos was probably introduced to the discourse of planetarity by Heidegger with whom he studied in the 1950s and who approached it from a distinctly philosophical angle. For Heidegger, Jünger's total mobilization is the final form of Western metaphysics, which is why Jünger accomplished the feat of a reversal of Platonism set out for by Nietzsche. In his book *The Worker: Domination and Gestalt*, Jünger fully wrests 'that which is' (the essence) from the transcendence it was couched in by Plato and invests his planetary worker avant-garde with it (cf. Jünger 2007; Heidegger 2004; for a reading of Jünger in the context of the avant-garde see Groys 1999). In this reversal – that Heidegger sees preconceived in Marx – transcendence becomes what he critically calls 'rescendence [*Reszendenz*]' (Heidegger 1996: 398). Instead of leading to a genuinely planetary form of thinking and action, Jünger's avant-garde fails to move beyond the horizon of globalization it meant to leave behind. For, by establishing the 'Gestalt of the Worker' as the epistemological lynchpin and the avant-garde agency of his *soi-disant* 'planetary' order, Jünger posits a central figure around which everything is made to revolve. In other words, Jünger's practices of envisioning and making the world are intent on generating a new solar system, except that now the central luminary is not a transcendent, but an earthly, and hence 'rescendent', figure.

This is where Axelos enters the debate. To be sure, besides pointing out that *The Worker* shows one facet only of a far more complex development (Axelos 1964: 307), Axelos has very little to say about Jünger – but all the more about Marx. And it is evident that his readings of Marx are inspired by Heidegger's critique of Jünger. For example, when characterizing Marx as the last philosopher because of his shift from a conventional ontology to a conception of 'techno-logy' (ibid.: 175), Axelos is obviously thinking in Heideggerian terms. Marx brings philosophy to a close because he sees the onto-theology of Western thought culminating in an ensemble of technologies that manage everything by means of autopoietic and self-regulatory cycles. This 'cyberneticization of thought' (ibid. 1964: 18) – and with it of economy and politics, culture and civilization – operates on a necessarily earth-encompassing scale. Thanks to the abstraction and dislocation behind this mobilization of earth itself, the circulation of cycles is not bound to a geographical centre or a concrete ideological framework anymore. Since globalization has, as it were, 'emptied' out everything – and in this sense Axelos will call it 'nihilistic' – it can be defined like Leonardo da Vinci's void: 'Its centre and circumference are nowhere and everywhere' (ibid.: 25).

And yet, Axelos stresses, the nexus of cybernetics and technology only apparently overcomes the onto-theological horizon circumscribed by globe and sun. Instead of moving beyond the Eurocentric system that implemented heliocentrism economically and politically, globalization needs to be understood as a specifically technological 'occidentalization of the world' (ibid.: 198).

Technology, in other words, does not free the planet from the circulation paradigm, it rather begins to 'corset the entire periphery of the planet that is precipitated into its rotating movement' (ibid.: 303f.): 'The circle seems vicious and magical' (ibid.: 17). Globalization admits of no outside anymore because, in universalizing itself, technology always already occupies any Archimedean point from where it could be called into question and thereby veils its onto-theological character as the objectivity of a system that has stripped off any empirical centre. Axelos's term for this objectiveness is 'dépouillement total' (ibid.: 283): the original meaning of 'dépouillement' being 'skinning'. Hence, by being predicated on the nexus of dislocation and abstraction, globalization's alleged 'total objectiveness' amounts to the pseudo-objectivity of a 'total skinning.'

In pointing this out, Axelos calls attention to the implicit philosophical presuppositions of globalization. Technology's cybernetic grip on the world is predicated on the Hegelian and Marxian dialectics of 'absolute truth' and 'total reality' (ibid.: 198), which assume that world history and the history of thought converge in a common teleological movement. This brings the end of history in Hegel's *Phenomenology of Spirit* to mind where absolute thinking divests itself of history and externalizes historical progress as 'a gallery of images' because it can come to itself in a 'circle that presupposes its beginning and only reaches it at the end' (Hegel 1977: 492, 802). Axelos sees this 'total and absolute spirit' (Axelos 1964: 198) spinning everything in cycles while absolving itself from any position within these cycles. Absolute thinking fully reflects itself in itself by, simultaneously, dispersing in what Hegel called a 'circle of circles' (Hegel 1991: § 15). A totality thus constituted by subtracting any localizable centre corresponds to technology's global grip on the planet. In a globalized framework – which has managed to seal itself off from any difference that could make a difference – progress is reduced to the ever-increasing technological and economic implementation of a dialectic that has, in principle, already come to fulfilment.

Axelos addresses the philosophical presuppositions of such a global discourse in an equally philosophical manner. This is why he urges that the *ego cogito* should not 'interpret itself as a sun, but rather as a planet' (Axelos 1964: 18). This paradigmatic shift would allow for a new understanding not only of the human being and human thinking but also of the world as a whole. It would thus perform the 'planetary … leap' (ibid.: 27) beyond the cyclical logic of rotation, circulation, revolution or feedback loops, which all tie into the onto-theological model of globe and solar system. Axelos was not the first, and will not be the last, to advocate a distinctly planetary thought. This call was already articulated in Heidegger's exhortation that Jünger follow through with a truly 'planetary thought' (Heidegger 1996: 424) and it will be echoed in Spivak's 'Imperatives' of 'Planet-thought' (Spivak 1999: 49): 'In our historical moment, we must try persistently to reverse and displace globalization into planetarity – an impossible figure' (Spivak 2005: 97).

The question is how to trace such an impossible figure if even the avant-garde remains trapped in a global horizon. Axelos tries to escape this problem by drawing a planetary 'trajectory' (Axelos 1964: 46) that follows an 'impossible necessity' (ibid.: 294). Such a trajectory cannot presuppose a central body for orientation or revolution. Instead, it has to conceive of a constellation of wandering stars forever erring through a decentralized universe, or better: *pluriverse*. This errancy of thought provides a continuity between conservative revolution and deconstructive postcolonialism that lays in more than the mere word 'planetary.' For, when Axelos speaks of planetarity's 'errant course' – a course which cannot, moreover, simply be understood as 'aberrant' – (ibid.: 46), he introduces a word that harks back to Heidegger's '*Irre*' (Heidegger 1996: 196f.) and anticipates the 'grounding errancy' that Spivak – by way of Derrida's *Politics of Friendship* (which, in its turn, is a critique of Schmitt's politics of enmity) – sees guiding her model of planetarity as well (Spivak 2005: 30). Achille Mbembe's (2016) study *Politiques de l'inimitié* (Politics of Enmity) also understands itself as an intervention in this planetary debate. Already in Heidegger, the grounding 'errancy' of human existence cannot be thought as an 'ab-errancy' because it is the precondition of 'truth,' not its opposite (Heidegger 1996: 197). Axelos – and after him Derrida and Spivak – will use the term to implode what is left of a metaphysical notion of truth in Heidegger's 1920s text. What Axelos will later say about planetary politics holds true for all things planetary: 'it is completely *errant*: its "truth" itself consists in errancy' (Axelos 1964: 310).

As the remarks on Hegel and Marx have shown, overcoming metaphysics implies distancing oneself from a dialectical logic of thinking and history. The errancy of planetary thought, in other words, has to shatter the teleological course implicit in globalization and thereby has to show that history cannot have a preordained end. Accordingly, Axelos calls for an abandonment of all hopes for an 'eschatology' (ibid.: 45) and supplants the dialectic of 'absolute truth' and 'total reality' by a never-ending 'dialogue' (ibid.: 29) of thinking and world. The word dialogue, however, is not meant to provide an answer or a solution. Instead, it marks 'a question and a problem' (ibid.: 29) and thus gestures towards the re-conceptualization of thought and world programmatically announced in the subtitle of *Vers la pensée planétaire*, a subtitle that rewrites a quotation from the early Marx: *Le devenir-pensée du monde et le devenir-monde de la pensée* ('the becoming-thought of the world and the becoming-world of thought').

In his dissertation on *The Difference between the Democritean and Epicurean Philosophy of Nature*, Marx speaks of the 'becoming-philosophical of the world' [*das Philosophisch-Werden der Welt*] and a concurrent 'becoming-worldly of philosophy' [*Weltlich-Werden der Philosophie*] (Marx 1975: 85, translation modified by the author). Marx uses the terms to critique the Hegelian school (including the avant-garde of *Junghegelianer*) that he sees showing an increasing tendency to dismantle itself. This observation leads Marx to posit a dialectic inherent in philosophy which equates its realization and self-destruction:

> By the way, I consider this unphilosophical turn in a large section of Hegel's school as a phenomenon which will always accompany the transition from discipline to freedom.
> It is a psychological law that the theoretical mind, once liberated in itself, turns into practical energy, and, leaving the shadowy empire of ... will, turns itself against the reality of the world existing without it. (From a philosophical point of view, however, it is important to specify these aspects better, since from the specific manner of this turn we can reason back towards the immanent determination and the universal historic character of a philosophy. We see here, as it were, its *curriculum vitae* narrowed down to its subjective point.) But the *practice* of philosophy is itself *theoretical*. It is the *critique* that measures the individual existence by the essence, the particular reality by the Idea. But this *immediate realisation* of philosophy is in its deepest essence afflicted with contradictions [...].
> The result is that as the world becomes philosophical, philosophy also becomes worldly, that its realisation is also its loss, that what it struggles against on the outside is its own inner deficiency, that in the very struggle it falls precisely into those defects which it fights as defects in the opposite camp, and that it can only overcome these defects by falling into them. That which opposes it and that which it fights is always the same as itself, only with factors inverted. (Marx 1975: 85; translation modified by the author)

In this process inside and outside, self and other, action and reflection, friend and foe implode – without leading to a final synthesis. The passage appeals to Axelos because it envisions an a-teleological encounter of philosophy and reality setting free an 'energy' that overrides the distinction of theory and practice. Here, Marx's own critical discourse opens the space for a thinking that withdraws the apparently safe foundations it relies upon. If all critique indeed leads to self-annihilation then this must also be true for Marx's critique of the Hegelian school. Axelos will follow the (impossible and yet necessary) 'trajectory' this insight opens for a thinking which is, in its own self-critical movement, already a political action that undermines a Schmittian distinction of friend and foe.

The importance Axelos attributes to the anti-dialectical tendencies at work in Marxian dialectics shows why Marx is a thoroughly ambiguous figure for him. Although his dialectical theory of historical progress has fostered Marxism and the totality and totalitarianism that this (both philosophical and political) ideology has led to, Axelos stresses that Marx himself escapes these tendencies and rather gives in to a fundamental errancy: 'Marx did not prepare a new philosophy and he did not believe in worldviews. The truth he took upon himself, which includes his errancy, can lead toward an open thinking that is not philosophy anymore' (Axelos 1964: 183). This is the reason Axelos engages with Marx in order to prepare the planetary leap away from globe and globalization, which means unleashing the practical energies theory contains for Marx in such a way as to swerve away from what is known as Marxian and Marxist philosophy. This is why Axelos rewrites Marx's *Feuerbach Theses*, amongst them the famous Eleventh Thesis. Where Marx stated that, instead of interpreting the world as the philosophers have always done, it is time 'to *change* it' (Marx 1976: 5), Axelos now holds that it is time 'to *think* it' (Axelos 1964: 177), with all the implications this has for Marx's 'theoretical mind' that is 'liberated in itself' (Marx 1975: 85).

Thus, reading Marx against Marx, Axelos develops the aporetic a-teleological movement of liberation (whose critique of self and other remains suspended between ideality and reality) into 'a unique becoming that carries and carries away ['porte et emporte'] world-and-thought' (Axelos 1964: 30) beyond a global horizon. For, the reason 'we cannot start with the world and reach thought, or gather élan from thought in order to encounter the world' is because this 'we' is always already 'at odds ['aux prises'] with the circularity and the sinusoidal movement' (ibid.: 30). Everything – from the economic model of circulation to the multiple astronomic rotations of the solar system, from the micro-technological feedback loops to the grand narratives of history and philosophy – loses its self-evidence in this becoming. It is a 'mystery' that is, at once, 'cosmic and ontological, gnoseo-logical and anthropo-logical' (Axelos

1964: 30). All these 'logical' disciplines are undone by what Axelos here and elsewhere calls the 'jeu du monde', the 'game' or 'play' of the world, that is, in which 'world' is what is, simultaneously, 'at stake' and 'at issue' ('l'enjeu') (ibid.: 20; for the 'jeu du monde' cf. Malette 2014).

It is no coincidence that Axelos' often playful language, which likes to engage in the game it speaks of, is reminiscent of Derrida. In fact, as the thinker of the 'game of the world' Axelos had a verifiable influence on nascent deconstruction. In its attempt to 'reach the point of a certain exteriority in relation to the totality of the age of logocentrism', *Of Grammatology* marginally refers to *Vers la pensée planétaire* and its 'game of the world' (Derrida 1998: 161, 326). The reason Derrida can name 'jeu' (game or play) 'the absence of the transcendental signified' (ibid.: 73) is that this concept tries to overcome the problem inherent in any attempt to gain access to a point external to logocentrism: that assuming such an outside reinforces logocentrism inasmuch as it implies an inside and a centre from which it tries to break away. It is only by suspending the difference between inside and outside, centre and periphery, Derrida holds, that one might be able to move away from logocentrism. Thus, Derrida is faced with a problem that is (at the very least) analogous to Axelos's problem and Derrida formulates his solution in terms that seem taken from *Vers la pensée planétaire*. The 'errancy' that *Of Grammatology* envisions follows an 'exorbitant' course and undermines the distinction of inside and outside, centre and periphery by managing to 'exceed the metaphysical orb in an attempt to get out of the orbit (*orbita*)' (ibid.: 161f.). That these parallels are more than coincidental comes to the fore when Derrida explains why his grammatology will never be able to attain the status of a science, because this would mean setting itself up as yet another transcendental signified. When calling attention to this impossibility Derrida again refers to Axelos, playfully and self-ironically founding grammatology on the 'game of the world' which, consequently, haunts every 'concept' such a pseudo- and para-science works with, first and foremost, its central category: the supplement. 'The supplement can only respond to the nonlogical logic of a game. That game is the play of the world' (ibid.: 259).

The stakes in Axelos's planetary thought are at least as high as those of Derrida's *Grammatology*. The, in its own right, 'exorbitant' claim of *Vers la pensée planétaire* is to seek an errancy that succeeds in remaining external to the horizon circumscribed by sun and globe. This is why Axelos – just like Derrida in his critique of logocentrism – does not critique globalization head-on ('caput'), as such a critique would itself get caught up in what it is critiquing. It would have to assume a stable position from where it could be voiced, falling into the rescendent trap of the avant-garde. Instead, Axelos develops a strategy of writing that inspires a new kind of thinking by trajectories found in the texts of others, prefiguring something that runs counter and askance to the apparent and official results of these texts. An effort to move beyond a global horizon, thus, relies on a performance of thinking animated by unforeseen encounters with others – and others' texts – that unsettles commonly held convictions in a much more radical way than a Jüngerian or Marxist avant-garde could. Since Axelos's errant thinking and world is put into practice in a reading and writing process, the performative aspects of his own textual trajectories already figure as an integral part of the political commitment he is advocating. It is by means of a specific 'performativity' of writing that a markedly planetary thought hopes to overcome what Spivak will call 'the logofratrocentric notion of collectivity' (Spivak 2005: 32).

From onto-theology to an onto-erotology

Given that he was writing in early 1960s France, it probably comes as no great surprise that Axelos turns to psychoanalysis in order to conceive of such an alternative notion of collectivity. *Vers la pensée planétaire* features a chapter-length rereading of Freud as an 'analyste de l'homme' (Axelos 1964: 243) which promises to prepare a shift from the onto-theological character of heliocentric metaphysics to an 'onto-erotology' (ibid.: 294) intended to overcome the philosophical fixation on the sun and, with it, the psychoanalytic fixation on the 'phallus' (ibid.: 291). The philosophical overtones of Eros are already present in Freud who once pointed out that 'the enlarged sexuality of psycho-analysis coincides with the Eros of the divine Plato' (Freud 1953a: 134). Planetary thought means swerving away from phallocentrism and heliocentrism alike, that is from the phallo-heliocentrism that inevitably emerges on the horizon of globe and globalization. Axelos's plea that the human being should 'not interpret itself as a sun, but rather as a planet' (Axelos 1964: 18) therefore involves a gender aspect. The French word for planet ('la planète') is feminine, while the word for sun ('le soleil') is masculine. Axelos is playing with this grammatical circumstance when he suggests that the world's (and, with it, thought's) gender 'is becoming female, if it is permissible to speak in this manner' (ibid.: 291). Spivak will take this game very seriously when she advises: 'let us all imagine anew imperatives that structure all of us, as giver and taker, female and male, planetary human beings' (Spivak 1999: 88).

Just like Marx before him, Freud plays a pivotal, but also extremely ambiguous, role in the passage from the global to the planetary. As an 'analyste de l'homme' (Axelos 1964: 243), Freud remains an 'analyst of man,' not an 'analyst of the human being' (the French word 'homme' means both). After all, Freud infamously holds 'that libido is invariably and necessarily of a masculine nature' (Freud 1953a: 219). Nevertheless, some passages of his writings can be read as invitations to veer away from the heliocentric cycles of globalization. Axelos here follows the path of *Civilization and its Discontents* where psychoanalytical concepts are employed to account for the complexities of modern society and its 'global malaise ['mal global']' (Axelos 1964: 243). In spite of this approach, Freud markedly abstains from offering a medical or psychological cure. This 'merit of renouncing any enterprise of social therapeutics' (ibid.: 271) allows Axelos to refer solely to the diagnosis which attracts him because it introduces another non-teleological becoming. For in his text Freud calls attention to an 'antagonism of forces within Eros' (ibid.: 268) tying it in a 'more than dialectical manner' to its 'opposing powers' (ibid.: 295). As elsewhere, Axelos again tries to release the 'energetic' potentials in this thought and is thus able to read Freud's interpretation of the 20th century's *global* malaise as the indication of a 'civilization about to become planetary' (ibid.: 262).

Civilization and its Discontents lends itself to such a strategy because it casts 'the dispute within the economics of the libido' (Freud 1953b: 141) in astrophysical terms. Before distinguishing it from the 'contradiction – probably an irreconcilable one – between the primal instincts of Eros and death' (ibid.: 141), Freud compares this 'dispute' to the movements within the solar system and, at one and the same time, introduces the possibility of calling this entire model into question:

> Just as a planet revolves around a central body as well as rotating around its own axis, so the human individual takes part in the course of the development of mankind at the same time as he pursues his own path in life. But to our dull eyes the play of forces in the heavens seems fixed in a never-changing order; in the field of organic life we can still see how the forces contend with one another, and how the effects of the conflict are continually changing. (ibid.: 141)

These sentences are indicative of how Axelos sees Freud employing natural phenomena in his arguments. At first, the natural order of the solar system seems to illustrate the forces at work in history, but the comparison with history ultimately serves to undermine the appearance of order in the natural world.

That their movements – or again 'trajectories' – unsettle conventional notions of history and nature alike is one of the most important reasons why Freud's writings appeal to Axelos. There are three things he gains by way of the passage in question. Besides tracing a path that is not dialectically oriented, Freud here suggests an 'energetic nucleus' of 'love' (Axelos 1964: 283) that constitutes itself as its own self-division, and he does this by mapping nature and culture onto each other in such a way as to undermine their distinction. In overriding the heliocentrism of the analogy, Axelos adds a fourth aspect that radicalizes Freud's anti-dialectical trajectory. From now on, the contention within Eros is not only supposed to suspend the fundamental empirical distinction of nature and culture, but also the fundamental logical distinction of individual and universal. Inspired by Freud, Axelos does not simply use the astrophysical language of constellations, suns, and wanderings stars in order to illustrate the erotic forces in history and society or to render them clearer by way of analogy. On the contrary, the way he brings the astrophysical model to bear involves a kind of 'backlash' that calls into question the status of the model itself. This backlash is supposed to undo a 'language that speaks in terms of predestination and reminiscence, of a terrestrial reprise of a celestial game' (ibid.: 281). To this end, Axelos unhinges the 'universal Eros' and the 'individual Eros' (ibid.: 288) from their association with the annual revolution (of earth around sun) and diurnal revolution (of earth around its own axis), making it unmistakably clear that the individual, or earthly, Eros does not revolve around a universal, celestial Eros. Instead, 'the 'celestial' and the 'common' guise ['visage'] of Eros' (ibid.: 288) infinitely mirror and multiply one another, dissociating into an infinite number of encounters with others. Eros is split into a constitutive tension between a 'universal Eros' and a 'particular, individual Eros'. Their conflictual interaction within Eros renders the 'fortune of humankind open. What is to come remains unpredictable' (ibid.: 288).

This movement of dispersal does more than simply change the interrelation of universe and individual, it calls into question what 'individual' or 'universe' can mean. Instead of envisioning an erotic solar system of global individuals revolving around the sun of a universal Eros, Axelos's planetary Eros moves within 'a play of centrifugal and centripetal forces' (ibid.: 279) that are 'not centred on' the *ego cogito*'s 'axis of subjectivity' (ibid.: 289). Drawing vectors between 'centering and decentering' (ibid.: 276), this play of forces can give rise to 'constellations' (e.g. ibid.: 275, 279) – but it can certainly also lead to 'disaster' (ibid.: 291), another astronomical pun since 'aster' is Greek for star.

Against a phallo-heliocentric melancholy

Axelos's 'onto-erotology' (Axelos 1964: 294) of wandering stars that do not revolve around a common centre or around themselves anymore goes a step further than Freud. For, despite his gestures toward the *devenir* of an onto-erotology, Freud does not abandon the onto-theological model of globe and sun. As he did Marx, Axelos is reading Freud against the grain. His ensuing critique of these two thinkers that are so crucial for him is modeled on Heidegger's critique of Jünger and Nietzsche (the two most prominent writers for the latter's take on planetarity). Inasmuch as Marx's and Freud's 'reversal of the perspective of metaphysics' remains 'beholden ['tributaire'] to metaphysics' (ibid.: 253) the reversal amounts to what Heidegger called a 'rescendence' (Heidegger 1996: 398) of transcendence: 'Marx socializes the *ego* of the *cogito*, the subject, and wants it to socialize the objects of the *res extensa*. Freud analyses the *ego*, descending into its unconscious and sees it at odds ['le voit aux prises'] with its objects' (Axelos 1964: 253). The consequences are a 'brutally anti-dualistic dualism' (ibid.: 253), which, in Marx's case, leads to a conception of the end of history in a class Armageddon and, in Freud's case, reintroduces a conception of social dynamics following a 'simple dialectic of love and hate' (ibid.: 283). Thus, the clear-cut distinction between friend and foe that Carl Schmitt did not cease to advocate re-enters the stage. Since neither Marx nor Freud follows the openings provided by their own texts, they always swerve back into the cyclical models they wanted to break away from and thus end up trying to reconstitute lines that could separate inside and outside, self and other, friend and foe. In this respect at least, they point back to Carl Schmitt's global and Eurocentric world where the 'Self' was still able to subtract itself from what it deemed to be a mere outside. Axelos's post-Freudian planetary Eros and post-Marxian planetary politics seek to undermine such distinctions, in the hope that this will overcome the melancholy haunting every avant-garde.

Axelos parts ways with psychoanalysis when he characterizes Freud as a 'melancholic' with 'anti-metaphysically metaphysical convictions' (ibid.: 263). While the latter knows that he is overcoming metaphysics, he does not know *what it is* that he is thus overcoming; just like the melancholic who knows '*whom* he has lost but not *what* he has lost in him' (Freud 1953c: 245). Freud's debunking of the *ego cogito* shows the 'ambivalence' (ibid.: 251) inherent in the way it models, and relates to, objects in the world (reifying everything including itself). But because he cannot move beyond his fixation on the (masculinely coded) I (to which he must always himself 'regress' – again just like a melancholic), Freud has to conceive of this ambivalence in the dualistic terms of 'narcissism' and 'sadism', 'love' and 'hate' (ibid.: 251). This also holds true for all avant-garde movements (such as the ones articulated in Marx or Jünger). Love (of the self, i.e. the either individual or collective identity) and hatred (for the either individual or collective other, the enemy) give rise to 'countless separate struggles ..., in which hate and love contend with each other' (ibid.: 256). The 20th century has globalized the repetition compulsion fuelling these conflicts by spinning the entire planet in an 'infernal cycle of revenge and resentment' (Axelos 1964: 278). Such a globalization compulsion would indeed be ruled by the Hobbesian 'maxim' Axelos attributes to Freud: '*homo homini lupus*' (ibid.: 259). The errant trajectories Axelos' text follows are meant to evade the civil war lurking on this horizon.

Such an eccentric errancy is necessary because Freud's critique of a globalized modernity rides on the implicit assumption of an essence of man (which is moreover defined as 'the wolf of the other'). In order to veer away from the dualisms of metaphysics, and the global conflicts such an assumption gives rise to, one has to jettison the concept of an essence altogether. And, since Freud's essence of the human is modelled on an alleged essence of man ('homme') – Axelos now argues with Lacan against Lacan – this will also mean conceiving of a 'phallus' that is 'owned' by no-one (ibid.: 291). Thinking will only be able to address the radically 'historical' character of any putative 'ontological essence of the human being' once the impossibility of 'fixing the essence of the male or the female' has blurred sexual difference, instead testifying to the 'fundamental bisexuality' of any human being (ibid.: 292). Jacques Lacan, whom Axelos knew personally, famously argues that the phallus is not an (albeit partial) object or a phantasm, but 'the signifier that is destined to designate meaning effects as a whole' (Lacan 2006: 579). This process of signification constitutes the barred subject of psychoanalysis by means of a 'not-having ['manque à avoir']' (ibid.: 582) that appears in males as the fear of castration and in females as penis envy. In the talk that Lacan gave on 'The Signification of the Phallus' in 1958 in Munich (and I am not sure whether Axelos knew this precise piece), he used an astrophysical term dear to Axelos to refer to the tension within the couple to which this *manque à avoir* gives rise. Every heterosexual relationship manifests 'a centrifugal tendency of the genital drive' (ibid.: 583) on both the male and the female side, demonstrating that Eros itself is not only defined by the centripetal tendency toward monogamy and monandry, but also by an opposite force toward polygamy and polyandry.

To conceive of a phallus owned by no-one means reappraising the role of this centrifugal tendency, and with it the role of lack, privation and negativity in Lacan's thought. To this end, Axelos propagates a 'negative onto-erotology where plenitude and void are not distinguished by the criteria of a massively positive reality or ideality' (Axelos 1964: 294). In an onto-erotological perspective, any 'fixation' would appear as one possible 'modality' of the 'fundamental errancy' of planetarity amongst others (ibid.: 294). Consequently, if the centrifugal und centripetal forces are articulated here in terms of 'a polygamous monogamy and a polyandrous monandry' (ibid.: 278f.), this is not only meant to emancipate women from a patriarchal paradigm, but also to reconsider the relation of Other, others, and selves. Instead of enabling all relationships to the self and to others, Lacan's Other is here dissolved into endless encounters with others that constellate, de-constellate, and re-constellate what could be called selves. In other words, the centripetal and centrifugal forces inspiring the planetary encounters in their ever-changing movements of (de- and re-)constellation are not directed toward the (phallic) sun, but toward a de-centralized pluriverse.

This is how, following certain trajectories of the Freudian text, Axelos is able to dissolve the heliocentric fixations of metaphysics without having to assume a rescendence. In an 'encounter with another being,' Axelos points out, 'it is *as if* we already knew what we are about to know and what we cannot know because we do not know it' (ibid.: 281). So far, this passage simply restates the paradox of seeking for knowledge formulated, for example, in Plato's *Meno*. However, since the planetary Eros has unmoored itself from the anamnetic fixation on the sun, it does not follow Plato in positing a past knowledge that could be retrieved in such a search. Instead, Axelos underscores that 'we cannot know' what we are on the verge of experiencing 'because we did not know it beforehand' (ibid.).

'Perhaps': the practical energies of planetary politics

Thus, the exorbitant claims planetarity is making should have become clearer. *Vers la pensée planétaire* sets out to unsettle the fundamental distinctions between nature and culture, individual and universe, self and other, man and woman, friend and foe. This is supposed to contribute to a new form of politics that might meet the challenges of a world where all cycles are turning into decentralized networks of technological feedback loops. Such a distinctly planetary thinking and politics are all the more necessary because the technological revolution that has swept away the classical Eurocentric global world order is in danger of reinforcing its onto-theological model of an absolute totality, and of thereby leading to new forms of totalitarianism based on what one might call a globalized 'white' ideology (cf. the 'white mythology' in Derrida 1974).

In order to meet the new and unforeseen challenges globalization poses, thought and politics 'must dare to be planetary' (Axelos 1964: 182). For Axelos, the only hope that they will indeed be 'in no way totalitarian' (ibid.) resides in the leap beyond the global horizon. A truly planetary thought comes to a (paradoxically self-beheading) head ('caput') in a political activity that unleashes the potentials granted by the dissolution of national borders and the end of Eurocentrism. This means engaging the technological ensemble of networks in ways that turn their graphs into open trajectories leading to encounters that cross all boundaries. In 'breaching the cape that still conceals the abstract landscape of the planetary era' (ibid.: 311) these encounters attest to a decentralized, trans-national, post-sovereign, a-teleological thought and world. When Axelos sketches the unforeseen opportunities the planetary leap will afford, he again refers to Freud's auto-antagonistic Eros. Genuinely planetary politics will have become possible, he argues,

> Once we remember that Eros is what connects the beings and things of the world by opening a conflict with opposing forces that are more than just dialectically tied to it, and once we establish – now already and in anticipation of what is to come – relations of camaraderie that are more profound and more trembling [*frémissante*] (in which terms can we still speak of friendship without lying?) between the men and women that we are and are becoming. (ibid.: 295)

Whatever Axelos's direct influence on Spivak might be, it is clear that the hybrid camaraderie outlined here prefigures what she will – with reference to Derrida's critique of Schmitt's notion of politics as a distinction of friend and foe – call a 'politics of friendship': 'I am not advocating the politicization of the discipline. I am advocating a depoliticization of the politics of hostility toward a politics of friendship to come' (Spivak 2005: 13).

Axelos sees this friendship stimulated by the aporetically 'practical energy' which, according to Marx' dissertation, 'accompan[ies] the transition' from theory to practice, 'from discipline to freedom' (Marx 1975: 85). That this energy does not fuel a new avant-garde, which would or could lead the way into a better future, brings up the issue of what status Axelos's own text has; how a book whose title reads 'toward planetary thinking' is involved in the 'planetary step and leap' (Axelos 1964: 27) it speaks of. Since *Vers la pensée planétaire* is admittedly geared to giving attention and articulation to the 'unique becoming that carries and carries away world-and-thought' (ibid.: 30), it thus in a sense, 'enacts' this *devenir*. This is why the constative and cognitive aspects of the text cannot be separated from its performative and rhetorical aspects. Here the full philosophical implications of the planetary Eros come into perspective. For, in order to articulate the ever-changing constellations of a planetary era, Axelos sees the need to 'prepare the way to a different language' (ibid.: 32), a language that has freed itself from the 'copula' just as Eros has freed itself from 'copulation' (ibid.: 296). This argument again alludes to Lacan for whom 'sexual intercourse ['copulation']' was signified by the phallus which, in its turn, stood in a close relation to the '(logical) copula' (Lacan 2006: 581). Deviating from the phallo-heliocentrism of the global model thus entails a conception of language that disperses the 'whole' of Lacan's 'meaning effects' (ibid.: 579). Instead of subsuming the specific under the general, the individual under the universal, (the 'global' under the 'solar'), Axelos breaks with a language that assumes subjects and objects brought in correlation by 'copulative judgements' (ibid.: 295).

Unmoored from their function within the totality of a universe meaningful in and of itself, the chains of 'signifiers' would open trajectories leading into the errancy of a decentred text (and in this movement the chains would cease to be 'signifiers'). In neither referring to a 'reality' nor signifying an 'ideality', such trajectories of language suspend the difference between literal and figurative sense, becoming what Axelos calls 'non-figurative figures' (Axelos 1964: 47), figures, that is, that are neither imaginary nor simply real. This is the language in which the always problematic and questionable 'dialogue' (Axelos 1964: 29) of world and thought could take place. Thus, Axelos's planetary trajectories are populated by figures defying the distinction of the rhetorical and imaginary on the one hand and the material and real on the other. They are supposed to invert and displace the onto-theological model that assumes a central being that could eminently embody being. Here it is the other way around: Planetary trajectories give rise to figures that are poised, and open, toward what is to come, but cannot be decoded as if there were a plaintext behind them. This is why the figures that populate such planetary trajectories are prefigurations gesturing toward a future – an *avenir* – that necessarily remains open. Or, one last time, in Spivak's words: 'The figure "is" irreducible' (Spivak 2005: 52).

The necessary self-defiguration of any prefiguration is why *Vers la pensée planétaire* will never establish a meta-discourse. Instead it sees itself – and the figure of planetarity it argues for – as one among many non-figurative figures. This is written into the figure of planetarity itself which, according to its own aporetic (Derrida might have said: supplemental) logic, brackets all its statements inasmuch as it shows that every apparent truth and reality is a mere prefiguration open to an other that is not phallo-heliocentric. This paradox is echoed in the tone of Axelos's book which questions and probes, suggests and alludes more than it pretends to give definitive answers. Entire paragraphs are mere catalogues of questions that may be maieutic, but are not supposed to serve the establishment of a philosophical system. And instead of giving closure to itself, *Vers la pensée planétaire* opens upon what is to come on its final pages. The book ends with an 'Interlude' (Axelos 1964: 321) of markedly 'Non-Final Remarks' (ibid.: 319).

The key word in the book might be the probing word 'perhaps' ('peut-être'). At least, one has to take Axelos's statement 'perhaps we are on our way to a planetary thought' (ibid.: 45) seriously. The we that is speaking here is not a *pluralis maiestatis*, it is the open place of encounter with others. Axelos invites his readers to the dangerous and endangered space opened by this shifter (or fader) because he hopes it can provide 'a hotspot ['foyer'] of resistance and attack' (ibid.: 277) against the self-veiling heliocentrism of the concept of globalization, a hotspot in which a multitude might conceive of 'a camaraderie' that is 'deeper and more trembling ['frémissante']' (ibid.: 295) than the self-veiling phallocentrism of a brotherhood of man.

Notes

[1] On 5 August 2020 the Süddeutsche Zeitung published a German translation of what was allegedly the text Mbembe was going to present at the Triennale. Its focus on Covid-19, however, makes it unlikely that this was in fact the original text (cf. Mbembe 2020b).

2   Since the book has not been translated into English yet, all translations from *Vers la pensée planétaire* are my own.

References

Aalberts, Tanja. 2016. 'Sovereignty'. In: Felix Berenskoetter (ed), *Concepts in World Politics*. London: SAGE Publications: 183–99.

Acosta, Alberto. 2009. 'Derechos de la naturaleza y buen vivir: Ecos de la Constitución de Motecristi'. *Pensamiento Jurídico* no. 25: 21–7.

Actas del Congreso de Cucuta. 1821. Tomos I, II y III (Obra completa). Retrieved from: http://www.bdigital.unal.edu.co/4546/1116/ACTAS_DEL_CONGRESO_DE_C%C3%9ACUTA%2C_1821.html [last accessed 30 August 2020].

Ahlwardt, Hermann. 1890. *Der Verzweiflungskampf der arischen Völker mit dem Judentum*. Berlin: Grobhäuser.

Ahmed, Sara. 2014. *The Cultural Politics of Emotion*. Edinburgh: Edinburgh University Press.

Akkaya, Ahmet Hamdi. 2013. 'Kürt Hareketi'nin Örgütlenme Süreci Olarak 1970'ler'. *Toplum ve Kuram* no. 127: 1–28.

Akkaya, Ahmet Hamdi. 2015. 'The "Palestinian Dream" in the Kurdish context'. *Kurdish Studies* 3(1): 47–63.

Akkaya, Ahmet Hamdi and Jongerden, Joost. 2010. 'The PKK in the 2000s. Continuity through breaks?' In: Marlies Casier and Joost Jongerden (eds), *Nationalisms and Politics in Turkey: Political Islam, Kemalism and the Kurdish Issue*. London: Routledge: 143–62.

Akopov, Sergei. 2020. 'Russia's "fortresses of solitude": Social imaginaries of loneliness after the fall of the USSR'. *Social Science Information*: Retrieved from: doi: 10.1177/0539018420925967 [last accessed 30 August 2020].

Alamán, Lucas. 2010 [1831]. 'Instructions from the Mexican Foreign Ministry to the extraordinary envoys near the republics that were once Spanish colonies' (3 June). In: Germán de la Reza (ed), *Documentos del Congreso Anfictiónico de Panamá*. Caracas: Fundación Biblioteca Ayacucho: 262–71.

Albert, Mathias. 2007. 'Past, against, or still before globalisation theory? Studying globalisation with social theory'. *International Political Sociology* 1(1): 165–82.

Albert, Mathias. 2009. 'Globalization and world society theory: a reply'. *International Political Sociology* 3(1): 126–8.

Albert, Mathias. 2016. *A Theory of World Politics*. Cambridge: Cambridge University Press.

Albrow, Martin. 1996. *The Global Age. State and Society beyond Modernity*. Cambridge: Polity Press.

Almarza, Ángel. 2009. 'Historia/Venezuela'. In: Javier Fernandez Sebastian (ed) *Diccionario Político del Mundo Iberoamericano*. Madrid: Centro de Estudios Políticos y Constitucionales: 681–91.

Aly, Götz. 2017. *Europa gegen die Juden. 1880–1945*. Frankfurt am Main: S. Fischer.

Anderson, Benedict. 1993. *Comunidades imaginadas. Reflexiones sobre el origen y la difusion del nacionalismo* Mexico City: Fondo de Cultura Económica.

Apter, Emily. 2006. '"Je ne crois pas beaucoup à la littérature comparée": Universal poetics and postcolonial comparatism'. In: Haun Saussy (ed), *Comparative Literature in the Age of Globalization*. Baltimore, MD: Johns Hopkins University Press: 54–62.

Arendt, Hannah. 1994. *The Origins of Totalitarianism*. Orlando, FL: A Harvest Book.

Arndt, Ernst Moritz. 1814. *Blick aus der Zeit auf die Zeit*. Germanien [Frankfurt]: Eichenberg.

Arrighi, Giovanni; Hopkins, Terence and Wallerstein, Imanuel. 1989. *Antisystemic Movements*. London: Verso.

Ashcroft, Bill; Griffiths, Gareth and Tiffin, Helen. 1989. *The Empire Writes Back*. London: Routledge.

Auer, Michael. 2013. *Wege zu einer planetarischen Linientreue? Meridiane zwischen Jünger, Schmitt, Heidegger und Celan*. Munich: Fink.

Axelos, Kostas. 1964. *Vers la pensée planétaire: Le devenir-pensée du monde et le devenir-monde de la pensée*. Paris: Minuit.

Bähr, Christiane; Homfeldt, Hans Günther; Schröder, Christian; Schröer, Wolfgang and Schweppe, Cornelia (eds). 2014. *Weltatlas Soziale Arbeit. Jenseits aller Vermessungen*. Weinheim: Beltz Juventa.

Ban Ki-moon. 2007. 'Address to inaugural global gorum on migration and development.' Retrieved from: https://www.un.org/sg/en/content/sg/

speeches/2007-07-10/address-inaugural-global-forum-migration-and-development [last accessed 30 August 2020].

Barak, Aharon. 2005. *Purposive Interpretation in Law*. Princeton, NJ: Princeton University Press.

Barfi, Barak. 2013. 'The fractious politics of Syria's Kurds'. *The Washington Institute*. Retrieved from: https://www.washingtoninstitute.org/policy-analysis/view/the-fractious-politics-of-syrias-kurds [last accessed 30 August 2020].

Bartelson, Jens. 1995. *A Genealogy of Sovereignty*. Cambridge: Cambridge University Press.

Bartelson, Jens. 2014. *Sovereignty as Symbolic Form*. London: Routledge.

Bartley, Allen and Beddoe, Liz (eds). 2018. *Transnational Social Work: Opportunities and Challenges of a Global Profession*. Bristol: Policy Press.

Basch, Linda; Glick Schiller, Nina and Szanton Blanc, Cristina. 1997. 'From immigrant to transmigrant: Theorizing transnational migration'. In: Ludger Pries (ed), *Transnationale Migration*. Baden-Baden: Nomos: 121–40.

Bastia, Tania and Skeldon, Ronald. 2020. 'Introduction'. In: Tania Bastia and Ronald Skeldon (eds), *Routledge Handbook of Migration and Development*. London: Routledge: 1–15.

Bateson, Gregory. 1987. *Steps to an Ecology of Mind*. Northvale, NJ: Jason Aranson.

Bauman, Zygmunt. 1998. 'On glocalization: Or globalization for some, localization for some others'. *Thesis Eleven* 54(1): 37–49.

Bayly, Christopher Alan. 2004. *The Birth of the Modern World, 1780–1914*. Oxford: Blackwell.

Beck, Ulrich. 2002. 'The cosmopolitan society and its enemies'. *Theory, Culture and Society* 19(1): 17–44.

Belis, José Maria et al. 2010 [1826]., 'Message from the municipality of the capital of the Isthmus to the installation of the congress' (22 June). Panama. In: Germán de la Reza (ed), *Documentos del Congreso Anfictiónico de Panamá*. Caracas: Fundación Biblioteca Ayacucho: 159–60.

Bell, Duncan. 2013. 'Making and taking worlds'. In: Samuel Moyn and Andrew Sartori (eds), *Global Intellectual History*. New York: Columbia University Press: 254–79.

Benhabib, Seyla. 2016. 'The new sovereigntism and transnational law. Legal utopianism, democratic skepticism and statist realism'. *Global Constitutionalism* 51(1): 109–44.

Benjamin, Walter. 1979. 'Theories of German Fascism: On the collection of essays *War and Warrior*, edited by Ernst Jünger'. *New German Critique* 17(1): 120–8.

Benz, Wolfgang. 2015. *Antisemitismus. Präsenz und Tradition eines Ressentiments*. Schwalbach: Wochenschau Verlag.

Berenskoetter, Felix. 2007 'Friends, there are no friends? An intimate reframing of the international'. *Millennium. Journal of International Studies* 35(3): 647–76.

Bergmann, Werner. 2002. *Die Geschichte des Antisemitismus*. München: C.H. Beck.

Bertola, Luis. 2016. 'Development patterns and welfare states in Latin America'. In: Alicia Barcena and Antonio Prado (eds), *Neostructuralism and Heterodox Thinking in Latin America and the Caribbean in the Early Twenty-first Century*. Santiago de Chile: Economic Commission for Latin America and the Caribbean (ECLAC): 239–68.

Beta, Ottomar. 1875. *Darwin, Deutschland und die Juden oder der Juda-Jesuitismus*. Berlin: Otto Dreyer.

Bhattacharya, Malini. 2017. 'The Russian revolution and the freedom struggle in India: Rabindranath Tagore's letters from Russia'. *Agrarian South: Journal of Political Economy* 6(2): 237–62.

Billig, Michael. 1995. *Banal Nationalism*. London: Sage.

Blaney, David L. and Tickner, Arlene B. 2017. 'International relations in the prison of colonial modernity'. *International Relations* 31(1): 71–5.

Blank, Beate; Gögercin, Süleyman; Sauer, Karin Elinor and Schramkowski, Barbara (eds). 2018. *Soziale Arbeit in der Migrationsgesellschaft. Grundlagen – Konzepte – Handlungsfelder*. Wiesbaden: Springer.

Blumenberg, Hans. 1987. *The Genesis of the Copernican World*. Cambridge, MA: MIT Press.

Bolívar, Simón 2010 [1822]. 'Invitation from the Liberator, President of Colombia to the governments of the new republics to sign a bilateral confederative treaty' (Lima, 8 and 9 January). In: Germán de la Reza (ed), *Documentos del Congreso Anfictiónico de Panamá*. Caracas: Fundación Biblioteca Ayacucho: 3–4.

Bolívar, Simón. 2010 [1824], 'Invitation from the Liberator of Colombia and the Supreme Commander of Peru to the Congress from Panama' (Lima 7 December). In: Germán de la Reza (ed), *Documentos del Congreso Anfictiónico de Panamá*. Caracas: Fundación Biblioteca Ayacucho: 40–2.

Bolívar, Simón. 2010 [1826]. 'A thought on the Congress of Panama'. In: Germán de la Reza (ed), *Documentos del Congreso Anfictiónico de Panamá*. Caracas: Fundación Biblioteca Ayacucho: 51–2.

Bolívar, Simón. 2012 [1813]. 'La Gaceta de Caracas. N° 30'. In: *Indalecio Liévano. Bolivarismo y monroísmo*. Bogotá: Universidad Nacional de Colombia: 36.

Bolívar, Simón. 2015 [1815]. *La Carta de Jamaica*. Caracas: Comisión presidencial para la conmemoración del bicentenario de la Carta de Jamaica.

Bonefeld, Werner. 2005. 'Nationalism and antisemitism in anti-globalization perspective: Social autonomy and the critique of capitalism'. In: Werner Bonefeld and Kosmas Psychopedis (eds), *Human Dignity*. New York: Routledge: 147–171.

Bordachev, Timofey. 2019. 'Russia and Europe: A problem of strategic intention. Valdai Club Expert Opinions'. Retrieved from: https://valdaiclub.com/a/highlights/russia-and-europe-problem-of-strategic-intentions/ [last accessed 30 August 2020].

Bozarslan, Hamit. 1997. *La Question Kurde: États et minorités au Moyen-Orient*. Paris: Presses de Sciences Po.

Bozarslan, Hamit. 2011. *Sociologie politique du Moyen-Orient*. Paris: La Découverte.

Bozarslan, Hamit. 2013. *Histoire de la Turquie*. Paris: Texto.

Braun, Christina von and Ziege, Eva-Maria. 2004. *Das 'bewegliche' Vorurteil*. Würzburg: Königshausen und Neumann.

Bunk, Benjamin; Kleibl, Tanja and Lutz, Ronald (eds). 2019. *Postcolonial Social Work and Local Knowledge*. Bielefeld: transcript.

Burr, Robert. 1955. 'The balance of power in nineteenth century South America: An exploratory essay'. *The Hispanic American Historical Review* 35(1): 37–60.

Butler, Judith. 1990. *Gender Trouble: Feminism and the Subversive of Identity*, London: Routledge.

Calhoun, Craig. 1997. *Nationalism*. Minneapolis, MN: University of Minnesota Press.

Capistrano [Otto Böckel]. 1886. *Die europäische Judengefahr*. Kassel: Werner.

Casier, Tom. 2016. 'From logic of competition to conflict: Understanding the dynamics of EU–Russia relations'. *Contemporary Politics* 22(3): 376–94.

Castles, Stephen. 2008. 'Comparing the experience of five major emigration countries'. In: Stephen Castles and Raul Delgado Wise (eds), *Migration and Development: Perspectives from the South*. Geneva: International Organization for Migration: 225–84.

Castles, Stephen and Delgado Wise, Raul. 2008. 'Introduction'. In: Stephen Castles and Raul Delgado Wise (eds): *Migration and Development: Perspectives from the South*. Geneva: International Organization for Migration: 1–16.

Castles, Stephen and Kosack, Godula. 1973. *Immigrant Workers and Class Structure in Western Europe*. Oxford: Oxford University Press.

Castles, Stephen and Ozkul, Derya. 2014. 'Circular migration: Triple win, or a new label for temporary migration?' In: Graziano Battistella (ed), *Global and Asian Perspectives on International Migration*. Cham: Springer: 27–49.

Castles, Stephen; de Haas, Hein and Miller, Mark. 2014. *The Age of Migration: International Population Movements in the Modern World*. New York: Guilford Press.

Caves, John. 2012. 'Backgrounder: Syrian Kurds and the Democratic Union Party (PYD).' Institute for the Study of War. Retrieved from: http://www.understandingwar.org/backgrounder/syrian-kurds-and-democratic-union-party-pyd [last accessed 30 August 2020].

Chaban, Natalia; Elgstrom, Ole and Gulyaeva, Olga. 2017. 'Russian images of the European Union: Before and after Maidan'. *Foreign Policy Analysis* 13(2): 480–99.

Chakrabarty, Dipesh. 2000. *Provincializing Europe: Postcolonial Thought and Historical Difference*. Princeton, NJ: Princeton University Press.

Charountaki, Marianna. 2015. 'Kurdish policies in Syria under the Arab uprisings: A revisiting of IR in the new Middle Eastern order.' *Third World Quarterly* 36(2): 337–56.

Cheah, Pheng. 2016. *What is a World? On Postcolonial Literature as World Literature*. Durham, NC: Duke University Press.

Chebankova, Elena. 2017. 'Russia's idea of the multipolar world order: Origins and main dimensions'. *Post-Soviet Affairs* 33(3): 217–34.

Chiaramonte, José Carlos. 2016. *Raíces Históricas del Federalismo Latinoamericano*. Buenos Aires: Penguin Random House.

Chilton, Paul. 1996. *Security Metaphors: Cold War Discourse from Containment to Common House*. Bern: Peter Lang.

Choudhry, Sujit. 1999. 'Globalization in search of justification: Toward a theory of comparative constitutional interpretation'. *Indiana Law Journal* 74(3): 819–92.

Chuji, Monica; Rengifo, Grimaldo; Gudynas, Eduardo. 2019. 'Buen Vivir'. In: Ashish Kothari; Ariel Salleh; Arturo Escobar; Federico Demaria and Alberto Acosta (eds), *Pluriverse. A Post-Development Dictionary*. New Delhi: Chaman: 111–4.

Cohn, Georg. 1888. 'Die Anfänge eines Weltverkehrsrechts'. In: Georg Cohn, *Drei Rechtswissenschaftliche Vorträge in Gemeinverständlicher Darstellung*. Heidelberg: Carl Winter Universitätsbuchhandlung: 76–149.

Conrad, Sebastian. 2016. *What is Global History?* Princeton, NJ: Princeton University Press.

Conrad, Sebastian. 2018. 'Nothing is the way it should be. Global transformations of the time regime in the nineteenth century'. *Modern Intellectual History* 15(3): 821–48.

Cox, Robert W. 1987. *Production, Power and World Order*. New York: Columbia University Press.

D'Ancona, Mathew. 2017. *Post-Truth: The New War on Truth and How to Fight Back*. London: Ebury Press.

Das, Sisir Kumar. 2015. *A History of Indian Literature 1911–1956: Struggle for Freedom: Triumph and Tragedy*. New Delhi: Sahitya Akademi.

de Haas, Hein. 2010. 'Migration and development: A theoretical perspective'. *International Migration Review* 44(1): 227–64.

de Haas, Hein. 2012. 'The migration and development pendulum: A critical view on research and policy.' *International Migration* 50(3): 8–25.

Delgado Wise, Raul. 2018. 'On the theory and practice of migration and development: A southern perspective'. *Journal of Intercultural Studies* 39(2): 163–81.

Delgado Wise, Raul and Márquez Covarrubias, Humberto. 2007. 'The theory and practice of the dialectical relationship between development and migration'. *Migracion y Desarrollo* 9(2): 5–24.

Delgado Wise, Raul and Veltmeyer, Henry. 2017. 'Aportes del pensamiento crítico Latinoamericano a la teoría y la práctica del desarrollo. Mundo Siglo XXI'. Retrieved from: https://www.researchgate.net/publication/316013949_Aportes_del_Pensamiento_Critico_Latinoamericano_a_la_Teoria_y_la_Practica_del_Desarrollo [last accessed 30 August 2020].

Derrida, Jacques. 1974. 'White mythology: Metaphor in the philosophical text'. *New Literary History* 6(1): 5–74.

Derrida, Jacques. 1992. *The Other Heading: Reflections on Today's Europe*. Bloomington: Indiana University Press.

Derrida, Jacques. 1998. *Of Grammatology*. Baltimore, MD: John's Hopkins University Press.

Dominelli, Lisa and Lorenz, Walter. 2017. *Beyond Racial Divides: Ethnicities in Social Work Practice*. London: Routledge.

Dorsen, Norman; Scalia, Antonin and Breyer, Stephen. 2005. 'The relevance of foreign legal materials in U.S. constitutional cases: A conversation between Justice Antonin Scalia and Justice Stephen Breyer'. *International Journal of Constitutional Law* 3(4): 519–41.

Ducoff, Louis J. et al. 1965 'The role of migration in the demographic development of Latin America'. *The Milbank Memorial Fund Quarterly* 43(4): 197–216.

Duscha, Annemarie. 2016. *Selbsthilfe von Migrantinnen in transnationalen Räumen. Eine brasilianische Migrantinnenorganisation in Deutschland*. Wiesbaden: Springer.

EC (European Commission). 2005. 'Migration and development: Some concrete orientations'. Retrieved from: https://eur-lex.europa.eu/legal-content/en/ALL/?uri=CELEX:52005DC0390 [last accessed 30 August 2020].

ECLAC (Economic Commission for Latin America and the Caribbean). 1957. 'Import substitution: Draft resolution approved by committee II on 25 May 1957'. Retrieved from: https://repositorio.cepal.org//bitstream/11362/13593/1/S5700191e.pdf [last accessed 30 August 2020].

ECLAC (Economic Commission for Latin America and the Caribbean). 1975. 'Prospects for action in the field of population in Latin America: The contribution of regional agencies'. Retrieved from: https://repositorio.cepal.org/bitstream/handle/11362/21639/S7500335_es.pdf?sequence=1 [last accessed 30 August 2020].

ECLAC (Economic Commission for Latin America and the Caribbean). 1990. 'Changing production patterns with social equality'. Retrieved from: https://repositorio.cepal.org/bitstream/handle/11362/29583/2/S9000090_en.pdf [last accessed 30 August 2020].

Ekurd Daily. 2014,). 'EUTCC Conference kicks off in Brussels'. Retrieved from: https://ekurd.net/eutcc-conference-on-eu-turkey-and-the-kurds-kicks-off-in-brussels-2014-12-11 [last accessed 30 August 2020].

ERFUKNI (Embassy of the Russian Federation to the United Kingdom of Great Britain and Northern Ireland). 2013. 'Concept of the Foreign Policy of the Russian Federation.'. Retrieved from: https://www.rusemb.org.uk/in1/ [last accessed 30 August 2020].

Epple, Angelika. 2007. 'Das Auge schmeckt Stollwerck. Uniformierung der Bilderwelt und kulturelle Differenzierung von Vorstellungsbildern in Zeiten des Imperialismus und der Globalisierung'. *Werkstatt Geschichte* 45: 13–31.

Epple, Angelika. 2018. 'Calling for a practice turn in global history: Practices as drivers of globalization/s'. *History and Theory* 57(3): 390–407.

Epple, Angelika. 2019. 'Comparing Europe and the Americas. The dispute of the New World between the sixteen and the nineteenth centuries'. In: Willibald Steinmetz (ed), *The Force of Comparison: A New Perspective on Modern European History and the Contemporary World*. Oxford: Berghahn Books: 137–63.

Epple, Angelika; Erhart, Walter and Grave, Johannes (eds). 2020. *Practices of Comparing: Towards a New Understanding of Fundamental Human Practice*. Bielefeld: Bielefeld University Press.

Epstein, Charlotte; Lindemann, Thomas and Sending, Ole Jacob. 2018. 'Frustrated sovereigns: the agency that makes the world go around'. *Review of International Studies* 44 (5): 787-804.

Erb, Rainer and Bergmann, Werner. 1989. *Die Nachtseite der Judenemanzipation. Antisemitismus und jüdische Geschichte*. Berlin: Metropol.

Faist, Thomas. 2018. 'The transnationalized social question. Migration and social inequalities'. In: Robert Scott; Stephen Kosslyn and Marlis Buchmann (eds), *Emerging Trends in the Social and Behavioral Sciences*. New York: John Wiley & Sons: 1–15.

Faist, Thomas and Fauser, Margit. 2011. 'The migration-development-nexus: Toward a transnational perspective'. In: Thomas Faist, Margit Fauser and Peter Kivisto (eds), *The Migration–Development Nexus: A Transnational Perspective*. Basingstoke: Palgrave Macmillan: 1–28.

Feize, Leyla and Gonzalez, John. 2018. 'A model of cultural competency in social work as seen through the lens of self-awareness'. *Social Work Education* 37(4): 472–89.

Fereidooni, Karim and El, Meral (eds). 2017. *Rassismuskritik und Widerstandsformen*. Wiesbaden: Springer.

Feres Júnior, Joao. 2009. 'El concepto de América en el mundo atlántico (1750–1850): Perspectivas teóricas y reflexiones sustantivas a partir de una comparación de múltiples casos.' In: Javier Fernandez Sebastian (ed), *Diccionario Político del mundo Iberoamericano*. Madrid: Fundación Carolina: 51–67.

Feres Júnior, Joao. 2017. 'O conceito de civilização: Uma análise transversal'. In: Javier Fernandez Sebastian (ed), *Diccionario politico y social del mundo iberoamericano II. Vol I*. Madrid: Centro de Estudios Políticos y Constitucionales: 85–106.

Fernandez Sebastian, Javier. 2007. 'Iberconceptos. Hacia una historia transnacionales de los conceptos políticos en el mundo iberoamericano'. *Revista de Filosofía Moral y Política* N 37: 165–76.

Fernandez Sebastian, Javier. 2009. 'Hacia una historia atlántica de los conceptos políticos'. In: Javier Fernandez Sebastian (ed), *Diccionario Político del mundo Iberoamericano*. Madrid: Fundación Carolina: 23–46.

Field, Roger. 2010. *Alex La Guma: A Literary & Political Biography*. Abingdon: Currey.

Foucault, Michel. 1991. *Der Wille zum Wissen*. Frankfurt am Main: Suhrkamp.

Frank, Andre G. 1967. *Capitalism and Underdevelopment in Latin America: Historical Studies of Chile and Brazil*. New York: Monthly Review Press.

Frank, Andre G. and Gills, Barry K. 1993. *The World System: Five Hundred Years or Five Thousand?* London: Routledge.

Frankenberg, Günter. 2018. 'Critical histories of comparative law'. In: Markus D. Dubber and Christopher L. Tomlins (eds), *The Oxford Handbook of Legal History*. Oxford: Oxford University Press: 43–62.

Freud, Sigmund. 1953a. 'Three essays on sexuality'. In: James Strachey (ed), *The Standard Edition of The Complete Psychological Works of Sigmund Freud*, Vol. 7. London: Hogarth.

Freud, Sigmund. 1953b. 'Civilization and its discontents'. In: James Strachey (ed), *The Standard Edition of The Complete Psychological Works of Sigmund Freud*, Vol. 21. London: Hogarth.

Freud, Sigmund. 1953c. 'Mourning and melancholia'. In: James Strachey (ed) *The Standard Edition of The Complete Psychological Works of Sigmund Freud*, Vol. 14. London: Hogarth.

Friesenhahn, Günther J. and Thimmel, Andreas. 2012. 'Soziale Arbeit weltweit: Große Erwartungen und gedämpfte Zuversicht. Einschätzungen zur Joint World Conference on Social Work and Social Development 2012 in Stockholm'. *Neue Praxis* 42(5): 511–9.

Fuchs, Ernst. 1970 [1910]. 'Freirechtlerei und soziologische Rechtslehre.' In: Ernst Fuchs, *Gesammelte Schriften über Freirecht und Rechtsreform*. Vol. 1. Aalen: Scientia Verlag: 457–72.

Furtado, Celso. 1973. 'The concept of external dependence in the study of underdevelopment'. In: Kenneth P. Jameson and Charles K. Wilber (eds), *The Political Economy of Development and Underdevelopment*. New York: Random House: 118–23.

Gängel, Andreas and Mollnau, Karl. 1992. 'Stationen der Methodenreformbewegung in Deutschland oder Richterabsolutismus contra Gesetzesabsolutismus.' In: Andreas Gängel and Karl Mollnau (eds), *Gesetzesbindung und Richterfreiheit. Texte zur Methodendebatte 1900–1914*. Freiburg: Haufe: 295–340.

Gauthier, Julie. 2005. 'Les événements de Qamichlo: Irruption de la question kurde en Syrie'. *Etudes Kurdes* 7: 97–114.

Gauvin, Albert. 2009. 'Kostas Alexos et la pensée planétaire. Sur des Oeuvres de Tiers'. Retrieved from: http://www.pileface.com/sollers/spip.php?article1056 [last accessed 30 August 2020].

Gerbi, Antonello. 1955. *La Disputa del Nuevo Mondo, Storia di una Polémica, 1750–1900*. Milano: Ricciardi.

Giebeler, Cornelia. 1998. 'Fremdheitserfahrung statt Fremdverstehen: Ein methodisches Verfahren der Kulturanalyse in der Sozialen Arbeit und Pädagogik. Theoretische und praktische Überlegungen zum professionellen Handeln in sozialer Realität'. *Zeitschrift für internationale erziehungs- und sozialwissenschaftliche Forschung des Deutschen Instituts für internationale pädagogische Forschung* 5(2): 339–57.

Giebeler, Cornelia. 2003. 'Global social work – Pedagogía Social Intercultural. Especialidad para el desarrollo de competencia gloabal e intercultural'. In: Gerardo Chacón and Heintz Neuser (eds), *Pedagogía Social en Latinoamérica. Estrategias en Educación Popular, Desarrollo, e Interculturalidad*. Quito: LAPSO/DAAD: 129-139.

Giebeler, Cornelia. 2008. 'Das Praktikum als Feldforschung in Ländern des Südens'. In: Cornelia Giebeler (ed), *Fallstudien und Fallverstehen. Beiträge zur interdisziplinären rekonstrukten Sozialarbeitsforschung*. Leverkusen: Barbara Budrich Verlag: 169–80.

Giebeler, Cornelia. 2009. '"Interkulturelle" Praxis'. In: Karin Bock and Ingrid Miethe (eds), *Handbuch Qualitative Forschungsmethoden*. Leverkusen: Beltz Juventa: 547–54.

Giebeler, Cornelia. 2019. 'La reflexión de la extrañeza como teoría y metodología de diálogos transculturales: Una propuesta para un camino decolonial'. In: Inés Cornejo and Cornelia Giebeler (eds), *Prójimos! Prácticas de investigación desde la horizontalidad*. Mexico City: UAM Cuajimalpa, División de Ciencias de la Comunicación y Diseño and FH Bielefeld, University of Applied Sciences.

Gill, Graeme. 2015. *Building an Authoritarian Polity. Russia in Post-Soviet Times*. Cambridge: Cambridge University Press.

Girard René. 1979. *Violence and the Sacred*. Baltimore, MD: Johns Hopkins University Press.

Goffman, Erving. 1986. *Frame Analysis: An Essay on the Organization of the Experience*. Boston, MA: Northeast University Press.

Goldhagen, Daniel J. 2013. *The Devil That Never Dies. The Rise and Threat of Global Antisemitism*. New York: Little Brown.

Gómez-Hernández, Esperanza. 2018. 'Das Menschsein des "Anderen" aus Perspektive der interkulturellen und dekolonialen Sozialen Arbeit'. In: Monika Pfaller-Rott, Esperanza Gómez-Hernández and Hilaria Soundari (eds), *Soziale Vielfalt. Internationale Soziale Arbeit aus interkultureller und dekolonialer Perspektive*. Wiesbaden: Springer: 13–23.

Gordley, James. 2006. 'Comparative law and legal history'. In: Mathias Reimann and Reinhard Zimmermann (eds), *The Oxford Handbook of Comparative Law*. Oxford: Oxford University Press: 754–73.

Grab, Walter. 1991. *Der deutsche Weg der Juden-Emanzipation 1879–1938*. München: Pieper.

Gray, Mel and Coates, John. 2011. 'Environmental ethics for social work: Social work's responsibility to the non-human world'. *International Journal of Social Welfare* 21(3): 239–47.

Greve, Jens and Heintz, Bettina. 2005. 'Die "Entdeckung" der Weltgesellschaft. Entstehung und Grenzen der Weltgesellschaftstheorie'. In: Bettina Heintz, Richard Münch and Hartmann Tyrell (eds), *Weltgesellschaft. Theoretische Zugänge und empirische Problemlagen*. Stuttgart: Lucius & Lucius: 89–119.

Groterath, Angelika. 2011. *Soziale Arbeit in internationalen Organisationen: Ein Handbuch zu Karrierewegen in den Vereinten Nationen und NGOs*. Opladen: Barbara Budrich.

Groupe France–Syrie. 2016. 'Entretien avec M. Khaled Issa, Représentant du Rojava en 'rance' (21 June). Retrieved from: https://www.senat.fr/international/groupes_amitie_cr/groupe_france_syrie_entretien_avec_m_khaled_issa_representant_du_rojava_en_france.html [last accessed 30 August 2020].

Groys, Boris. 1999. 'Ernst Jünger's technologies of immortality'. *Jahrbuch für Philosophie des Forschungsinstituts für Philosophie Hannover* 10: 233–42.

Gruzinsky, Serge. 2010. *Las cuatro partes del mundo. Historia de una mundialización*. Mexico City: Fondo de Cultura Económica.

Guadalupe, Victoria. 2010 [1827]. 'Report by Guadalupe Victoria at the opening of the sessions of Congress' (Mexico, 1 January) In: Germán de la Reza (ed), *Documentos del Congreso Anfictiónico de Panamá*. Caracas: Fundación Biblioteca Ayacucho: LX.

Gual, Pedro. 2010 [1821]. 'Instructions from the government of Colombia given to Joaquin Mosquera and Miguel Santamaría for their mission to the States of Peru, Chile, Buenos Aires and Mexico' (Cúcuta, 10 and 11 October). In: Germán de la Reza (ed), *Documentos del Congreso Anfictiónico de Panamá*. Caracas: Fundación Biblioteca Ayacucho: 5–10.

Guarnizo, Luis E. 2017. 'The migration–development nexus and the changing role of transnational immigrant organizations.' *Ethnic and Racial Studies* 40(3): 457–65.

Gudynas, Eduardo. 2011. 'Buen vivir: Germinando alternativas al desarrollo' *América Latina en Movimiento* 462: 1–20.

Gunes, Cengiz. 2013. 'Explaining the PKK's mobilization of the Kurds in Turkey: Hegemony, myth and violence'. *Ethnopolitics* 12(3): 247–67.

Gunes, Cengiz and Lowe, Robert. 2015. 'The impact of the Syrian war on Kurdish politics across the Middle East'. *Chatham House*. Retrieved from: https://www.chathamhouse.org/publication/impact-syrian-war-kurdish-politics-across-middle-east [last accessed 30 August 2020].

Halliday, Fred. 1999. *Revolution and World Politics: The Rise and Fall of the Sixth Great Power*. London: Macmillan.

Halliday, Fred. 2005. *The Middle East in International Relations*. Cambridge: Cambridge University Press.

Halmai, Gábor. 2012. 'The use of foreign law in constitutional interpretation'. In: Michael Rosenfeld and András Sajó (eds), *The Oxford Handbook of Comparative Constitutional Law*. Oxford: Oxford University Press: 1328–48.

Halmai, Gábor. 2017. 'The Hungarian constitutional court and constitutional identity. Retrieved from: https://verfassungsblog.de/the-hungarian-constitutional-court-and-constitutional-identity/ [last accessed 30 August 2020].

Hamnet, Brian. 2013. 'Themes and tensions in a contradictory decade: Ibero-America as a multiplicity of states'. In: Matthew Brown and Gabriel Paquette (eds), *Connections after Colonialism: Europe and Latin America in the 1820s*. Tuscaloosa: University of Alabama Press: 29–45.

Hanssen, Beatrice. 2006. 'Benjamin or Heidegger: Aesthetics and politics in an age of technology'. In: Andrew Benjamin (ed), *Walter Benjamin and Art*. London: Continuum: 73–92.

Hardt, Michael and Negri, Antonio. 2000. *Empire*. Cambridge, MA: Harvard University Press.

Harket, Hakon. 2019. 'Deutschland. In der Gewalt des Denkens'. In: Trond Berg Eriksen, Hakon Harket and Einhart Lorenz (eds), *Judenhass*. Göttingen: Vandenhoeck und Ruprecht: 183–210.

Harrison, Gai. 2006. 'Broadening the conceptual lens on language in social work: Difference, diversity and English as a global language'. *British Journal of Social Work* 36(3): 401–18.

Harvey, David. 2007. 'Neoliberalism as creative destruction'. *The Annals of the American Academy of Political and Social Science* 610(21): 21–44.

Hasse, Raimund and Schmidt, Lucia. 2010. 'Unternehmertum, Arbeit, Sprache. Zur Mikrofundierung des Neo-Institutionalismus'. *Sociologia Internationalis* 48(1): 1–28.

Haukkala, Hiski. 2015. 'From cooperative to contested Europe? The conflict in Ukraine as a culmination of a long-term crisis in EU–Russia relations'. *Journal of Contemporary European Studies* 23(1): 25–40.

Haury, Thomas. 2002. *Antisemitismus von links*. Hamburg: Hamburger Edition.

Healy, Lynn M. and Hall, Nigel. 2009. 'Internationale Organisationen der Sozialen Arbeit'. In: Leonie Wagner and Ronald Lutz (eds), *Internationale Perspektiven Sozialer Arbeit*. Wiesbaden: VS Verlag für Sozialwissenschaften.

Hegel, Georg Wilhelm Friedrich. 1977. *Phenomenology of Spirit*. Oxford: Oxford University Press.

Hegel, Georg Wilhelm Friedrich. 1991. *The Encyclopedia Logic*. Indianapolis, IN: Hackett.

Heidegger, Martin. 1996. *Wegmarken*. Frankfurt am Main: Klostermann.

Heidegger, Martin. 2004. *Zu Ernst Jünger*. Frankfurt am Main: Klostermann.

Heintz, Bettina and Werron, Tobias. 2011. 'Wie ist Globalisierung möglich? Zur Entstehung globaler Vergleichshorizonte am Beispiel von Wissenschaft und Sport'. *Kölner Zeitschrift für Soziologie und Sozialpsychologie* 63(3): 359–94.

Hettling, Manfred; Müller, Michael and Hausmann, Guido. 2013. *Die 'Judenfrage' – ein europäisches Phänomen?* Göttingen: Metropol.

Hevian, Rodi. 2013. 'The resurrection of Syrian Kurdish politics'. *Middle East Review of International Affairs* 17(3): 45–56.

Hitchins, Keith. 2000. 'Kurdish Elites and Nationhood in Anatolia, 1890s–1938'. In: Hamit Bozarslan and Clemence Scalbert-Yucel (eds), *Joyce Blau. L'Eternelle chez les Kurdes*. Bibliothèque (électronique) de l'IFEA: 81–99.

Holz, Klaus. 2000. 'Die Figur des Dritten in der nationalen Ordnung der Welt'. *Soziale Systeme* 6(2): 269–90.

Holz, Klaus. 2001. *Nationaler Antisemitismus*. Hamburg: Hamburger Edition.

Holzer, Boris; Kastner, Fatima and Werron, Tobias. 2015. 'Introduction. From globalization to world society'. In: Boris Holzer, Fatima Kastner and Tobias Werron (eds) *From Globalization to World Society: Neo-Institutional and Systems-Theoretical Perspectives*. London: Routledge: 1–19.

Hortzitz, Nicoline. 1988. *Früh-Antisemitismus in Deutschland (1789–1871/72)*. Tübingen: Niemeyer.

Hundt-Radowsky, Hartwig. 1821. *Judenspiegel*. Ulm: Wagner.

Hutchison, Emma and Bleiker, Roland. 2014. 'Theorizing emotions in world politics'. *International Theory* 6(3): 491–514.

Hutchison, Emma. 2016. *Affective Communities in World Politics: Collective Emotions After Trauma*. Cambridge: Cambridge University Press.

IASSW (International Association of Schools of Social Work). 2018. 'Global social work statement of ethical principles (IASSW)'. Retrieved from: https://www.iassw-aiets.org/wp-content/uploads/2018/04/Global-Social-Work-Statement-of-Ethical-Principles-IASSW-27-April-2018.pdf [last accessed 30 August 2020].

ICG (International Crisis Group). 2014. 'Flight of Icarus? The PYD's Precarious Rise in Syria.'. Retrieved from: https://www.crisisgroup.org/middle-east-north-africa/eastern-mediterranean/syria/flight-icarus-pyd-s-precarious-rise-syria [last accessed 30 August 2020].

IFSW (International Federation of Social Workers). 2014. 'Global Definition of Social Work.' Retrieved from: https://www.ifsw.org/global-definition-of-social-work/ [last accessed 30 August 2020].

Istôczy, Gyozo. 1882. 'Manifest an die Regierungen und Völker der durch das Judenthum gefährdeten christlichen Staaten laut Beschluss des Ersten Internationalen Antijüdischen Kongresses zu Dresden am 11. und 12. September 1882'. Retrieved from http://germanhistorydocs.ghi-dc.org/pdf/deu/417_Manifest_Antijuedischen%20Kongresses_118.pdf [last accessed 30 August 2020].

Ivanov, Igor. 2018. 'Entering 2019: Challenges and opportunities.' *Russian International Affairs Council (RIAC)*. Retrieved from: https://russiancouncil.ru/en/analytics-and-comments/analytics/entering-2019-challenges-and-opportunities/ [last accessed 30 August 2020].

Ivanov, Igor. 2019. 'Geopolitics and relations among major powers'. *Russian International Affairs Council (RIAC)*. Retrieved from: https://russiancouncil.ru/en/analytics-and-comments/analytics/geopolitics-and-relations-among-major-powers/?sphrase_id=33792711 [last accessed 30 August 2020].

Jackson, Vicki C. 2005. 'Constitutional comparisons: convergence, resistance, engagement'. *Harvard Law Review* 119(1): 109–28.

Jacobs, Susie. 2011. 'Globalisation, anti-globalisation and the Jewish "question"'. *European Review of History* 18(1): 45–56.
Jamin, Christophe. 2010. 'Dix-neuf cent: Crise et renouveau dans la culture juridique'. In: Denis Alland and Stéphane Rials (eds), *Dictionnaire de la Culture Juridique*. Paris: Presses Universitaires de France: 380–4.
Jenkins, Rhys. 2013. 'Raul Prebisch'. In: Barry R. J. Jones (ed): *Routledge Encyclopaedia of International Political Economy*. Hoboken: Taylor and Francis: 1264–5.
Jhering, Rudolf v. 1866. *Geist des Römischen Rechts auf den Verschiedenen Stufen Seiner Entwicklung*. Vol. 1. Leipzig: Breitkopf und Härtel.
Jones, David N. (ed). 2018. *Global Agenda for Social Work and Social Development: Third Report. Promoting Community and Environmental Sustainability'*. Rheinfelden: IFSW.
Jünger, Ernst. 1930. 'Die Totale Mobilmachung'. In: Ernst Jünger (ed), *Krieg und Krieger*. Berlin: Junker und Dünnhaupt: 9–30.
Jünger, Ernst. 1948. *The Peace*. Hinsdale, IL: Henry Regnery.
Jünger, Ernst. 2007. *Der Arbeiter: Herrschaft und Gestalt*. Stuttgart: Klett-Cotta.
Kandylaki, Agapi and Kallinikaki, Theano. 2018. 'Critical, anti-oppressive and human rights social work in the "rough pathways" of the Muslim Roma neighbourhoods in Thrace: Towards inclusion in education'. *British Journal of Social Work* 48(6): 1559–75.
Karaganov, Sergei. 2015. 'The 21st-century concert of Vienna'. *Valdai Discussion Club Expert Opinions*. Retrieved from: https://valdaiclub.com/a/highlights/the_21st_century_concert_of_vienna/ [last accessed 30 August 2020].
Karaganov, Sergei and Suslov, Dmitry. 2018. 'A new world order: A view from Russia'. *Russia in global affairs*. Retrieved from: https://eng.globalaffairs.ru/articles/a-new-world-order-a-view-from-russia/ [last accessed 30 August 2020].
Karayılan, Murat. 2014. *Bir Savaşın Anatomisi: Kürdistan'da Askeri Çizgi*. Diyarbakır: Aram.
Katz, Jacob. 1971. 'A state within a state, the history of an antisemitic slogan.' *Israel Academy of Sciences and Humanities Proceedings* 4(3): 29-58.
Katz, Jacob. 1980. *From Prejudice to Destruction. Antisemitism, 1700–1933*. Cambridge, MA: Harvard University Press.
Kay, Cristobal. 1989. *Latin American Theories of Development and Underdevelopment*. London: Routledge.

Kay, Cristobal. 2018. 'Critical development theory: Results and prospects'. In: Henry Veltmeyer and Paul Bowles (eds), *The Essential Guide to Critical Development Studies*. London: Routledge: 71–83.

Kay, Cristobal and Gwynne, Robert N. 2000. 'Relevance of structuralist and dependency theories in the neoliberal period: A Latin American perspective'. *Journal of Developing Societies* 16(1): 49–69.

Kaya, Zeynep and Whiting, Matthew. 2017. 'Sowing division: Kurds in the Syrian war'. *Middle East Policy*, 24(1): 79–91.

Kennedy, Duncan. 2006. 'Three globalizations of law and legal thought: 1850–2000'. In: David Trubek and Alvaro Santos (eds), *The New Law and Economic Development. A Critical Appraisal*. Cambridge: Cambridge University Press: 19–73.

Khoshnaw, Hemin. 2012. 'Interview: FSA Commander: We won't allow formation of federal regions in Syria'. (14 August). Retrieved from: http://www.mesop.de/interview-fsa-commander-we-wont-allow-formation-of-federal-regions-in-syria/ [last accessed 30 August 2020].

Kindleberger, Charles. 1967. *Europe's Postwar Growth. The Role of Labour Supply*. Cambridge, MA: Harvard University Press.

King, Russell and Collyer, Michael. 2016. 'Migration and development framework and its links to integration'. In: Blanca Garces-Mascarenas and Rinus Penninx (eds), *Integration Processes and Policies in Europe. Contexts, Levels and Actors*. Cham: Springer Open: 167–88.

Kirchner, Stefan; Krüger, Anne; Meier, Frank and Meyer, Uli. 2015. 'Wie geht es weiter mit dem soziologischen Neo-Institutionalismus? Eine kritische Auseinandersetzung'. In: Maja Apelt and Uwe Wilkesmann (eds), *Zur Zukunft der Organisationssoziologie*. Wiesbaden: Springer VS: 191–204.

Knorr-Cetina, Karin and Bruegger, Urs. 2002. 'Global microstructures: the virtual societies of financial markets'. *American Journal of Sociology* 107(4): 905–50.

Kohler, Josef. 1886. 'Über die Interpretation von Gesetzen'. *Zeitschrift für das Privat- und Öffentliche Recht der Gegenwart* 13: 1–61.

Kohler, Josef 1905 [1900] 'De la méthode du droit comparé'. In: *Congrès International de Droit Comparé Tenu à Paris du 31 Juillet au 4 Août 1900. Procès-Verbaux des Séances et Documents*. Vol. 1. Paris: Librairie générale de droit et de jurisprudence: 227–37.

König, Mareike and Schulz, Oliver. 2019. *Antisemitismus im 19. Jahrhundert aus internationaler Perspektive*. Göttingen: V&R Press.

Kortunov, Andrey. 2018a. 'Russia and the European Union: Four scenarios for the new cycle'. *Russian International Affairs Council* (RIAC). Retrieved from: https://russiancouncil.ru/en/analytics-and-comments/analytics/europe-and-russia-four-scenarios-for-the-new-cycle/ [last accessed 30 August 2020].

Kortunov, Andrey. 2018b. 'Why the world is not becoming multipolar.' *Russian International Affairs Council* (RIAC). Retrieved from: https://russiancouncil.ru/en/analytics-and-comments/analytics/why-the-world-is-not-becoming-multipolar/ [last accessed 30 August 2020].

Kortunov, Andrey. 2019a. 'An unforeseeable Europe'. *Russia in Global Affairs*. Retrieved from: https://eng.globalaffairs.ru/articles/an-unforeseeable-europe/ [last accessed 30 August 2020].

Kortunov, Andrey. 2019b. 'Russia is winning, but here is the catch.' *Russian International Affairs Council* (RIAC). Retrieved from: https://russiancouncil.ru/en/analytics-and-comments/analytics/russia-is-winning-but-here-s-the-catch/ [last accessed 30 August 2020].

Krastev, Ivan and Leonard, Mark. 2014. *The New European Disorder*. London: European Council on Foreign Relations.

Kremlin. 2013. 'Meeting of Valdai international discussion club'. Retrieved from http://en.kremlin.ru/events/president/news/19243 [last accessed 30 August 2020].

Kremlin. 2016. 'Meeting of Valdai international discussion club. Retrieved from: http://en.kremlin.ru/events/president/news/53151 [last accessed 30 August 2020].

Kremlin. 2017. 'St Petersburg international economic forum plenary meeting'. Retrieved from http://en.kremlin.ru/events/president/news/54667 [last accessed 30 August 2020].

Kremlin. 2018. 'World Russian people's council'. Retrieved from: http://en.kremlin.ru/events/president/news/59013 [last accessed 30 August 2020].

Kremlin. 2019a. 'Monument to Yevgeny Primakov unveiled in Moscow'. Retrieved from: http://en.kremlin.ru/events/president/news/61929 [last accessed 30 August 2020].

Kremlin. 2019b. 'Vladimir Putin (Interests)'. Retrieved from: http://en.putin.kremlin.ru/interests/page-2 [last accessed 30 August 2020].

Küçük, Bülentl and Özselçuk, Ceren. 2016. 'The Rojava experience: Possibilities and challenges of building a democratic life'. *South Atlantic Quarterly*, 115(1): 184–96.

La Guma, Alex. 1978. *A Soviet Journey*. Moscow: Progress Publishers.

Lacan, Jacques. 2006. 'The signification of the phallus'. In: Jacques Lacan, *Écrits*. New York: Norton: 575–84.

Laclau, Ernesto. 2000. 'Identity and hegemony: The role of universality in the constitution of political logics'. In: Judith Butler, Ernesto Laclau and Slavoj Žižek (eds), *Contingency, Hegemony, Universality: Contemporary Dialogues on the Left*. London: Verso: 44–89.

Lagarde, Paul de. 1920 [1881]. *Gesamtausgabe letzter Hand*. Göttingen: Nabu Press.

Lakoff, George. 2006. 'Simple framing. An introduction to framing and its uses in politics' (February 14). *Rockridge Institute*. Retrieved from: http://archives.evergreen.edu/webpages/curricular/2006-2007/languageofpolitics/files/languageofpolitics/Simple%20Framing%20Rockridge%20Institute.pdf [last accessed 30 August 2020].

Lakoff, George and Johnson, Mark. 1980. *Metaphors We Live By*. Chicago, IL: University of Chicago Press.

Lambert, Edouard. 1900. 'Une réforme nécessaire des études de droit civil.' *Revue Internationale de l'Enseignement* 40: 216–43.

Lambert, Edouard. 1905 [1900]. 'Conception générale et définition de la science du droit comparé, sa méthode, son histoire; Le droit comparé et l'enseignement du droit.' In: *Congrès International de Droit Comparé Tenu à Paris du 31 Juillet au 4 Août 1900. Procès-Verbaux des Séances et Documents*. Vol. 1. Paris: Librairie générale de droit et de jurisprudence: 26–60.

Lange, Matthew. 2011. 'Goldene Internationale'. In: Wolfgang Benz (ed), *Handbuch des Antisemitismus*. Bd. 3. Berlin: de Gruyter: 111–2.

Lavrov, Sergey. 2014. 'Foreign Minister of the Russian Federation Sergey Lavrov's interview with TV Channel France 24', (16 December). *Ministry of Foreign Affairs of the Russian Federation*. Retrieved from https://www.mid.ru/en/posledniye_dobavlnenniye/-/asset_publisher/MCZ7HQuMdqBY/content/id/848819 [last accessed 30 August 2020].

Lavrov, Sergey. 2018a. 'Acting Foreign Minister Sergey Lavrov's interview with the journal Russian Business Guide – Italian-Russian Chamber of Commerce' (May 18). *Ministry of Foreign Affairs of the Russian Federation*. Retrieved from: https://www.mid.ru/en/press_service/minister_speeches/-/asset_publisher/7OvQR5KJWVmR/content/id/3228219 [last accessed 30 August 2020].

Lavrov, Sergey. 2018b. 'It is not Russia that is shaping this world, it is history'. *Russia in Global Affairs*. Retrieved from: https://eng.globalaffairs.ru/arti

cles/it-is-not-russia-that-is-shaping-this-world-order-it-is-history/ [last accessed 30 August 2020].
Lavrov, Sergey. 2018c. 'Russia's foreign policy in a historical perspective: Musings at a new stage of international development'. *Russia in Global Affairs*. Retrieved from: https://eng.globalaffairs.ru/articles/russias-foreign-policy-in-a-historical-perspective-2/ [last accessed 30 August 2020].
Law, John. 2011. 'What's wrong with a one-world world'. *Heterogeneities*. Retrieved from: http://www.heterogeneities.net/publications/Law2011Whats WrongWithAOneWorldWorld.pdf [last accessed 30 August 2020].
Lawson, George. 2016. 'Within and beyond the 'fourth generation' of revolutionary theory'. *Sociological Theory* 34(2): 106–27.
Lawson, George. 2019. *Anatomies of Revolution*. Cambridge: Cambridge University Press.
Leal, Carole. 2010. 'El concepto de orden en tiempos de transición: Venezuela (1770–1850)'. *Bulletin de l'Institut français d'Études Andines* 39(10): 37–61.
Leal, Carole. 2017. 'El concepto orden en Iberoamérica. El orden entre dos voluntades: divina y humana'. In: Javier Sebastian Fernandez (ed), *Diccionario Politico y Social del Mundo Iberoamericano II*. Vol VI. Madrid: Centro de Estudios Políticos y Constitucionales: 15–51.
Lentin, Alana. 2004. *Racism and Anti-Racism in Europe*. London: Pluto Press.
Lentin, Alana. 2019. 'White supremacy, white innocence and inequality in Australia'. *AlanaLentin.Net*. Retrieved from: http://www.alanalentin.net/2019/03/22/white-supremacy-white-innocence-and-inequality-in-australia-2/ [last accessed 30 August 2020].
Levy, Richard S. 1975. *The Downfall of the Antisemitic Political Parties in Imperial Germany*. New Haven, CT: Yale University Press.
Lo, Bobo. 2018. 'Going Legit? The foreign policy of Vladimir Putin: Putin's foreign policy will remain grounded in long-standing assumptions about Russia, the West, and international order'. *Lowy Institute for International Policy*. Retrieved from: https://www.lowyinstitute.org/publications/going-legit-foreign-policy-vladimir-putin [last accessed 30 August 2020].
Luhmann, Niklas. 1987. 'The evolutionary differentiation between society and interaction.' In: Jeffrey Alexander, Richard Münch, Bernhard Giesen and Neil Smelser (eds). *The Micro-Macro Link*. Berkeley: University of California Press: 112–31.
Luhmann, Niklas. 1991 [1971]. 'Die Weltgesellschaft'. In: Niklas Luhmann: *Soziologische Aufklärung 2. Aufsätze zur Theorie der Gesellschaft*. Opladen: VS Verlag für Sozialwissenschaften: 51–71.

Lukyanov, Fyodor. 2014a. 'Russia and the European Union: A rethinking'. *Russian International Affairs Council (RIAC)*. Retrieved from: https://russiancouncil.ru/en/analytics-and-comments/comments/russia-and-the-european-union-a-rethinking/ [last accessed 30 August 2020].

Lukyanov, Fyodor. 2014b. 'What the world needs is "19th century behavior"'. *Russia in Global Affairs*. Retrieved from: https://eng.globalaffairs.ru/articles/what-the-world-needs-is-19th-century-behavior [last accessed 30 August 2020].

Lutz, Helma. 2007. *Vom Weltmarkt in den Privathaushalt: Die neuen Dienstmädchen im Privathaushalt*. Leverkusen: Barbara Budrich.

Lutz, Ronald. 2018. 'Eine Geschichte der Sozialen Arbeit als grenzüberschreitendes Projekt'. In: Gunther Graßhoff, Anna Renker and Wolfgang Schröer (eds), *Soziale Arbeit. Eine elementare Einführung*. Wiesbaden: Springer: 287–99.

Lynch, John. 1986. *The Spanish American Revolutions 1808–1826*. New York: Norton.

Lyons, Karen. 2016. *International Social Work: Themes and Perspectives*. London. Routledge.

Mafile'o, Tracie and Vakalahi, Halaevalu F Ofahengaue. 2018. 'Indigenous social work across borders: Expanding social work in the South Pacific'. *International Social Work* 61(4): 537–52.

Malette, Michel. 2014. *Kostas Axelos et le jeu du monde: Le destin planétaire en question*. Montreal: Nota bene.

Malinova, Olga. 2012. 'Simvolicheskaya politika: kontury problemnogo polya', In: Malinova Olga (ed): *Simvolicheskaya politika*. Moscow: Institute of Scientific Information on Social Sciences of the Russian Academy of Sciences: 5–16.

Mann, Michael. 1997. 'Has globalization ended the rise and rise of the nation-state?' *Review of International Political Economy* 4(3): 472–96.

Marini, Ruy M. 1973. *Dialectica de la dependencia*. Mexico City: Ediciones Era.

Markesinis, Basil and Fedtke, Jorg. 2006. 'The judge as comparatist'. *Tulane Law Review* 80(1): 11–168.

Martin, Philip L. 2016. 'Migration, trade and remittances: low- and high-skilled workers'. *Remittances Review* 1(1): 37-52.

Marx, Karl. 1975. 'The difference between the democritean and epicurean philosophy of nature'. In: Karl Marx and Friedrich Engels, *Collected Works*. Vol. 1. New York: International Publishers.

Marx, Karl. 1976. 'Theses on Feuerbach'. In: *Karl Marx and Friedrich Engels, Collected Works*. Vol. 5. New York: International Publishers.

Marx, Karl. 2000. *Selected Writings: Revised Edition*. Oxford: Oxford University Press.

Marx, Karl. 2008 [1852]. *The Eighteenth Brumaire of Louis Bonaparte*. New York: Cosimo.

Massey, Douglas S.; Arango, Joaquin; Hugo, Graeme; Kouaouci, Ali; Pellegrino, Adela and Taylor, Edward, J. 1998. *Worlds in Motion. Understanding International Migration at the End of the Millennium*. Oxford: Clarendon Press.

Massing, Paul. 1949. *Rehearsal for Destruction: A Study of Political Antisemitism in Imperial Germany*. New York: Harper.

Mayall, James. 1990. *Nationalism and International Society*. Cambridge: Cambridge University Press.

Mbembe, Achille. 2016. *Politiques de l'inimitié*. Paris: La Découverte.

Mbembe, Achille. 2020a. 'Reflections on planetary living'. *Ruhrtriennale*. Retrieved from: https://www.ruhrtriennale.de/en/agenda/262/ACHILLE_M BEMBE/Reflections_On_Planetary_Living [last accessed 30 August 2020].

Mbembe, Achille. 2020b. 'Die Leben wägen' (5 August). *Süddeutsche Zeitung*: 9.

McDowall, David. 1996. *A Modern History of the Kurds*. London: I.B.Tauris.

McKay, Ben; Nehring, Ryan and Walsh-Dilley, Marygold. 2014. 'The "state" of food sovereignty in Latin America: Political projects and alternative pathways in Venezuela, Ecuador and Bolivia'. *The Journal of Peasant Studies* 41(6): 1175–200.

Melo Ferreira, Fátima de Sá e. 2009. 'Entre viejos y nuevos sentidos:"Pueblo" y "Pueblos" en el mundo Iberoamericano entre 1750 y 1850'. In: Javier Sebastian Fernandez (ed), *Diccionario Político del Mundo Iberoamericano*. Madrid: Fundación Carolina: 1117–38.

Mezhuev Boris. 2012. 'Danilevskii: zabytyi genii Russkoi filosofii' [Danilevsky: Forgotten Genius of Russian Philosophy.] Forum discussion 'Chto Delat?' [What to do?]. Retrieved from: https://tvkultura.ru/video/show/brand_id/ 20917/episode_id/181279/video_id/181279/ [last accessed 30 August 2020].

MFARF (Ministry of Foreign Affairs of the Russian Federation). 2016. 'Foreign Policy of the Russian Federation (approved by President of the Russian Federation Vladimir Putin' (30 November). Retrieved from: https://www.mid.ru/en/foreign_policy/official_documents/-/asset _publisher/CptICkB6BZ29/content/id/2542248 [last accessed 30 August 2020].

Midgley, James. 2016. 'Promoting reciprocal international social work exchanges: Professional imperialism revisited'. In: Mel Grey, John Coates and Michale Yellow Birds (eds), *Indigenous Social Work around the World*. London: Routledge: 59–74.

Monteagudo, Bernardo de. 1825. *Ensayo sobre la necesidad de una federación jeneral entre los estados hispano-americanas: y plan de su organización*. Lima: Imprenta del Estado por J. Gonzales.

Monteagudo, Bernardo de and Mosquera, Joaquín. 2010 [1822], 'Treaty of union, league and perpetual confederation between the Republic of Colombia and the State of Peru' (Lima, 6 July). In: Germán de la Reza (ed), *Documentos del Congreso Anfictiónico de Panamá*. Caracas: Fundación Biblioteca Ayacucho: 11–4.

Moustakas, Clark and Moustakas, Kerry. 2004. *Loneliness, Creativity and Love: Awakening Meanings in Life*. Philadelphia, PA: Xlibris.

Moyn, Samuel and Sartori, Andrew. 2013. 'Approaches to global intellectual history'. In: Samuel Moyn and Andrew Sartori (eds), *Global Intellectual History*. New York: Columbia University Press: 3–30.

Muy, Sebastian. 2018. 'Über Widersprüche Sozialer Arbeit in Sammelunterkünften für Asylsuchende'. In: Johannes Stehr; Roland Anhorn and Kerstin Rathgeb (eds), *Konflikt als Verhältnis – Konflikt als Verhalten – Konflikt als Widerstand. Widersprüche der Gestaltung Sozialer Arbeit zwischen Alltag und Institution*. Wiesbaden: Springer: 155–67.

Nagy, Andrea; Klein, Alex and Schmid, Christine. 2019. 'International kooperative Studiengänge als Beitrag zur notwendigen Internationalisierung innerhalb der Sozialen Arbeit'. *Soziales_kapital* 21: 22–30.

Nehru, Jawaharlal. 1994. *The Discovery of India*. New Delhi: Oxford University Press.

Neuser, Heinz; Chacón, Gerardo, (Eds). 2003. *Pédagogía Social en Latinoamérica: Estrategias en educadión popular, desarrollo e interculturalidad*. Quito/Bonn: DAAD.

Nyberg-Sørensen, Nina. 2012. 'Revisiting the migration–development nexus: from social networks and remittances to markets for migration control.' *International Migration* 50(3): 61–76.

Nyberg-Sørensen, Nina; Van Hear, Niklas and Engberg-Pedersen, Poul. 2002. 'The migration–development nexus: Evidence and policy options'. *International Migration* 40(5): 49–73.

Obregón, Liliana. 2006. 'Between civilization and barbarism: Creole interventions in international law'. *Third World Quarterly*, 27(5), 815–32.

Öcalan, Abdullah (n.d.) *Nasıl Savaşmalı* (Vols. 1 & 2). (Place of publication unknown): Bilim ve Aydinlanma Yayinlari.
Öcalan, Abdullah. 1995. *Nasıl Yaşamalı* (Vols. 1 & 2). (Place of publicaion unknown): Weşanên Serxwebûn.
Öcalan, Abdullah. 2003. *Özgür İnsan Savunması*. Cologne: Mezopotamya Yayınları.
Öcalan, Abdullah. 2013a. *Demokratik Uygarlık Manifestosu (Vol. 3): Özgürlük Sosyolojisi Üzerine Deneme*. Neuss: Mezopotamya Yayınları.
Öcalan, Abdullah 2013b *Demokratik Uygarlık Manifestosu (Vol. 5): Kürt Sorunu ve Demokratik Ulus Çözümü*. Neuss: Mezopotamya Yayınları.
OECD (Organisation for Economic Co-operation and Development). 1978. *Migration, Growth and Development*. Paris: OECD.
OECD (Organisation for Economic Co-operation and Development). 2006. *International Migration Outlook*. Paris: OECD.
Oteíza, Enrique. 1971. 'Emigración de profesionales, técnicos y obreros calificados argentinos a los Estados Unidos'. *Desarrollo Económico* 10: 429–454.
Özkirimli, Umut. 2010. *Theories of Nationalism*. Basingstoke: Palgrave.
Özoğlu, Hakan. 2001. '"Nationalism" and Kurdish notables in the late Ottoman – early Republican era'. *International Journal of Middle East Studies* 33(3): 383–409.
Paasch, Carl. 1892. *Eine jüdischdeutsche Gesandtschaft und ihre Helfer. Geheimes Judenthum, Nebenregierungen und jüdische Weltherrschaft*. Leipzig: C. Minde.
Paasche, Till F. 2015. 'Syrian and Iraqi Kurds: Conflict and cooperation'. *Middle East Policy* 22(1): 77–88.
Pando, Jose María. 2010 [1826], 'Third instructions from the Council of Governments of Peru to its delegates' (Lima, 25 May). In: Germán de la Reza (ed), *Documentos del Congreso Anfictiónico de Panamá*. Caracas: Fundación Biblioteca Ayacucho: 62–73.
Paulus, Heinrich Eberhard Gottlob. 1831. *Die Jüdische Nationalabsonderung nach Ursprung, Folgen und Besserungsmitteln*. Heidelberg: C. F. Winter.
Pawar, Manohar. 2017. 'Reflective learning and teaching in social work field education in international contexts'. *British Journal of Social Work* 47(1): 198–218.
Perez Caldentey, Eesteban. 2016. 'A time to reflect on opportunities for debate and dialogue between (neo)structuralism and heterodox schools of thought'. In: Alicia Barcena and Antonio Prado (eds), *Neostructuralism and Heterodox Thinking in Latin America and the Caribbean in the Early Twenty-First*

Century. Santiago de Chile: Economic Commission for Latin America and the Caribbean (ECLAC): 31–83.

Perju, Vlad. 2012. 'Constitutional transplants, borrowing, and migrations'. In: Michael Rosenfeld and András Sajó (eds), *The Oxford Handbook of Comparative Constitutional Law*. Oxford: Oxford University Press: 1304–27.

Petersen, Mark and Schultz, Carsten-Andreas. 2018. 'Setting the regional agenda: A critique of post-hegemonic regionalism'. *Latin American Politics and Society*, 60(1), 102–7.

Petras, James F. and Veltmeyer, Henry. 2011. *Social Movements in Latin America. Neoliberalism and Popular Resistance*. New York: Palgrave Macmillan.

Pfahl-Traughber, Armin. 2002. *Antisemitismus in der deutschen Geschichte*. Opladen: Leske + Budrich.

Piper, Ernst. 2005. *Alfred Rosenberg, Hitlers Chefideologe*. München: Karl Blessing.

Podbrey, Pauline. 1993. *White Girl in Search of the Party*. Pietermaritzburg: Hadeda Books.

Polanyi, Karl. 1973 [1944]. *The Great Transformation: Politische und Ökonomische Ursprünge von Gesellschaften und Wirtschaftssystemen*. Frankfurt am Main: Suhrkamp.

Pombo, Miguel de. 2010 [1811] 'Discurso sobre los principios y ventajas del Sistema federativo'. In: Carlos Valderrama (ed), *La propuesta federal. Biblioteca Centenario*. Vol 4. Bogotá: Universidad Nacional de Colombia: 19–60.

Portes, Alejandro. 1978. 'Migration and underdevelopment'. *Politics & Society* 8(1): 1-4.

Poslanie Prezidenta. 2005. 'Poslanie Prezidenta RF Federal'nomu Sobraniyu' (25 April). *Consultant Plus*. Retrieved from: http://www.consultant.ru/document/cons_doc_LAW_53088/#dst0 [last accessed 30 August 2020].

Poslanie Prezidenta. 2018. 'Poslanie Prezidenta RF Federal'nomu Sobraniyu' (01 March) *Consultant Plus*. Retrieved from: http://www.consultant.ru/document/cons_doc_LAW_291976/#dst0 [last accessed 30 August 2020].

Posner, Richard A. 2005. 'The Supreme Court, 2004 Term'. *Harvard Law Review* 119: 28–102.

Powell, Walter and Colyvas, Jeannette. 2008. 'Microfoundations of institutional theory'. In: Royston Greenwood, Christine Oliver, Kerstin Sahlin and Roy Suddaby (eds), *The Sage Handbook of Organizational Institutionalism*. Thousand Oaks, CA: Sage: 276–98.

Prasad, Nivedita. 2019. 'Menschenrechtsbasierte Theorie und Praxis Sozialer Arbeit. Menschenrechte als Orientierungshilfe bei Mandatskonflikten'. *BdW Blätter der Wohlfahrtspflege* 166(2): 51–3.

Prashad, Vijay. 2007. *The Darker Nations: A People's History of the Third World*. New York: The New Press.

Prebisch, Raul. 1950. 'The economic development of Latin America and its principal problems'. *United Nations Department of Economic Affairs*. Retrieved from: https://repositorio.cepal.org//bitstream/11362/29973/1/002_en.pdf. [last accessed 30 August 2020].

Pries, Ludger. 2002. 'Transnationalisierung der Sozialen Welt?' *Berliner Journal für Soziologie* 12(2), 263–72.

Primakov, Yevgeny. 1996. 'Mejdunarodnie otnosheniya nakanune XXI veka: Problemi, perspektivi' [International relations at the turn of XXI century: problems, perspectives]. *Mejdunarodnaya jizn*10: 3–13.

Pryke, Sam. 2009. *Nationalism in a Global World*. Basingstoke: Palgrave.

Pulzer, Peter. 2004. *Die Entstehung des politischen Antisemitismus in Deutschland und Österreich 1867–1914*. Göttingen: V&R.

Purschewitz, Anne. 2013. 'Von der „bürgerlichen Verbesserung" zur „Judenfrage". Die Formierung eines Begriffs zwischen 1781 und 1843'. In: Manfred Hettling, Michael Müller and Guido Hausmann, (eds), *Die „Judenfrage" – ein europäisches Phänomen?* Göttingen: Metropol: 23–53.

Putin, Vladimir. 2007. 'Speech at the Munich Conference on Security Policy' (10 February). Retrieved from: http://en.kremlin.ru/events/president/transcripts/24034 [last accessed 30 August 2020].

Putin, Vladimir 2010. 'Von Lissabon bis Wladiwostok'. *Süddeutsche Zeitung*. Retrieved from https://www.sueddeutsche.de/wirtschaft/putin-plaedoyer-fuer-wirtschaftsgemeinschaft-von-lissabon-bis-wladiwostok-1.1027908 [last accessed 30 August 2020].

Putin, Vladimir. 2014. 'Address by President of the Russian Federation' (18 March). Retrieved from: http://en.kremlin.ru/events/president/news/20603 [last accessed 30 August 2020].

Quijano, Anibal and Wallerstein, Inmanuel. 1992. 'La americanidad como concepto o América en el moderno sistema mundial'. *Revista Internacional de Ciencias Sociales* 134, 583–92.

Rabinovici, David; Speck, Ulrich and Sznaider, Nathan (eds). 2005. *Neuer Antisemitismus? Eine globale Debatte*. Frankfurt am Main: Suhrkamp.

Rehklau, Christine and Lutz, Ronald. 2009. 'Partnerschaft oder Kolonisation? Thesen zum Verhältnis des Nordens zur Sozialarbeit des Südens'. In:

Leonie Wagner and Ronald Lutz (eds), *Internationale Perspektiven Sozialer Arbeit. Dimensionen – Themen – Organisationen*. Wiesbaden: VS Verlag für Sozialwissenschaften: 33–53.

Revenga, José. 2010 [1825]. 'General instructions of the Secretary of Foreign Affairs of Colombia to its delegates'. (Bogotá, 22 September). In: Germán de la Reza (ed), *Documentos del Congreso Anfictiónico de Panamá*. Caracas: Fundación Biblioteca Ayacucho: 74–9.

Reza, Germán de la (ed). 2010. *Documentos del Congreso Anfictiónico de Panamá*. Caracas: Fundación Biblioteca Ayacucho.

Richter, Dirk. 1996. *Nation als Form*. Opladen: Westdeutscher Verlag.

Riesman, David; Glazer, Nathan and Denney, Reuel. 2001. *The Lonely Crowd: A Study of the Changing American Character*. New Haven, CT: Yale University Press.

Robertson, Roland. 1998. 'Glokalisierung: Homogenität und Heterogenität in Raum und Zeit'. In: Ulrich Beck (ed), *Perspektiven der Weltgesellschaft*. Frankfurt am Main: Suhrkamp: 192–220.

Robertson, Roland. 2009. 'Differentiational reductionism and the missing link in Albert's approach to globalization theory.' *International Political Sociology* 3(1): 119–22.

Roldán Vera, Eugenia. 2017 [1831]. 'El orden en México/ Nueva España' (27 February). In: Javier Sebastian Fernandez (ed) *Diccionario político y social del mundo iberoamericano II*. Vol IV. Madrid: Centro de Estudios Políticos y Constitucionales: 159–72.

Rosenberg, Alfred. 1924. 'Jüdische Weltpolitik'. *Der Weltkampf* 1: 1–17.

Rosenberg, Justin. 2006. 'Why is there no international historical sociology?' *European Journal of International Relations* 12(3): 307–40.

Roudometof, Victor. 2015. 'Theorizing glocalization: Three interpretations'. *European Journal of Social Theory* 19(3), 391–408.

Rürup, Reinhard. 1975. *Emanzipation oder Antisemitismus*. Göttingen: V&R.

Saed. 2017. 'From the October Revolution to revolutionary Rojava: An ecosocialist reading.' *Capitalism, Nature, Socialism* 28(4): 3–20.

Sahni, Bhisham. 2015. *Today's Pasts: A Memoir*. London: Penguin.

Said, Edward. 1978. *Orientalism*. New York, NY: Pantheon.

Sakwa, Richard. 2015. 'The death of Europe? Continental fates after Ukraine'. *International Affairs* 91(3): 553–79.

Saleilles, Raymond. 1905 [1900]. 'Conception et objet de la science du droit comparé'. In: *Congrès International de Droit Comparé Tenu à Paris du 31 Juillet au 4 Août 1900. Procès-Verbaux des Séances et Documents.* Vol. 1. Paris: Librairie générale de droit et de jurisprudence: 167–89.

Salin, Pavel. 2011. 'Russia and Asia, or Russia within Asia? Prospects for Russian policy in the Asia-Pacific Region'. *Russia in Global Affairs*. Retrieved from: https://eng.globalaffairs.ru/articles/russia-and-asia-or-russia-within-asia/ [last accessed 30 August 2020].

Sałustowicz, Piotr. 2009. 'Internationale Soziale Arbeit zwischen Kolonialisierung, Ethnisierung und Transnationalisierung'. In: Leonie Wagner and Ronald Lutz (eds), *Internationale Perspektiven Sozialer Arbeit*. Wiesbaden: VS Verlag für Sozialwissenschaften: 55–72.

Salzborn, Samuel. 2012. 'Weltanschauung und Leidenschaft. Überlegungen zu einer integrativen Theorie des Antisemitismus'. *Zeitschrift für Politische Theorie* 3(2) 187–203.

Salzborn, Samuel. 2020. *Globaler Antisemitismus. Eine Spurensuche in den Abgründen der Moderne*. Weinheim: Beltz Juventa.

Samokhvalov, Vsevolod. 2017. *Russian–European Relations in the Balkans and Black Sea Region. Great Power Identity and the Idea of Europe*. London: Palgrave.

Sandwith, Corinne. 2013. '"Yours for socialism": communist cultural discourse in early apartheid South Africa'. *Safundi* 14(3): 283–306.

Sassen, Saskia. 2001. *The Global City: New York, London, Tokyo*. Princeton, NJ: Princeton University Press.

Sassen, Saskia. 2007. *A Sociology of Globalization*. New York: Norton.

Sauer, Stefanie and Wießmeier, Brigitte. 2016. 'Verlauf von Auslandsadoptionen – die Entwicklung von sicheren Eltern–Kind-beziehungen in Adoptivfamilien mit einem im Ausland adoptierten Kind'. *Institut für Innovation und Beratung an der Evangelischen Hochschule Berlin e. V.* Retrieved from: https://www.inib-berlin.de/images/doc/Auslandsadoption_Sauer.pdf [last accessed 30 August 2020].

Schelsky, Helmut. 1980 [1972]. 'Das Jhering-Modell des sozialen Wandels durch Recht. Ein Wissenschaftsgeschichtlicher Beitrag'. In: Helmut Schelsky, *Die Soziologen und das Recht. Abhandlungen und Vorträge zur Soziologie von Recht, Institution und Planung*. Wiesbaden: VS Verlag für Sozialwissenschaften: 147–86.

Schirilla, Nausikaa. 2018. 'Transnationale Perspektiven auf Soziale Arbeit'. In: Beate Blank; Süleyman Gögercin; Karin Elinor Sauer and Barbara Schramkowski (eds), *Soziale Arbeit in der Migrationsgesellschaft. Grundlagen – Konzepte – Handlungsfelder*. Wiesbaden: Springer: 199–208.

Schmitt, Carl. 1997. *Land and Sea*. Corvallis, OR: Plutarch Press.
Schmitt, Carl. 1999. 'The way to the total state'. In: Carl Schmitt, *Four Articles 1931-1938*. Corvallis, OR: Plutarch Press: 1–18.
Schmitt, Carl. 2003. *The Nomos of the Earth in the International Law of the Jus Publicum Europaeum*. New York: Telos.
Schröder, Jan. 1985. *Gesetzesauslegung und Gesetzesumgehung. Das Umgehungsgeschäft in der Rechtswissenschaftlichen Doktrin von der Spätaufklärung bis zum Nationalsozialismus*. Paderborn: Ferdinand Schöningh.
Schröer, Wolfgang and Schweppe, Cornelia. 2013. 'Die Transnationalität sozialer Dienstleistungen. Die Herstellung von Handlungsfähigkeit (Agency) als Grenzarbeit in transnationalen Alltagswelten'. In: Gunther Graßhoff (ed), *Adressaten, Nutzer, Agency. Akteursbezogene Forschungsperspektiven in der Sozialen Arbeit*. Wiesbaden: Springer: 243–53.
Schulin, Ernst. 1999. 'Doppel-Nationalität?' In: Peter Alter, Claus-Ekkehard Bärsch and Peter Berghoff (eds), *Die Konstruktion der Nation gegen die Juden*. München: Fink: 243–59.
Schulz, Johann Heinrich. 1784. *Philosophische Betrachtungen über Theologie und Religion überhaupt und über die jüdische Besonderheit*. Frankfurt and Leipzig [no publisher given].
Secretary-General. 2006. 'International migration and development (No. 60/871)'. *United Nation General Assembly*. Retrieved from: https://www.refworld.org/docid/44ca2d934.html [last accessed 30 August 2020].
SENPLADES (Secretaría Nacional de Planificación y Desarrollo) 2010. *National Plan for Good Living 2009-2013*. Quito: SENPLADES.
Shevtsova, Lilia. 2010. *Lonely Power: Why Russia Has Failed to Become the West and the West is Weary of Russia*. Washington, DC: Carnegie Endowment for International Peace.
Singh, Ram. 1991. 'Loneliness: Dynamics, dimensions and many faces'. *International Review of Modern Sociology*, 21(1): 109–20.
Skocpol, Theda. 1979. *States and Social Revolutions: A Comparative Analysis of France Russia and China*. Cambridge: Cambridge University Press.
Slaughter, Anne-Marie. 2004. *A New World Order*. Princeton, NJ: Princeton University Press.
Solovyov, Vladimir. 2018. 'The world order 2018. The Russian side of the story'. Film by Vladimir Solovyov. Retrieved from https://www.youtube.com/watch?v=gcWoVnYDa84; (accessed 8 May 2020; no longer available as of 10 September 2020).

Spitzer, Helmut. 2019. 'Globale Herausforderungen und internationale Soziale Arbeit'. *soziales_kapital* 21(0): 42–58.
Spivak, Gayatri Chakravorty. 1999. *Imperative zur Neuerfindung des Planeten: Imperatives to Re-Imagine the Planet*. Vienna: Passagen.
Spivak, Gayatri Chakravorty. 2005. *Death of a Discipline*. New York: Columbia University Press.
Spyer, Jonathan. 2013. 'Fragmented Syria: The balance of forces as of late 2013'. *Middle East Review of International Affairs (Online)* 17(3). Retrieved from: https://www.questia.com/library/journal/1P3-3214952101/fragmented-syria-the-balance-of-forces-as-of-late [last accessed 30 August 2020].
Stanchev, Petar. 2015. 'From Chiapas to Rojava: Seas divide us, autonomy binds us.' *Roar*. Retrieved from https://roarmag.org/essays/chiapas-rojava-zapatista-kurds/ [last accessed 10 September 2020].
Staub-Bernasconi, Silvia. 2003. 'Soziale Arbeit auf dem Weg zur Weltgesellschaft. Implikationen für die Sozialarbeitswissenschaft'. (Talk delivered at the 'Fachtagung der Hochschule für Soziale Arbeit Zürich', 30 Oct-01 Nov). Retrieved from: https://docplayer.org/29589339-Soziale-arbeit-auf-dem-weg-zur-weltgesellschaft-implikationen-fuer-die-sozialarbeitswissenschaft.html [last accessed 30 August 2020].
Staub-Bernasconi, Silvia. 2007. 'Vom beruflichen Doppelmandat zum professionellen Triplemandat. Wissenschaft und Menschenrechte als Begründungsbasis der Profession Soziale Arbeit'. *Schwerpunkt* S02(07): 8–18.
Staub-Bernasconi, Silvia. 2008. 'Menschenrechte in ihrer Relevanz für die soziale Arbeit als Theorie und Praxis. Oder: Was haben Menschenrechte überhaupt in der Sozialen Arbeit zu suchen?' *Widersprüche* 107: 9–32.
Steinmetz, Willibald. 2005. 'Introduction: towards a comparative history of legal cultures, 1750-1950.' In: Willibald Steinmetz (ed), *Private Law and Social Inequality in the Industrial Age. Comparing Legal Cultures in Britain, France, Germany and the United States*. Oxford: Oxford University Press: 1–41.
Stêrk, Zilar. 2018. 'The feminization of Kurdish politics: A guerrilla's sociological analysis' (November 16). *Komun Academy*. Retrieved from https://komun-academy.com/2018/11/16/the-feminization-of-kurdish-politics-a-guerrillas-sociological-analysis/ [last accessed 30 August 2020].
Sterling, Eleonore. 1969. *Judenhass. Die Anfänge des politischen Antisemitismus*. Frankfurt am Main: Europäische Verlagsanstalt.
Stichweh, Rudolf. 2000. *Die Weltgesellschaft*. Frankfurt am Main: Suhrkamp.

Stichweh, Rudolf. 2019. 'World society'. In: Ludger Kühnhardt and Tilman Mayer (eds), *The Bonn Handbook of Globality*. Vol. 1. Wiesbaden: Springer: 515–26.

Stoetzler, Marcel. 2008. *The State, the Nation & the Jews: Liberalism and the Antisemitism Debate in Bismarck's Germany*. Lincoln: University of Nebraska Press.

Stögner, Karin and Schmidinger, Thomas. 2010. 'Antisemitismus und die Transformation des Nationalen'. *Östereichische Zeitschrift für Politikwissenschaft* 39(4): 387–92.

Strang, David and Meyer, John. 1993. 'Institutional conditions for diffusion'. *Theory and Society* 22(4), 487–511.

Sunkel, Oswaldo. 1993. *Development from Within: Toward a Neostructuralist Approach for Latin America*. Boulder, CO: Lynne Rienner Publishers.

Surkov, Vladislav. 2018. 'The loneliness of the half-breed'. *Russia in Global Affairs*. Retrieved from: https://eng.globalaffairs.ru/articles/the-loneliness-of-the-half-breed/ [last accessed 30 August 2020].

Tagore, Rabindranath. 1960. *Letters from Russia*. Calcutta: Visva-Bharati.

Tejel, Jordi. 2009. *Syria's Kurds. History, Politics and Society*. London: Routledge.

Tejel, Jordi. 2014. 'Les paradoxes du printemps Kurde en Syrie'. *Politique Étrangère* 2: 51–61.

Tejel, Jordi. 2017. 'Le Rojava: heurs et malheurs du Kurdistan (2004–2015)'. *Anatoli* 8: 133–49.

Tezcür, Güneş M. 2015. 'Violence and nationalist mobilization: The onset of the Kurdish insurgency in Turkey'. *Nationalities Papers* 43(2): 248–66.

Thiersch, Hans; Grunwald, Klaus; Köngeter, Stefan. 2012. 'Lebensweltorientierte Soziale Arbeit'. In: Werner Thole (ed), *Grundriss Soziale Arbeit*. Wiesbaden: VS Verlag für Sozialwissenschaften: 175-196.

Treitschke, Heinrich von. 1879. 'Unsere Aussichten'. *Preußische Jahrbücher* 44(5): 559–76.

Trenin, Dmitri. 2018. 'Rossiya i Yevropa: k chemu stremitsya i chto delat'?' [Russia and Europe: what is to be aspired to and what is to be done?]. *Moscow Carnegie Center*. Retrieved from: https://carnegie.ru/2018/03/29/ru-pub-75938 [last accessed 30 August 2020].

Trenin, Dmitri. 2019. 'Russia Facing Europe: A Provisional Road Map'. *Moscow Carnegie Center*. Retrieved from: https://carnegie.ru/commentary/80014 [last accessed 30 August 2020].

Tretyakov, Vitaly. 2012. 'Danilevskii: zabytyi genii Russkoi filosofii' [Danilevsky: Forgotten Genius of Russian Philosophy.] Forum discussion 'Chto Delat?' [What to do?]. Retrieved from: https://tvkultura.ru/video/show/brand_id/20917/episode_id/181279/video_id/181279/ [last accessed 30 August 2020].

Tsygankov, Andrei. 2016. 'Crafting the state-civilization Vladimir Putin's turn to distinct values'. *Problems of Post-Communism* 63(3): 146–58.

Tsygankov, Pavel. 2018. 'A rapidly changing reality: The nature of the world order and crisis through the eyes of leading experts in International Relations'. *Russia in Global Affairs* (no 3/2018). Retrieved from https://eng.globalaffairs.ru/articles/a-rapidly-changing-reality/ [last accessed 13 September 2020].

Tushnet, Mark. 2006. 'Essay: Referring to foreign law in constitutional interpretation. An episode in the culture wars'. *University of Baltimore Law Review* 35(3): 299–312.

UNECE (United Nations Economic Commission for Europe). 1963. *Economic Survey of Europe 1962*. Geneva: United Nations.

Unver, H. Akin. 2016. 'Schrödinger's Kurds: Transnational Kurdish geopolitics in the age of shifting borders'. *Journal of International Affairs* 69(2): 65.

Vali, Abbas. 1998 'The Kurds and their "others": Fragmented identity and fragmented politics'. *Comparative Studies of South Asia, Africa and the Middle East* 18(2): 82–95.

Vanegas, Isidro. 2009. 'Opinión Pública. Colombia'. In: *Diccionario Político del mundo Iberoamericano*. Madrid: Iberconceptos, Fundación Carolina: 1037–49.

Vanhulst, Julian and Beling, Adrian. E. 2014. 'Buen Vivir: Emergent discourse within or beyond sustainable development?' *Ecological Economics* 101: 54–63.

Veltmeyer, Henry and Petras, James F. 2000. *The Dynamics of Social Change in Latin America*. London: Palgrave Macmillan.

Vidaurre, Manuel 2010 [1826]. 'Discourse of the Peruvian plenipotentiary Manuel Vidaurre'. (La Gaceta del istmo, Panama. 22 June). In: Germán de la Reza (ed), *Documentos del Congreso Anfictiónico de Panamá*. Caracas: Fundación Biblioteca Ayacucho: 184–90.

Villalba, Unai. 2013. 'Buen Vivir vs development: A paradigm shift in the Andes?' *Third World Quarterly* 34(8): 1427–42.

Virilio, Paul´. 1995. *The Art of the Motor*. Minneapolis: University of Minnesota Press.

Wagner, Leonie. 2009. 'Soziale NGOs und die EU – Zivilgesellschaftliche Akteure und der Zivile Dialog'. In: Leonie Wagner and Ronald Lutz (eds),

Internationale Perspektiven Sozialer Arbeit. Dimensionen – Themen – Organisationen. Wiesbaden: VS Verlag für Sozialwissenschaften: 227–42.

Wagner, Leonie and Lutz, Ronald. 2018. 'Internationale Soziale Arbeit zwischen Kolonialismus und Befreiung. Eine Einleitung'. In: Leonie Wagner, Ronald Lutz, Christine Rehklau and Friso Ross (eds), *Handbuch Internationale Soziale Arbeit*. Weinheim: Beltz Juventa: 7–21.

Waldron, Jeremy. 2005. 'Foreign law and the modern ius gentium'. *Harvard Law Review* 119(1): 129–47.

Walker, Rob B.J. 1993. *Inside/Outside: International Relations as Political Theory*. Cambridge: Cambridge University Press.

Wallerstein, Immanuel. 2004. *World-Systems Analysis: An Introduction*. Durham, NC: Duke University Press.

Wallerstein, Immanuel. 2014. 'Antisystemic movements, yesterday and today'. *Journal of World-Systems Research* 20(2): 158–72.

Watson, Andrea. 2019. 'Collision: An opportunity for growth? Māori social workers' collision of their personal, professional, and cultural worlds and the values and ethical challenges within this experience'. *Journal of Social Work Values and Ethics* 16(2): 28–39.

Weber, Cynthia. 1992. 'Reconsidering statehood: Examining the sovereignty/intervention boundary'. *Review of International Studies* 18(3): 199–216.

Weber, Cynthia. 1998. 'Performative states'. *Millennium: Journal of International Studies* 27(1): 77–95.

Webman, Esther. 2011. *The Global Impact of The Protocols of the Elders of Zion. A Century-old Myth*. London: Routledge.

Weil, Bruno. 1924. *Die jüdische Internationale*. Berlin: Verlag für Politik und Wirtschaft.

Weitzman, Mark. 2017. *Magical Logic: Globalization, Conspiracy Theory, and the Shoah*. Jerusalem: Vidal Sassoon International Center for the Study of Antisemitism.

Wellman, Barry. 1999. *Networks in the Global Village: Life in Contemporary Communities*. Boulder, CO: Westview Press.

Werron, Tobias. 2005. 'Der Weltsport und sein Publikum. Weltgesellschaftstheoretische Überlegungen zum Zuschauersport'. In: Bettina Heintz, Richard Münch and Hartmann Tyrell (eds), *Weltgesellschaft. Theoretische Zugänge und Empirische Problemlagen*. Stuttgart: Lucius & Lucius: 260–89.

Werron, Tobias. 2008. '"World Series": Zur historischen Genese eines Weltereignisses'. In: Stefan Nacke; Tobias Werron; and Rene Unkelbach (eds),

Weltereignisse. Theoretische und empirische Perspektiven. Wiesbaden: VS Verlag für Sozialwissenschaft: 101–40.

Werron, Tobias. 2012. 'Schlüsselprobleme der Globalisierungs- und Weltgesellschaftstheorie'. *Soziologische Revue* 35(2): 99–118.

Werron, Tobias. 2015. 'What do nation-states compete for?' In: Boris Holzer, Fatima Kastner and Tobias Werron (eds), *From Globalization to World Society: Neo-Institutional and Systems-Theoretical Perspectives*. London: Routledge: 85–106.

Werron, Tobias. 2021. 'Nationalism as a global institution'. In: Mathias Albert and Tobias Werron (eds), *What in the World. Understanding Global Social Change*. Bristol: Bristol University Press: 157-76.

Werron, Tobias and Boris Holzer. 2009. '"Public otherhood". World society, theorization, and global systems dynamics' (Institute for World Society Studies Working Paper no. 2). Bielefeld: Institute for World Society Studies.

Weyand, Jan. 2016. *Historische Wissenssoziologie des modernen Antisemitismus*. Göttingen: Wallstein.

Wilmanns, Carl [Karl]. 1876. *Die 'goldene' Internationale und die Nothwendigkeit einer socialen Reformpartei*. Berlin: Niendorf.

Wimmer, Andreas and Feinstein, Yuval. 2010. 'The rise of the nation-state across the world, 1816–2001'. *American Sociological Review* 75(5): 764–90.

Winker, Gabriele. 2018. 'Care Revolution, interviewed by Brigitte Aulenbacher and Birgit Riegraf'. *Diversity and Inclusion* 37(4): 420–28.

Wohlfahrt, Irving. 2002. 'Walter Benjamin and the idea of a technological eros: A tentative reading of Zum Planetarium'. *Benjamin Studien/Studies* 1: 64–109.

World Bank. 2007. *World Development Report 2008: Agriculture for Development*. Washington, DC: The World Bank.

World Bank. 2018. *Migration and Remittances: Recent Developments and Outlook* Washington, DC: The World Bank

Wyrwa, Ulrich. 2009. 'Die Internationalen Antijüdischen Kongresse von 1882 und 1883 in Dresden und Chemnitz. Zum Antisemitismus als europäischer Bewegung'. *Themenportal Europäische Geschichte*. Retrieved from: www.europa.clio-online.de/essay/id/fdae-1481 [last accessed 30 August 2020].

Yeni Özgür Politika. 2013. 'PYD hêza gel e' (17 December). Retrieved from https://yeniozgurpolitika.net/pyd-heza-gel-e/

Yetkin, Murat. 2004. *Kürt Kapanı: Şam'dan İmralı'ya Öcalan.* Istanbul: Remzi Kitabevi.

Zermeño Padilla, Guillermo. 2017 [2009]. 'Historia, experiencia y modernidad en Iberoamérica, 1750–1850' In: Javier Sebastian Fernandez (ed) *Diccionario Político del mundo Iberoamericano.* Madrid: Iberconceptos. Fundación Carolina: 551–79.

Zitelmann, Ernst. 1905 [1900]. 'Des différents rôles et de la portée à attribuer au droit comparé.' In: *Congrès International de Droit Comparé Tenu à Paris du 31 Juillet au 4 Août 1900. Procès-Verbaux des Séances et Documents.* Vol. 1. Paris: Librairie Générale de Droit et de Jurisprudence: 189–98.

Zweigert, Konrad. 1970. 'Jherings Bedeutung für die Entwicklung der Rechtsvergleichenden Methode'. In: Franz Wieacker (ed), *Jherings Erbe.* Göttingen: Vandenhoeck & Ruprecht: 240–51.

Zweigert, Konrad and Kötz, Hein. 1998. *Introduction to Comparative Law.* Oxford: Clarendon Press.

Zweigert, Konrad and Siehr, Kurt. 1971. 'Jhering's influence on the development of comparative legal method'. *The American Journal of Comparative Law* 19(2): 215–31.

Notes on Contributors

Sergei Akopov is Professor of Political Science and International Relations at the Higher School of Economics of the National Research University in St. Petersburg. He holds a doctoral degree from the Institute of Philosophy of the Russian Academy of Science and conducted post-doctoral work in Sweden, Denmark and Hungary. His current fields of interest include Russia's identity and ontological security in world politics, intellectual history, transnational intellectuals, and 'politics of loneliness'. Among his latest publications are: (2020) 'Russia's 'fortresses of solitude': Social imaginaries of loneliness after the fall of the USSR.' *Social Science Information*. 59(2): 288-309; (2019) 'The concept of "Russian Europeans" in an Anti-War Film "The Cuckoo"'. In: U. Hamenstädt (ed), *The Interplay Between Political Theory and Movies: Bridging Two Worlds*. Berlin: Springer: 63-78.

Mustafa Aksakal is the scientific coordinator of the Research Training Group 'World Politics' at the Faculty of Sociology of Bielefeld University. In his habilitation project, he focuses on the multi-level analysis of the relation between the international migration of highly-skilled people and inequalities. He also works on the methodologies of migration research. He has co-edited and co-authored several works on the policies and processes of the Asian-European migration system as well as on migration and crisis in Latin America.

Mathias Albert is Professor of Political Science at Bielefeld University. He has published widely on world society, globalization, International Relations' theory, youth studies and polar research. His latest book publications include: (2016) *A Theory of World Politics*, Cambridge: Cambridge University Press; (ed with A.F. Lang) (2019) *The Politics of International Political Theory*, London: Palgrave Macmillan; (with K. Hurrelmann et al.) (2019) *Jugend 2019. 18. Shell Ju-*

gendstudie, Weinheim: Beltz; (ed with T. Werron) (2021) *What in the World? Understanding Global Social Change*, Bristol: Bristol University Press.

Michael Auer is Assistant Professor of German Studies and Comparative Literature at the LMU in Munich. He is currently acting full professor there. He conducted research on the discourse of planetarity maps in the No-Mans-Land between literature, international law, and the history and theory of technology. His publications include (2013) *Wege zu einer planetarischen Linientreue? Meridiane zwischen Jünger, Schmitt, Heidegger und Celan*, Munich. Fink; (2014) 'Präfigurationen des Planetarischen: Ernst Jünger, Gayatri Spivak und die typologische Lektüre'. In: C. Moser and L. Simonis (eds): *Figuren des Globalen. Weltbezug und Welterzeugung in Literatur, Kunst und Medien*. Bonn: Bonn University Press: 73-84.

Aziz Elmuradov obtained his PhD as a member of the Research Training Group 'World Politics' at Bielefeld University. He studied International Relations, Diplomacy, Peace and Security Studies. His research covers Russian foreign policy, relations between Russia and the EU, and political processes in post-Soviet space. His current research interests include political sociology, historical sociology, and most recently political psychology.

Lucy Gasser is a lecturer in Anglophone Studies at the University of Potsdam. She obtained her PhD as a member of the Research Training Group 'Minor Cosmopolitanisms' there. She also holds a Masters degree from the University of Cape Town and has taught at universities in South Africa and Germany. She is one of the founding editors of pocolit.com, a bilingual platform for postcolonial literatures, and has published on world literature and postcolonial studies.

Cornelia Giebeler is professor for the Theory and Methodology of Social and Educational Sciences at the University of Applied Sciences Bielefeld. She holds a PhD in sociology and is interested in feminism, childhood, decolonial and transformative processes, indigenous movements, strangeness experiences in Global Social Work, and research epistemology/methodology. She conducted projects in Venezuela, Mexico, Chile and Ecuador, including 'The women merchants of Juchitán, Mexico', 'Social pedagogics in Latin America', 'Kitas des buen vivir in Ecuador', and 'Entangled Americas – migration processes in Mexico'. Her latest publications include: (ed with I. Cornejo) (2019) *Prójimos*.

Prácticas de investigación desde la horizontalidad. Mexico City and Bielefeld: UAM Mexico and FH Bielefeld; (ed with C Rademacher and E Schulze) (2013) *Intersektionen von race, class, gender, body*. Opladen: Barbara Budrich.

Sandra Holtgreve is a doctoral researcher and a member of the Research Training Group 'World Politics' at Bielefeld University. She studied Social Work, Sociology, and Inter-American Studies. Her doctoral research concerns knowledge sociology and Social Work education. The project analyses the consolidation of knowledge of post- and decolonial theory in Social Work curricula in Germany, Mexico, and Ecuador. Her main interests include Social Work education in a global world, in organizational aspects of universities, theories in sociology and in Social Work, as well as the diffusion and dynamics of scientific knowledge and theories in the social sciences and humanities.

Marc Jacobsen is a doctoral researcher and a member of the Research Training Group 'World Politics' at Bielefeld University. He currently works on his dissertation on 'anti-Semitism in world society'. The project analyzes modern Jew hatred as a specific form of observing globalization based on anti-Jewish conspiracy myths. His research interests also include nationalism, globalization, and (early) critical theory.

Karlson Preuß is a doctoral researcher and a member of the Research Training Group 'World Politics' at Bielefeld University. He studied Sociology, Philosophy, French Philology and Comparative Constitutional Law. Working at the interface of legal sociology, legal history and historical sociology, his doctoral research concerns the mutual influences of jurisprudence and sociology since the late 19th century.

Yasin Sunca obtained his PhD as a member of the Research Training Group 'World Politics' at Bielefeld University, in a joint degree with the University of Ghent. His work intersects international historical sociology, revolutionary politics, radical political theory, and conflict analysis/transformation with a geographical focus on West Asia. He has published in the fields of nationalism and peace. Previously, he advised European institutions and NGOs on the relations between the EU, Turkey and the Kurds. He currently co-leads a research agenda on the decolonial practices of peace at the DEMOS research association (Ankara).

Gladys Vásquez is a doctoral researcher at Bielefeld University and a member of the Research Training Group 'World Politics'. She studied Social Sciences and History with a major in Andean Studies and Latin American history. She was an associate lecturer of Critical History at the *Universidad Peruana de Ciencias Aplicadas* and conducted research for private and public institutions in various cultural and academic projects. Her doctoral research focuses on the construction of international relations in Spanish America at the beginning of the 19th century.

Tobias Werron is Professor of Sociological Theory at Bielefeld University. His main research interests include competition, nationalism and globalization. Among his recent publications are: (2020) 'Global publics as catalysts of global competition: A sociological view'. In: V Huber and J Osterhammel (eds), *Global Publics. Their Power and Their Limits, 1870-1990*). Oxford: Oxford University Press: 343-66; (2018) (together with Jelena Brankovic und Leopold Ringel) 'How rankings produce competition. The case of global university rankings'. Zeitschrift für Soziologie, 47(4): 270-88; (2018) *Der globale Nationalismus*, Berlin: Nicolai Publishing.

Social Sciences

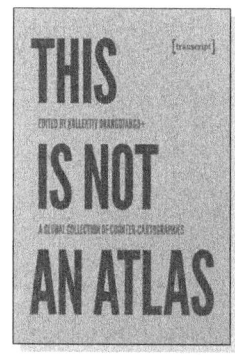

kollektiv orangotango+ (ed.)
This Is Not an Atlas
A Global Collection of Counter-Cartographies

2018, 352 p., hardcover, col. ill.
34,99 € (DE), 978-3-8376-4519-4
E-Book: free available, ISBN 978-3-8394-4519-8

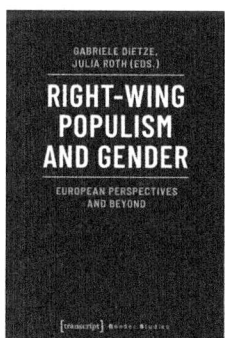

Gabriele Dietze, Julia Roth (eds.)
Right-Wing Populism and Gender
European Perspectives and Beyond

April 2020, 286 p., pb., ill.
35,00 € (DE), 978-3-8376-4980-2
E-Book: 34,99 € (DE), ISBN 978-3-8394-4980-6

Mozilla Foundation
Internet Health Report 2019
2019, 118 p., pb., ill.
19,99 € (DE), 978-3-8376-4946-8
E-Book: free available, ISBN 978-3-8394-4946-2

All print, e-book and open access versions of the titles in our list are available in our online shop www.transcript-verlag.de/en!

Social Sciences

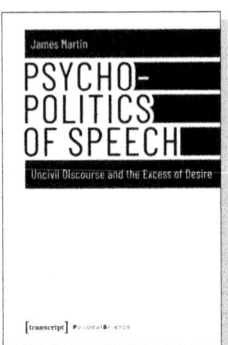

James Martin
Psychopolitics of Speech
Uncivil Discourse and the Excess of Desire

2019, 186 p., hardcover
79,99 € (DE), 978-3-8376-3919-3
E-Book: 79,99 € (DE), ISBN 978-3-8394-3919-7

Michael Bray
Powers of the Mind
Mental and Manual Labor
in the Contemporary Political Crisis

2019, 208 p., hardcover
99,99 € (DE), 978-3-8376-4147-9
E-Book: 99,99 € (DE), ISBN 978-3-8394-4147-3

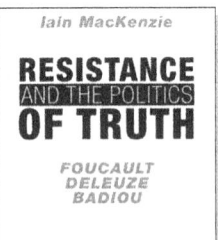

Iain MacKenzie
Resistance and the Politics of Truth
Foucault, Deleuze, Badiou

2018, 148 p., pb.
29,99 € (DE), 978-3-8376-3907-0
E-Book: 26,99 € (DE), ISBN 978-3-8394-3907-4
EPUB: 26,99 € (DE), ISBN 978-3-7328-3907-0

**All print, e-book and open access versions of the titles in our list
are available in our online shop www.transcript-verlag.de/en!**